# Learn AutoCAD!

## Mechanical Drawing
## Using AutoCAD® 2017

## David Martin

## Dedication

I would like to dedicate this book to my AutoCAD students, both past and present.

---

# Table of Contents

INTRODUCTION ........................................................................................................ 3

**PROJECTS – 2D VERSIONS** ............................................................................... 11

PROJECT #1 – ABSOLUTE COORDINATE EXERCISE .................................................. 11
PROJECT #2 – RELATIVE COORDINATE EXERCISE ................................................... 37
PROJECT #3 – BRACKET .......................................................................................... 43
PRINTING YOUR DRAWING ....................................................................................... 69
PROJECT #4 – PLATE ............................................................................................... 75
PROJECT #5 – SAW HANDLE .................................................................................... 95
PROJECT #6 – GUIDE ............................................................................................. 109
PROJECT #7 – GASKET ........................................................................................... 125
PROJECT #8 – GENEVA CAM ................................................................................... 133
PROJECT #9 – HOLE GUIDE .................................................................................... 145
PROJECT #10 – COVER PLATE ................................................................................ 159
PROJECT #11A – WELD SYMBOLS .......................................................................... 175
PROJECT #11B – WELDMENT ................................................................................. 183

**PROJECTS – 3D VERSIONS** ............................................................................. 193

PROJECT #1 – 3D – ABSOLUTE COORDINATE EXERCISE ....................................... 195
PROJECT #2 – 3D – RELATIVE COORDINATE EXERCISE ......................................... 205
PROJECT #3 – 3D – BRACKET ................................................................................ 207
USING A 3D SOLID TO CREATE ORTHOGRAPHIC VIEWS .......................................... 217
PROJECT #4 – 3D – PLATE ..................................................................................... 233
PROJECT #5 – 3D – SAW HANDLE .......................................................................... 237
PROJECT #6 – 3D – GUIDE ..................................................................................... 247
PROJECT #7 – 3D – GASKET ................................................................................... 255
PROJECT #8 – 3D – GENEVA CAM ASSEMBLY ........................................................ 259
PROJECT #9 – 3D – HOLE GUIDE ........................................................................... 287
PROJECT #10 – 3D – COVER PLATE ........................................................................ 297
PROJECT #11 – 3D – WELDMENT ........................................................................... 305

**CONCLUSION** .................................................................................................... 313

**GLOSSARY** ....................................................................................................... 315

# Introduction

## AutoCAD Students:

Welcome to **Learn AutoCAD!: Mechanical Drawing Using AutoCAD 2017**. This book is designed to give you an introduction to Mechanical Drawing using the AutoCAD 2017 software. These projects were originally developed based on the projects used for my Introduction to AutoCAD course at Glendale Community College in Glendale, California.

The operating system used for these projects is Windows® 10. The book is divided into two parts: 2D Tutorials and 3D Tutorials of the projects. All of these projects have step-by-step procedures, screenshots, and demonstration videos on the companion website at: **www.mechdrawautocad.com**. The videos will also provide additional instruction of the tools and techniques being used for each project. It is recommended that you view these either before or during the drawing of the projects.

**Please Note:** *Access to the videos and support files require a Google Account. If you would prefer to access the files using a different method, please contact the author at mechdrawautocad@gmail.com so that different arrangements for file access can be made.*

You will receive an introduction to the 3D portion of the software and complete the projects using this portion of the program. Once you have completed the tutorials, you may wish to print your drawings and assemble them into a portfolio. You should have a general knowledge of orthographic projection, linetypes, vellum and border sizes, welding symbology, and dimensioning practice.

It is my hope that you will find this process an enjoyable and informative one. Once you have completed the book please feel free to email me with any suggestions and/or compliments about the book.

Enjoy,

David Martin
**mechdrawautocad@gmail.com**
**www.mechdrawautocad.com**

## Before Beginning to Draw

Each project has set of procedures that will aid you in drawing the project. The units that are used are either in inches or millimeters. Before beginning the project, be sure to set up the file with the appropriate drawing units and layers. As the book projects progress, the setup for new projects will change.

A good strategy is to use a previous project that is similar to the current project to aid in the set-up of the file. If a template does not exist, create one from a completed drawing.

Before beginning the projects, it is recommended to print out the PDF versions of the completed projects. This way you will have a reference for the measurements and locations of the features of each part. High-resolution files of the PDF versions of the projects are available on the book website.

## Video Tutorials

There are on-line video tutorials available for student use at:

**www.mechdrawautocad.com**

Permission to access these files will be given as part of book purchase. The author may be contacted by email at **mechdrawautocad@gmail.com**. You will also be required to create a Google Account or contact the author for other methods to access the files. This account and the associated email account will be used to access the tutorial videos. After the email is sent, you will receive instructions on how to access the tutorials and support files.

## Title Blocks and Other Support Files

Title Blocks and other support files will be provided on the book website. Student should copy these files to their local drive and/or flash drive.

## File Management

One of the most important issues while learning a computer-based skill is the management of the various files created. Always create a backup copy of your working files. Students should use folders to organize their work. A recommended method to do this will be covered during the first project.

## AutoCAD Educational License

Autodesk Inc. provides free educational licenses of their software. To download the software, registration on the Autodesk site is required. Access the Download Trial link at the web address below:

**http://www.autodesk.com/education/free-software/all**

If you are a student or teacher at an academic institution, you are eligible to receive a variety of products for free from the Autodesk site. Please visit the Autodesk.com site for terms and conditions.

## Mechanical Drawing Layer Setup

Use this guide for the Layer Setup for the drawings. The procedure to setup the levels for the drawing will be covered later in the book.

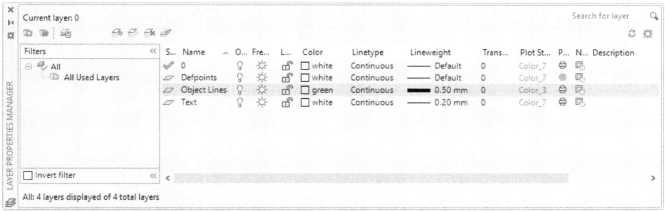

**Layer Properties Manager Dialog Box**

Use the following level setup for both imperial and metric drawings:

| Layer Name | Color | Linetype | Lineweight |
|---|---|---|---|
| Object Lines | Green (2) | 0 | 2 |
| Hidden Lines | White (0) | (Hidden) | 0 |
| Centerlines | White (0) | (Center) or (Center-Short) | 0 |
| Dimensions | White (0) | 0 | 0 |
| Text | White (0) | 0 | 0 |
| Hatching | Red (3) | 0 | 0 |
| Border Lines* | Yellow (4) | 0 | 2 |
| Points* | Magenta (5) | 0 | 6 |
| Tags* | White (0) | 0 | 0 |

*Used for A-Size and B-Size Border Files.

## Drawing Setup for the 2D Projects

Please watch the Tutorial Video for Project #1 for information of drawing setup. The steps are also covered in the tutorial for the projects.

This chart shows the drafting settings for the 12 projects.

| Project # | Drawing Scale | Plot Scale | Text Size | Dimension Scale | Linetype Scale Factor | Grid Dot Spacing | Paper Size |
|-----------|---------------|------------|-----------|-----------------|-----------------------|------------------|------------|
| **1,2** | None | 1:2 | .2500 | 1.0000 | N/A | .2500 | ANSI A |
| **3,4** | 1:1 | 1:1 | .1250 | 1.0000 | 1.000 | .2500 | ANSI A |
| **5-8** | 1:1 | 1:1 | .1250 | 1.0000 | 1.000 | .2500 | ANSI B |
| **9** | 1:1 | 1:1 | 3.175 | 25.4000 | 25.4000 | 5.0000 | ISO A3 |
| **10** | 1:2 | 1:2 | .2500 | 2.0000 | 2.000 | .5000 | ANSI B |
| **11a** | None | 1:1 | .1250 | N/A | 1.000 | .2500 | ANSI B |
| **11b** | 1:2 | 1:2 | .2500 | 2.0000 | 2.000 | .5000 | ANSI B |

## Project Volumes for 3D Projects

AutoCAD can measure the volume of the 3D projects that you will be drawing. This provides an easy way of determining if you drew the object the correct size and shape.

Use these volumes as a guide when calculating the volumes of the 3D versions of your projects.

Use the VOLUME key-in command to measure the volume of your project.

| Project # | Volume | Units |
|-----------|--------|-------|
| 1 | 32.8393 | Cubic Inches |
| 2 | 9.4599 | Cubic Inches |
| 3 | 3.0664 | Cubic Inches |
| 4 | 5.7910 | Cubic Inches |
| 5 | 12.4649 | Cubic Inches |
| 6 | 9.5502 | Cubic Inches |
| 7 | 1.7920 | Cubic Inches |
| 8 (Cam) | 2.2996 | Cubic Inches |
| 8 (Drive Wheel) | 2.2619 | Cubic Inches |
| 8 (Base) | 10.9718 | Cubic Inches |
| 8 (Shaft) | 0.1474 | Cubic Inches |
| 8 (Key) | 0.0097 | Cubic Inches |
| 9 | 163987.3199 | Cubic Millimeters |
| 10 | 6.8571 | Cubic Inches |
| 11* | 13.5996 | Cubic Inches |

**Note:**
To check the volume of Project #11, create a copy of the parts and then union them together.

# Part One

## Projects
## 2D Versions

# Projects – 2D Versions

## Project #1 – Absolute Coordinate Exercise

**Filename:** PROJ-01.dwg
Note: All screenshots are from the Autodesk® AutoCAD® software.

**Description:** This is the first project of the book. It is designed to introduce you to the AutoCAD interface and to give you practice in the use of the Absolute Coordinate system. A completed version of the project is shown at the end of the tutorial.

You will also be introduced to the Move, Copy, Offset, and Text tools and the use of the various commands to control the font, size, and the spacing of the various text elements in the drawing.

<u>Setting up a Folder Structure and Downloading the Support Files</u>

1.  Before beginning to draw, you will set up a folder structure to save and organize your drawing and support files.

2.  On your desktop, open your File Explorer window.

3.  On the drive/location of your choice, create a folder called AutoCAD Projects. All your files used and created while using this book will be contained in this folder.

4.  Within this folder, create a set of sub-folders as shown.

    More folders will be created later on in the book.

    **Note:** In this case the folders were created on the Desktop. If you are using different computers and wish for you files to be mobile, you may wish to use a Flash Drive instead.

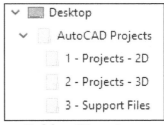

**Folder Structure**

5.  Open the website for the text book located at <u>www.mechdrawautocad.com</u>.

    Find and download the Support Files from the Google Drive folder and copy the files into your Support Files folder on your local drive.

    **Note:** This folder contains all the files you will need to complete the book projects.

Starting the AutoCAD Software

1. Find and double-click on the AutoCAD 2017 icon to start the software.

   The icon should be located on the desktop.

**AutoCAD 2017 Icon**

2. The splash screen will appear. Wait for the software to open and for the opening screen to appear.

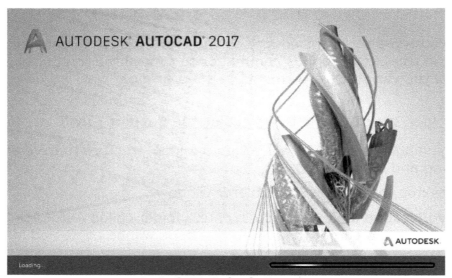

**AutoCAD Splash Screen**

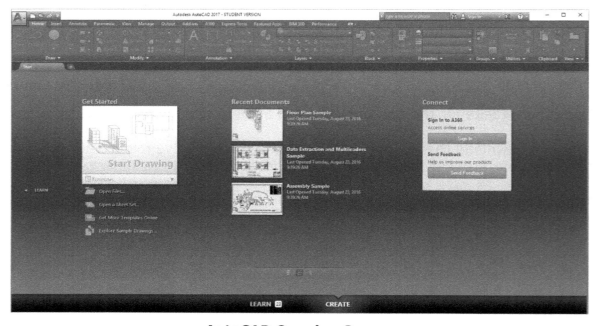

**AutoCAD Opening Screen**

3. Click on the Start Drawing icon on the left side of the screen.

**Start Drawing**

4. A new drawing file will open.

   AutoCAD will automatically use the acad.dwt file as the template file.

5. This is the user interface.

   At the top is the Ribbon panel that contains the tools you will use to complete the projects.

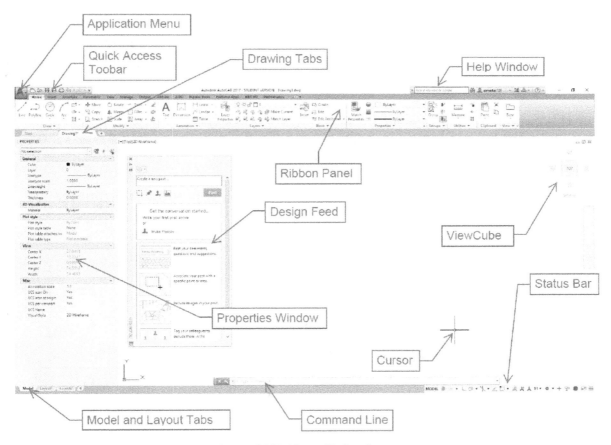

**AutoCAD User Interface**

**Note:**
The tools and other parts of the user interface will be discussed in greater detail as you progress through the book.

Beginning the Project

1.  Click on the Save tool in the Quick Access Toolbar at the top left of the screen.

    Save the file as: PROJ-01.

    The file should be saved in your Projects – 2D folder.

    **Note:** You should save the file regularly (approx. every 15-20 minutes) while you are working on the project.

**Save Tool**

2.  Click on the line tool in the Home Tab, Draw Panel.

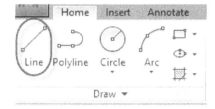

**Line Tool**

3.  Next to the drawing cursor you will see the coordinates for the start of the line.

    For this first project you will be using the keyboard to key-in the coordinates for the endpoints of the lines.

    **Note:** If you cannot see the coordinates appear when adding the line, make sure that the Dynamic Input variable is turned on. Type DYNMODE and set it to 3.

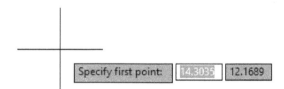

**Endpoint Coordinates**

4.  Type 0,0 to place the first endpoint. You will see that the start point is located at the origin of the drawing marked with an X and Y.

    The X and Y symbol is also known as the UCS (Universal Coordinate System) Icon.

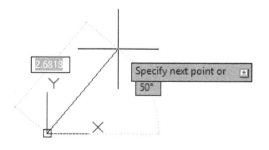

**Start Point and UCS Icon**

5.  For the next point type in the
    coordinates as shown in the
    example.

    This will place the endpoint 1.50 up
    and 1.50 to the right of the 0,0
    coordinate.

    **Note:** You do not need to type in the
    trailing zeros.

Specify next point or   [±] [#] [1.5] [🔒] [1.5]

**# Sign Used to Indicate
Absolute Coordinates**

When typing in the coordinates, include the number sign "#" before the numbers.

This sign indicates that the coordinates are Absolute Coordinates and are measured
from the Origin.

Use the chart in the next step as reference for the coordinates for each of the line
endpoints.

**Note:** AutoCAD uses the Cartesian Coordinate System (X,Y) for the coordinate entry.

6.  Work your way through the chart for the outside
    shape of the drawing.

    When you get to point to Point K, close the
    shape by typing in #0,0 to end the line back at
    Point A.

    Press the ESC key to end the command.

    **Note:** As you are adding the lines you may need
    to adjust the view of the drawing. Use your
    Mouse Wheel to zoom in and out. To pan the
    view, hold the wheel down and drag your
    mouse.

| POINT | ABSOLUTE COORDINATES | |
|---|---|---|
| | X | Y |
| A | 0.00 | 0.00 |
| B | 1.75 | 1.75 |
| C | 1.75 | 6.50 |
| D | 4.25 | 6.50 |
| E | 5.25 | 3.50 |
| F | 4.70 | 2.25 |
| G | 8.00 | 2.25 |
| H | 8.00 | 0.00 |
| J | 7.00 | −1.75 |
| K | 4.75 | −0.50 |
| L | 2.50 | 5.75 |
| M | 3.75 | 5.75 |
| N | 3.75 | 2.75 |
| P | 2.50 | 2.75 |
| Q | 4.25 | 1.00 |
| R | 6.50 | 0.25 |

**Project #1
Absolute Coordinate Chart**

7.  Next you will draw the rectangular shape.

    Resume the Line tool and begin by entering the first coordinate at point L (2.50,5.75). Continue around the rectangle and back to point L.

**Completed Rectangle**

8.  Next you will place the hexagon.

    Begin by clicking on the Polygon tool.

    This tool is found in the Draw Panel.

    You may access the tool by clicking on the arrow next to the Rectangle tool and selecting the Polygon tool.

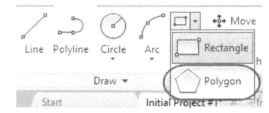

**Polygon Tool**

9.  Enter the number of sides as 6 and press Enter.

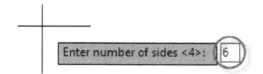

**Entering Number of Sides**

10. Specify the center of the polygon at point Q (4.25, 1.00)

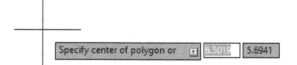

**Specify Center of Polygon**

11. Press Enter to accept the option as "Inscribed in circle".

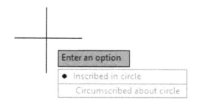

**Inscribed in Circle Option**

12. Type .75 as the radius of the circle that the hexagon will be contained in.

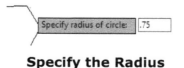

**Specify the Radius**

13. Press the Enter key to place the hexagon.

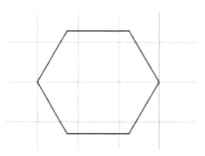

**Hexagon is Placed**

14. The procedure to place the Circle is similar.

    Click on the Circle tool in the Draw Panel.

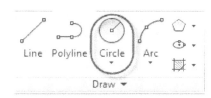

**Circle Tool**

15. Enter the center point at point R then specify the radius at .75.

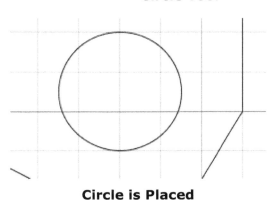

**Circle is Placed**

16. This completes the shape of the object.

    Next you will set up the layers for the drawing.

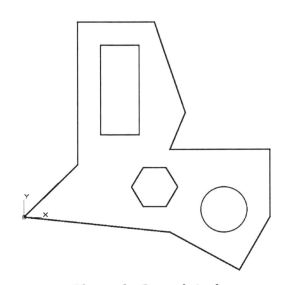

**Shape is Completed**

Setting up the Layers

Layers are used to organize the drawing. By categorizing the different types of objects on a drawing into layers, you can control their appearance and visibility on the drawing. Every drawing will have its own layer set-up and will depend on the type of project you are drawing.

1.  Click on the Layer Properties tool in the Layers panel.

**Layer Properties Tool**

2.  The Layer Properties Manager dialog box will open.

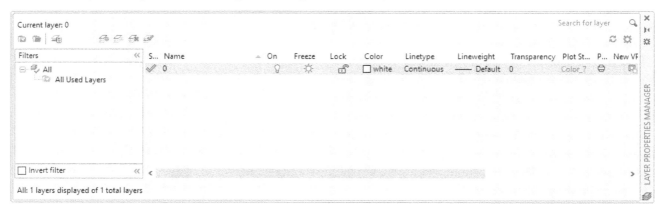

**Layer Properties Manager**

The Layer Properties Manager dialog box is used to control different attributes of a layer. These are the ones that we will be concerned with at this point:

**Status** – Shows which layer is the current one being used.

**Name** – The name given to the layer.

**On or Off** – Whether the layer is visible or not visible.

**Color** – The color of the layer. (If white is used it will be the opposite of the background.)

**Linetype** – The style of the line in the layer (i.e. dashed, dotted).

**Lineweight** – The thickness of the line in millimeters.

3.  Click on the New Layer tool within the dialog box.

    This will add a new layer to the drawing.

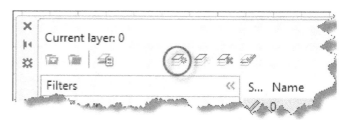

**New Layer Tool**

4.  Type in the new name of the layer as "Object Lines".

    Set the color to Green.
    Keep the linetype as Continuous
    Set the lineweight to .50mm

**Object Lines Layer Properties**

5.  Add another layer called Text. Set the color to White, the Linetype to Continuous, and the Lineweight to .20mm.

6.  Close the Layer Properties Manager dialog box.

Setting the Drawing Grids, Snap Settings, and Polar Setting

Drawing Grids are the lines that are on the background of the drawing. These lines are used to help estimate size on the drawing and to help line up elements on the screen. These lines are similar to lines on a sheet of grid paper. You will change the grids to a new setting.

Snaps are used to lock the cursor onto existing elements. You may have noticed that while you were drawing the shape for Project #1 that the lines were occasionally locking onto other elements. You will review and change the snap settings for the drawing.

1.  Before opening the Drafting Settings dialog box, you will need to turn on the pulldown menus.

    Click on the down arrow next to the Quick Access Toolbar.

    **Note:** You may also use this pulldown to customize the toobar.

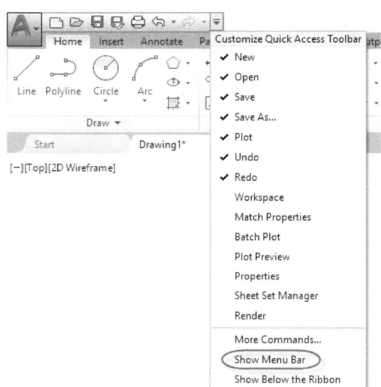

**Down Arrow**

2.  Click on the Tools menu and select Drafting Settings.

**Drafting Settings**

3.  The Drafting Settings
    dialog box opens.

    Set the Grid X and Y
    spacing to .25 and the
    Major line setting to 4.

    This will set the distance
    of the Major Lines every
    1 inch.

    Press the OK button to
    close the dialog box.

    You should see that the
    grids lines are now
    approximately half the
    distance that they were
    before.

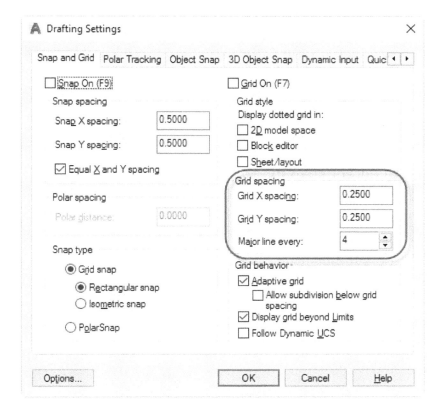

**Drafting Settings Dialog Box**

4.  Some commands also have keyboard shortcuts
    called aliases.

    The keyboard shortcut for the Drafting Settings
    dialog box is DS.

    **Note:** Whenever a key is pressed, a suggestion
    will appear for possible keyboard shortcuts.

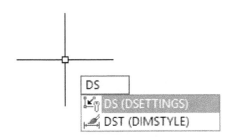

**Keyboard Shortcut**

5.  Re-open the Drafting
    Settings dialog box
    and click on the Object
    Snap tab at the top.

    Verify that the
    checkboxes next to the
    Midpoint, Geometric
    Center, Node, and
    Quadrant snap modes
    are checked.

    The small symbols
    next to the names are
    the symbols that
    appear when you snap
    on an object using that
    mode.

    Press OK to close the
    dialog box.

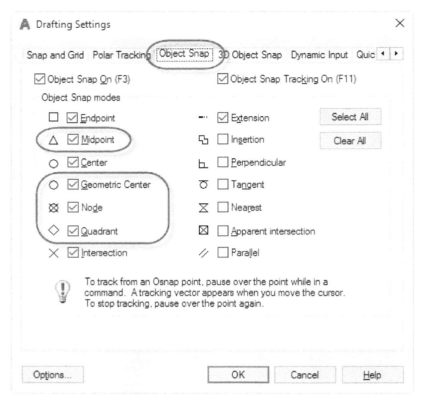

**Object Snap Settings**

6.  Click the Polar
    Tracking tab.

    Set the Incremental
    Angle setting to 90.00.

    This will set the Polar
    Tracking line to every
    90 degrees when
    placing lines and other
    elements.

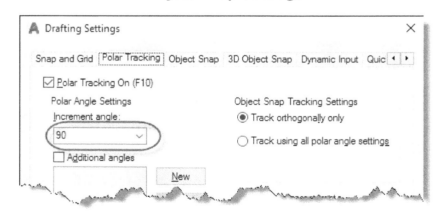

**Polar Tracking Set to 90 Degrees**

7.  At this point you have set up the drawing to draw the remaining objects.

## Changing the Layer of the Elements

1. Before drawing the table you will move the lines that you have already drawn to the Object Lines layer.

2. Select the elements by quickly clicking and holding at the top left of the shape.

   Drag to the right and down. You should see a light blue box appear and enclose the shape.

   This box is known as a Fence.

   Click again at the lower right corner to select the elements.

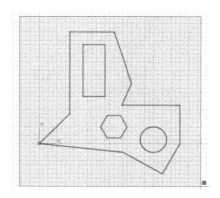

**Fence Placed**

3. After the fence disappears, you will see blue boxes on the individual elements.

   These are handles and can be used to modify the individual elements.

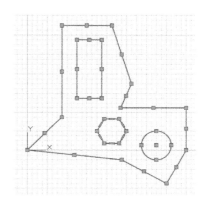

**Elements Selected**

4. Click on the down arrow next to the layer. Select the Object Lines layer.

   You will see the lines of the shape change to a green color.

5. Next you will turn on the lineweight toggle to see the thicker lines.

   Press the ESC key a few times to clear the selection.

   Type LW to see the keyboard shortcut options.

   Select the LWDISPLAY variable then chose Yes to see the thicker lineweights.

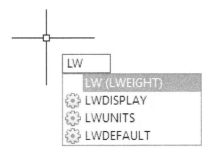

**LWDISPLAY Variable**

Drawing the Lines for the Table

1.  Draw the table using the dimensions as shown.

2.  Begin by drawing a horizontal line at 4.50 inches long.

3.  Using the Snap function, snap a line from the left end and draw the vertical line 9.50 inches long.

4.  Repeat for the right side.

    **Note:** The lines in the book screenshots will appear monochrome. Your version will appear with color. If you wish to view the screenshots in this book in color, use the Kindle version of this book.

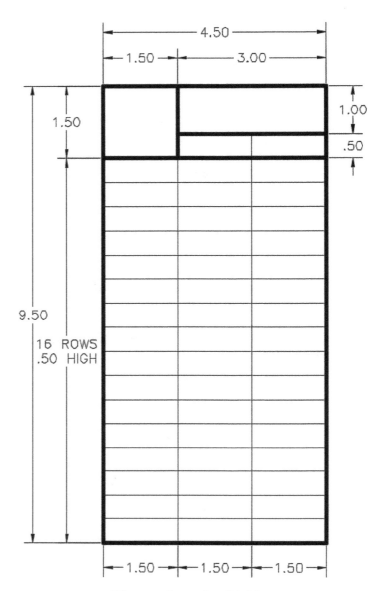

**Dimensions for Table**

5.  To add the other horizontal and vertical lines, you will use the Offset tool.

    This tool is used to copy lines from an existing line or arc at a specific distance.

**Offset Tool**

6.  Click on the Offset tool and set the distance to 1.5 inches.

    Click the Vertical line and copy to the right twice.

    Offset the top horizontal line down 1.00 then .50.

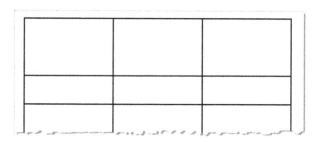

**Lines Offset**

7.  Next you will trim the lines to create the boxes for the text.

    Click on the Trim tool in the Modify panel.

    Press Enter to select all the objects in the drawing.

    Click on the portion of the lines that you want to trim.

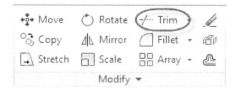

**Trim Tool**

CLICK THESE LINES.

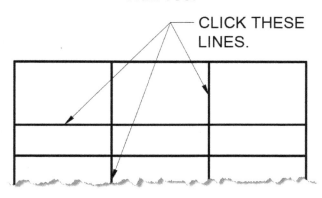

**Lines to Trim**

8.  When trimming the right line, click on the top of the line first and then below.

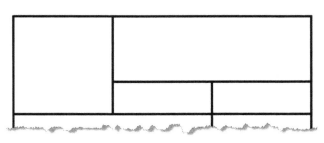

**Lines Trimmed**

9. Offset the lower horizontal line down .50.

   After the first offset change the line to the text level.

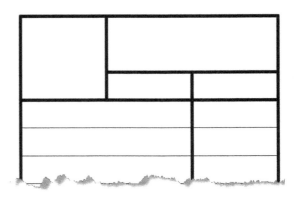

**Layer Changed and Lines Offset**

10. To complete the lines for the table, change the vertical line to the text layer and add a new vertical line as shown in the example.

    When drawing the vertical line, you will see an alignment line appear to show that the new line is locked vertically.

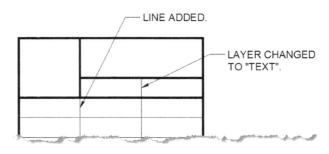

**Lines for Table Completed**

Adding the Text Elements and Outside Border

1. Begin by adding the text to the top two boxes.

   Click on the Multiline Text tool in the Annotation panel.

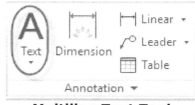

**Multiline Text Tool**

2. Draw a small box for the text off to the side of the table.

**Multiline Text Box**

3. Type the word "Point" in the editor box.

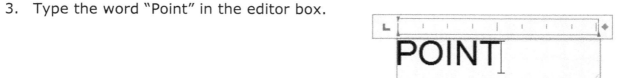

**Text Editor Box**

4. The default setting for the text is Arial for the font and .200 for the height.

   Highlight the text and change the font to "Romans" in the Formatting panel and the height to .1875 in the Style panel.

**Font Changed**

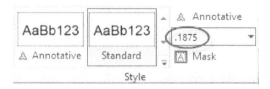

**Text Height Changed**

5. With the text still selected, click on the Justification tool in the Paragraph panel and set it to Middle Center.

   Click outside the text editor box to complete the changes.

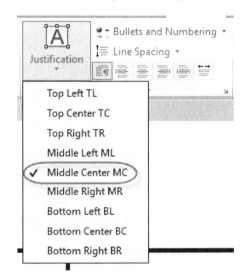

**Justification Changed to Middle Center**

6. To place the word in the center of the box in the table, draw a line diagonally through the box. Use the Snap function lock onto the corners of the box.

   Click on the text and grab it by the blue handle in the center of the word and drag to the midpoint of the line.

   You should see a green triangle appear and the word Midpoint.

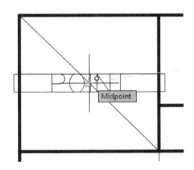

**Text at Midpoint of the Line**

7. Repeat the process for the words "Absolute Coordinates". Instead of creating new text use the Copy tool to copy the first line of text to the new location.

   Click the tool, select the text, click at the start point of the copy, and finish at the location of the copy.

**Copy Tool**

8. To edit the copied text, double-click on the text and edit in the text editor box.

   Delete the diagonal lines when finished.

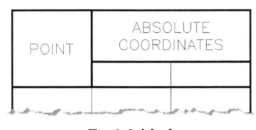

**Text Added**

9. Next, you will add the three columns of text.

   Copy the word "Point" and place away from the table.

10. Double-click on the text to edit.

11. Make the following changes to the text:

    Set the height to .25.

    Set the Justification to Top Center.

    You will also need to set the line spacing to 1.200x. This will be done in the Paragraph setting for the text.

    Click on the small arrow at the lower right corner of the panel to open the dialog box.

    Set the Line spacing to Multiple and the setting to 1.200x.

    This will give you a line spacing of .50 inches.

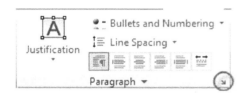

**Paragraph Settings**

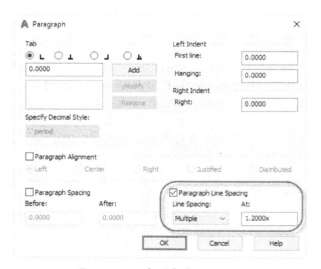

**Paragraph Dialog Box**

12. After changing the text settings, select the text and drag to the upper left corner of the first cell.

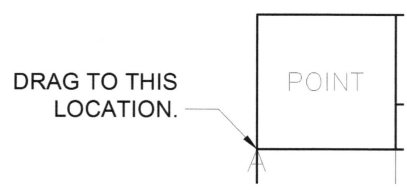

**Text Column Location**

13. Select the text column and then click the Move tool in the Modify panel.

    Enter the following coordinates for the move: @.75,-.125

    **Note:** The "@" is used to indicate relative coordinates instead of absolute.

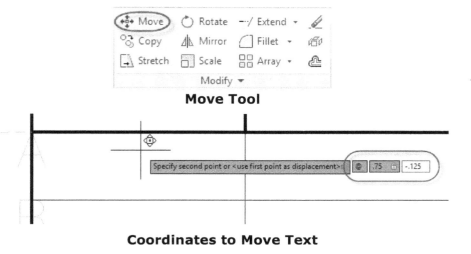

**Move Tool**

**Coordinates to Move Text**

14. The text is now moved.

    Copy the column twice to the other two locations.

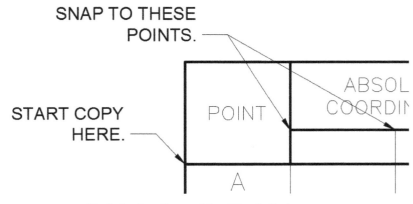

**Points to Copy the Text Column**

15. Edit the text as shown in the example.

    If the line spacing setting changes, set it again to 1.200x.

| POINT | ABSOLUTE COORDINATES | |
|---|---|---|
| | X | X |
| A | 0.00 | 0.00 |
| B | 1.75 | 1.75 |
| C | 1.75 | 6.50 |

**Text Placed and Edited**

16. Add the border using the Rectangle Tool.

    Use the coordinates -1.50, -3.50 for the start point at the lower left corner.

    Use 18.50, 10.25 for the upper right corner.

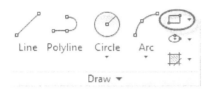

Line  Polyline  Circle  Arc

Draw ▾

**Rectangle Tool**

17. The outside border is placed.

    The lines will be on the Object Lines layer.

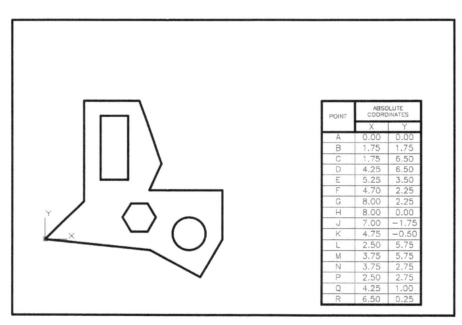

| POINT | ABSOLUTE COORDINATES | |
|---|---|---|
| | X | Y |
| A | 0.00 | 0.00 |
| B | 1.75 | 1.75 |
| C | 1.75 | 6.50 |
| D | 4.25 | 6.50 |
| E | 5.25 | 3.50 |
| F | 4.70 | 2.25 |
| G | 8.00 | 2.25 |
| H | 8.00 | 0.00 |
| J | 7.00 | -1.75 |
| K | 4.75 | -0.50 |
| L | 2.50 | 5.75 |
| M | 3.75 | 5.75 |
| N | 3.75 | 2.75 |
| P | 2.50 | 2.75 |
| Q | 4.25 | 1.00 |
| R | 6.50 | 0.25 |

**Outside Border Placed**

18. Add the remaining text.

    Use the settings as shown.

    Estimate the location of the text based off the completed example.

    When underlining the text, select the text and press the Underline toggle in the Formatting panel.

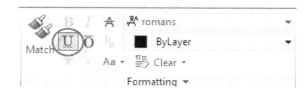

**Underline Toggle**

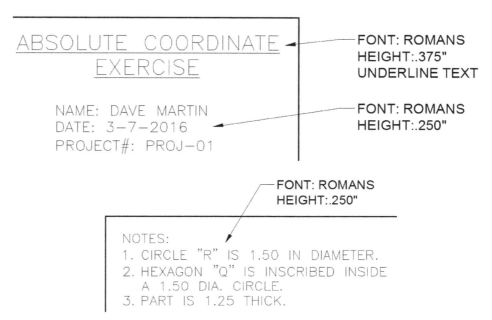

**Text Setting for Remaining Text**

19. To add the note for the origin at the bottom left of the shape, you will use the Leader tool located in the Annotation panel.

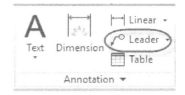

**Leader Tool**

20. Before using the tool you will need to modify the style of the leader.

    Click the down arrow next to the word Annotation in the panel. This will expose options for the tools in the panel.

    Then click on the Multileader Style tool.

    **Note:** When using other tools in AutoCAD, this down arrow will be available for additional options.

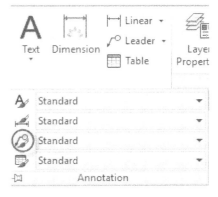

**Multileader Style**

21. The Multileader Style
    Manager dialog box
    opens.

    You will be creating a
    new style based off the
    Standard style.

    Click the New... button to
    start the process.

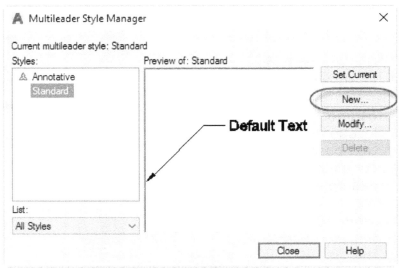

**Multileader Style Manager Dialog Box**

22. The Create New Multileader Style
    dialog box opens.

    Name the new style "Mechanical" then
    click the Continue button.

**Create New Multileader Style Dialog Box**

23. The Modify
    Multileader Style
    dialog box opens.

    The name of the
    new style is also
    shown in the title
    bar.

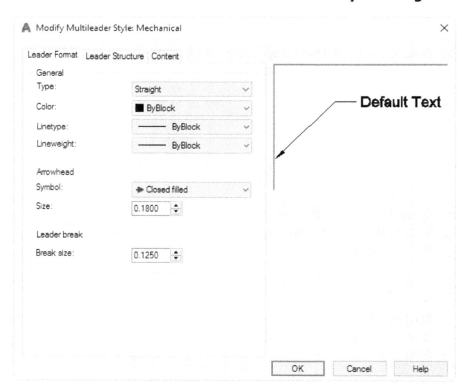

**Modify Multileader Style Dialog Box**

24. Make the following changes to the style:

   In the Leader Format tab, change the arrowhead size to .2500.

   In the Leader Structure tab, change the landing distance to .3750.

   In the Content tab, change the text height to .2500.

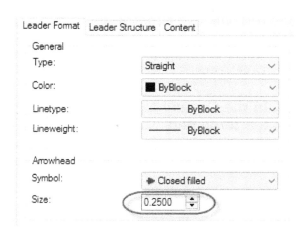

**Arrowhead Setting Changed**

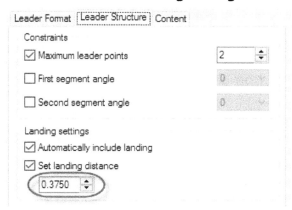

**Landing Distance Changed**

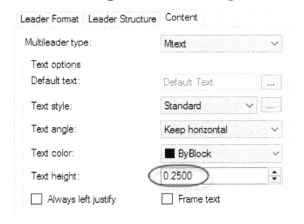

**Text Height Changed**

25. You will also change the Font of the text.

    This will involve changing the Standard Text style.

    In the Content tab, click the button with the three dots "…" next to the Standard text style.

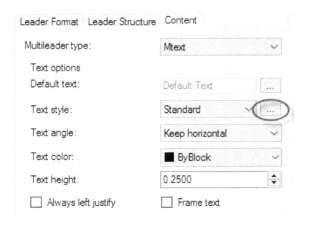

26. The Text Style dialog box opens.

    Change the font name setting to Romans.shx.

    **Note:** Leave the height of the text set to 0.0000. The text height will be controlled by the Multileader settings.

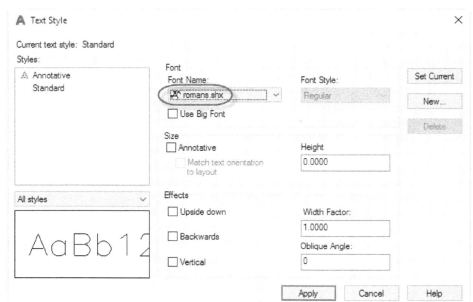

**Text Style Font Name Changed**

27. Click the Apply button then the Close button to close the Text Style dialog box.

    Then click the OK button to close the Modify Multileader Style dialog box.

    Confirm that the Mechanical Style is your current style and click the Close button to close the Multileader Style Manager dialog box.

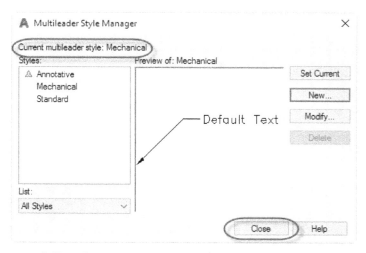

**Multileader Style: Mechanical Set to Current**

28. To add the leader, click on the
Leader tool and snap on Point A to
place the arrowhead.

Click the second point to locate the
text.

Type in the words for the note.

Click outside the text editor box to
complete the process.

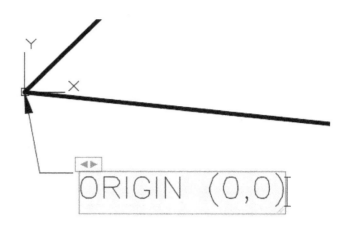

**Adding the Text**

29. Click on the leader and move the
text by grabbing the blue handle to
the left of the text.

Place the leader text as shown in
the example.

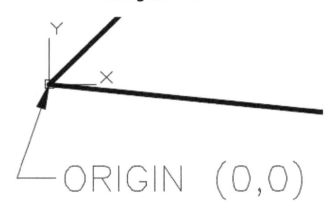

**Final Location of the Text**

30. Add the letters for the point
locations.

Use the same font and size as the
leader text.

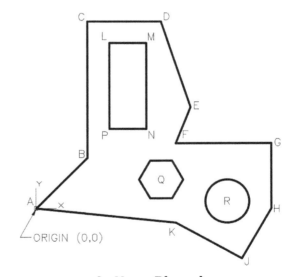

**Letters Placed**

31. Save the project. This concludes the tutorial.

In a later tutorial you will plot the drawing to paper and as a PDF file.

# ABSOLUTE COORDINATE
## EXERCISE

NAME: DAVE MARTIN
DATE: 8-28-2016
PROJECT#: PROJ-01

| POINT | ABSOLUTE COORDINATES | |
|---|---|---|
| | X | Y |
| A | 0.00 | 0.00 |
| B | 1.75 | 1.75 |
| C | 1.75 | 6.50 |
| D | 4.25 | 6.50 |
| E | 5.25 | 3.50 |
| F | 4.70 | 2.25 |
| G | 8.00 | 2.25 |
| H | 8.00 | 0.00 |
| J | 7.00 | -1.75 |
| K | 4.75 | -0.50 |
| L | 2.50 | 5.75 |
| M | 3.75 | 5.75 |
| N | 3.75 | 2.75 |
| P | 2.50 | 2.75 |
| Q | 4.25 | 1.00 |
| R | 6.50 | 0.25 |

NOTES:
1. CIRCLE "R" IS 1.50 IN DIAMETER.
2. HEXAGON "Q" IS INSCRIBED INSIDE A 1.50 DIA. CIRCLE.
3. PART IS 1.25 THICK.

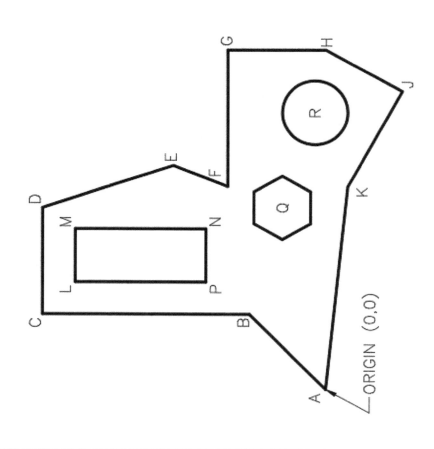

ORIGIN (0,0)

# Project #2 – Relative Coordinate Exercise

**Filename:** PROJ-02.dwg
Note: All screenshots are from the Autodesk® AutoCAD® software.

**Description:** Now that you have been introduced to some of basic the AutoCAD tools and techniques, you will continue with a similar project. This project will continue with the use of coordinate entry to place lines but will use relative coordinates instead of absolute. Instead of starting from a new file, you will use PROJ-01.dwg as your starting file.

Creating the New File and Drawing the Shape

1.  Open PROJ-01.dwg and save the drawing as PROJ-02.dwg.

    **Note:** If you are immediately starting the project just after completing PROJ-01, save the file before using the Save As... command to save as PROJ-02.

2.  Keep and use the same layer setup as PROJ-01.

    In the Layers panel, set Object Lines as your current layer.

3.  Select and move the shape to the left of the border. You will use some of the elements for the new project.

4.  Since the points for this project are using relative coordinates, you will place the first point with the mouse.

5.  After placing the first point, use the coordinate display for point B.

    Type the "@" symbol before the coordinates.

    After typing in the length, type the "<" symbol to indicate that the next value will be an angle measurement.

    The symbol will disappear after the angle in entered.

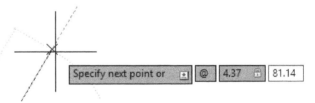

**Coordinate for Point A**

6. Continue with the next point until the shape is complete.

   If you lose your place, snap the line endpoint at the previous point to continue.

   When you get to point L, snap the line back to point A.

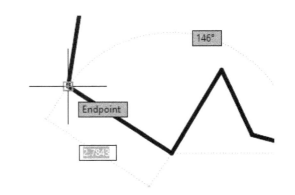

**Snap the Line Endpoint to Point A**

7. To check the line from point L to point A for accuracy, select the line and right-click Properties to open the Properties Window.

   You should keep the Properties window open while drawing the projects.

   **Note:** You may also open the Properties window at any time by using the PROPS key-in command.

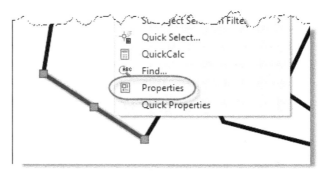

**Opening the Properties Window**

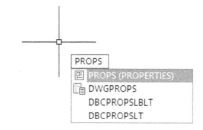

**PROPS Key-in Command**

8. To see the precision of the angle of the line to two decimal places, open the Drawing Units dialog box and change the Angle Precision setting to 0.00.

   **Note:** Use the DDUNITS key-in to open the dialog box.

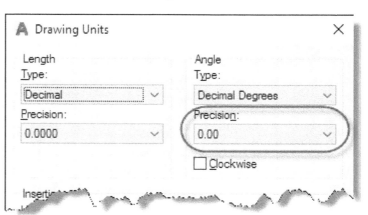

**Angle Precision Changed to 0.00**

9.  The length and angle values for the
    line are in the Geometry portion of
    the Properties window.

    **Note:** The other values will be
    different for your drawing.

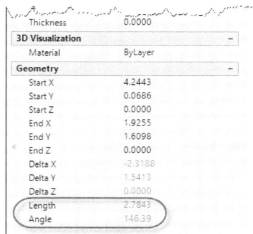

**Length and Angle for Line L to A**

## Modifying the Table

1.  You will need to stretch the width of
    the columns before editing the text.

    The original width of the three
    columns is 1.500.

    You will use the Stretch tool to
    change the width of each column to
    2.000.

**Stretch Tool**

2.  Click on the Stretch tool.

    Select the objects on the left side of the table using the fence
    option.

    Start the fence on the right side of the line to place a crossing
    fence.

    The color of the fence will be light green.

    Click the second point below and to the left of the bottom left
    corner of the table.

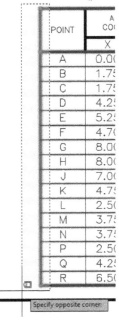

**Fence Placed**

3.  Press the Enter key to accept the selection.

4. Click a point near the table for the first point of displacement and drag the cursor to the left.

   Make sure that polar tracking is keeping the second location horizontal.

   Type .5 for the second point. You will see the fence stretch to the left.

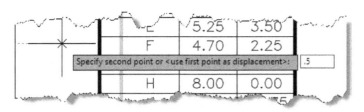

**Second Point .5 from the First Point**

5. The column is now stretched .5 to the left.

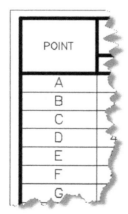

**Column Stretched**

6. To re-center the text in the column, move the text half the distance stretched, or .25 to the left.

**Text Re-centered**

7. Stretch the other two columns to 2.000 wide and re-center the text.

   When stretching the other columns, complete enclose the first column so that the width is not changed.

| POINT | |
|---|---|
| A | 0 |
| B | 1 |
| C | 1 |
| D | 4 |
| E | 5 |
| F | 4 |
| G | 8 |
| H | 8 |
| J | 7 |
| K | 4 |
| L | 2 |
| M | 3 |
| N | 3 |
| P | 2 |
| Q | 4 |
| R | 6 |

Specify opposite corner or

**Fence Location for Stretching the Second Column**

8. The columns are now at their correct width.

| POINT | ABSOLUTE COORDINATES | |
|---|---|---|
| | X | Y |
| A | 0.00 | 0.00 |
| B | 1.75 | 1.75 |
| C | 1.75 | 6.50 |

**Columns at 2.000 Width**

9. Double-click on the text to edit it to match the example.

   When editing the columns, do not delete all of the text. Leave the first line of text to maintain the spacing that was set up in the previous project.

   You will also need to increase the width of the text column to accommodate the text.

   Click and drag the upper right side of the window to the right.

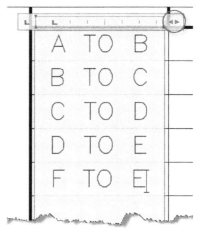

**Adding the Text and Increasing the Width**

10. Edit the remaining text to match the example.

11. Add the text for the points. Use the same size as in the previous project.

12. Save the project. This concludes the tutorial.

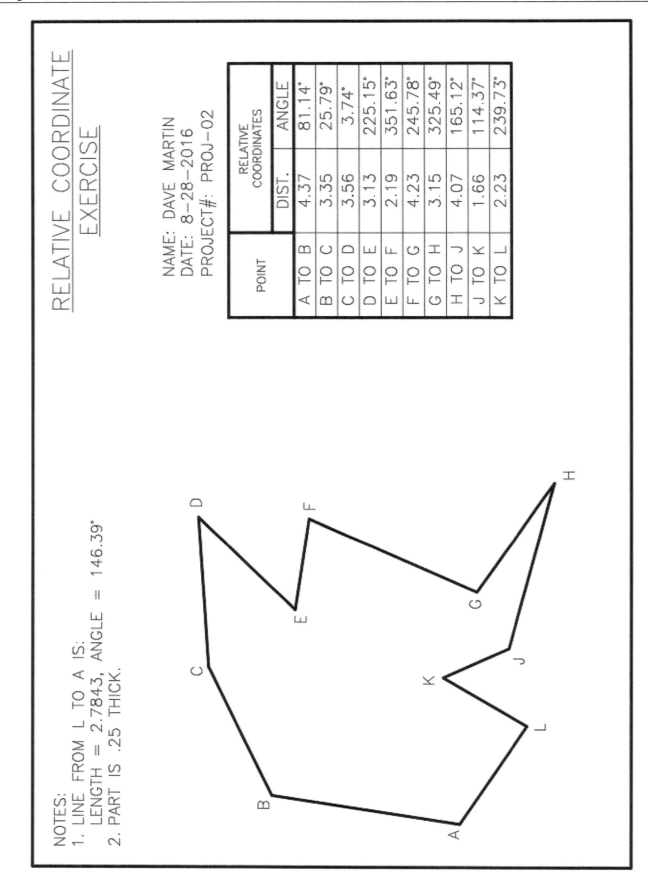

RELATIVE COORDINATE
EXERCISE

NAME: DAVE MARTIN
DATE: 8-28-2016
PROJECT#: PROJ-02

| POINT | RELATIVE COORDINATES | |
|---|---|---|
| | DIST. | ANGLE |
| A TO B | 4.37 | 81.14° |
| B TO C | 3.35 | 25.79° |
| C TO D | 3.56 | 3.74° |
| D TO E | 3.13 | 225.15° |
| E TO F | 2.19 | 351.63° |
| F TO G | 4.23 | 245.78° |
| G TO H | 3.15 | 325.49° |
| H TO J | 4.07 | 165.12° |
| J TO K | 1.66 | 114.37° |
| K TO L | 2.23 | 239.73° |

NOTES:
1. LINE FROM L TO A IS:
   LENGTH = 2.7843, ANGLE = 146.39°
2. PART IS .25 THICK.

# Project #3 – Bracket

**Filename:** PROJ-03.dwg
Note: All screenshots are from the Autodesk® AutoCAD® software.

**Description:** This project will use orthographic projection and the miter line technique to create the views. You will create a dimension style to dimension the views and additional layers and linetypes will be used.

Beginning the Project

1.  Open PROJ-02.dwg and save the drawing as PROJ-03.dwg.

    **Note:** If you are immediately starting the project just after completing PROJ-02, save the file before using the Save As... command to save as PROJ-03.

2.  Delete all the objects in the file. You will not need any elements from the previous project.

Loading the Custom Linetypes and Creating the New Layers

1.  Before creating the layers, you will load the custom linetype from the support files on the website.

    The name of the file is "acad-md.lin" (the letters "md" stand for mechanical drawing). Before continuing, download this file to your local drive.

    **Note:** This file was modified from the original linetype file (acad.lin) that came with the program.

2.  Type LINETYPE and then press Enter in the command line to open the Linetype Manager dialog box.

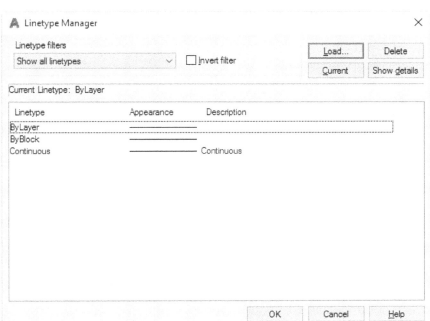

**Linetype Manager Dialog Box**

3.  Click the Load... button to load the new linetypes.

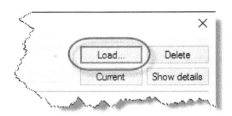

**Load... Button**

4.  The Load or Reload Linetypes dialog box opens.

    Click on the File... button and navigate to where you saved the acad-md.lin file from the website.

    **Note:** Your file location path will be different.

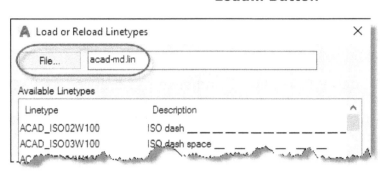

**Custom Linetype File Selected**

5.  Choose the following linetypes in the Available Linetypes window:

    CENTER
    CENTER-Short
    CENTER-X-Short
    HIDDEN
    PHANTOM
    PHANTOM-Short
    PHANTOM-X-Short

    **Note:** You may select multiple linetypes by using the mouse button with the Ctrl key pressed.

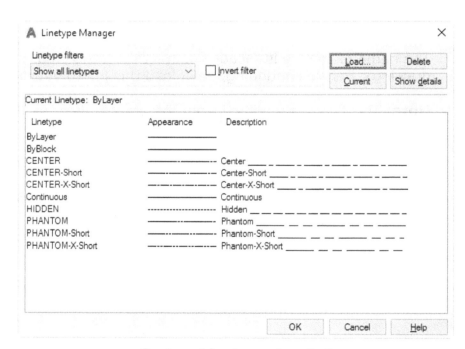

**Custom Linetypes Loaded**

6.  Press OK to close the dialog box.

    Open the Layer Properties Manager dialog box.

7. Refer to the layer setup page at the beginning of the book for the layers to create and their properties. There will be additional levels added to this drawing. You may also refer to the diagram below for their names and properties.

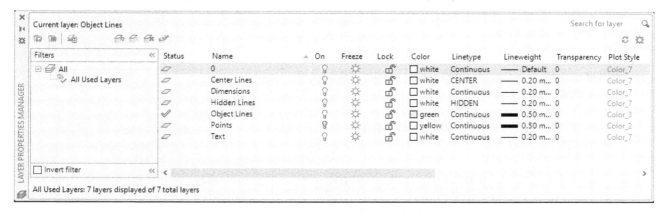

**Layer Setup for Project #3**

8. The Layers and Linetypes are setup. When starting the next project, you will use this file as your starting file. This way, you will not need to repeat this process.

## Copying and Pasting the Title Block

1. As stated at the beginning of project PROJ-01, you are provided with the border files you will need for the projects in this book.

   If you have not done so already, download and open the A-Size border file (A-Size Border.dwg) located in the Support Files portion of the website.

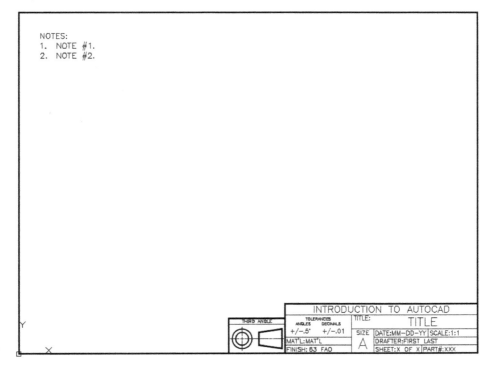

**A-Size Border**

2.  Select the entire border and copy to clipboard.

    Use the Copy Clip tool located in the Home tab, Clipboard panel.

**Copy Tool**

3.  Switch to the PROJ-03 file and paste the title block into your file.

    When pasting, use the Paste to Original Coordinates option.

    This will locate the elements at the same location relative to the origin (0,0) of the drawing.

    **Note:** When switching to another drawing try using the Drawing Tabs at the top left of the drawing area.

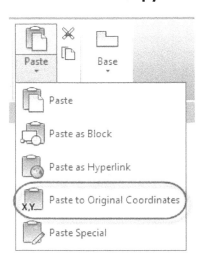

**Paste to Original Coordinates Option**

**Drawing Tabs**

Beginning the Drawing (Front View)

1.  Begin with the front view.

    Refer to the sample drawing for sizes.

    Other sizes will be on the top and right side views.

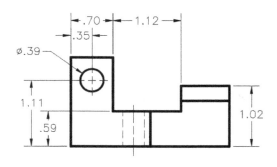

**Completed Front View**

2.  Begin by drawing the overall width and height.

    The width of the part is 2.63 and the height is 1.51. These dimensions are shown on other views.

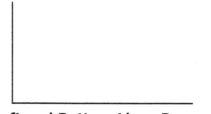

**Left and Bottom Lines Drawn**

3.  Snap a line to the top and draw .70 to the right.

    Use the Offset tool to copy the bottom line .59 up.

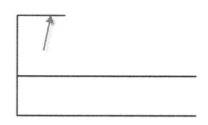

**Line Offset**

4.  Draw a 1.02 vertical line on the left side from the bottom.

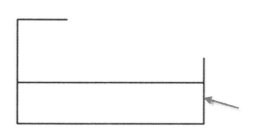

**Vertical Line Added**

5.  Draw and vertical line from the end of the top horizontal line. Use approximately .50 for the length.

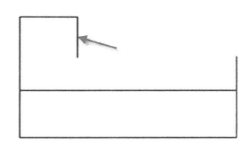

**Line Added**

6.  Use the Fillet tool to trim the line to the upper horizontal line.

    By default the Fillet tool is set to a zero radius.

    This tool is also used to create rounded corners.

**Fillet Tool**

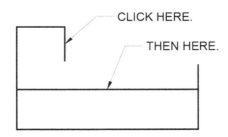

CLICK HERE.

THEN HERE.

**Lines Picked to Fillet**

7.  The corner is trimmed.

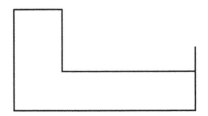

**Lines Trimmed**

8.  Offset the second vertical line 1.12 to the right and add a horizontal line from the top of the right vertical line.

    Use Fillet to trim the corners as shown.

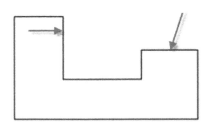

**Line Added and Corners Trimmed**

9.  To add the circle, you will use two different methods.

    In the first method you will offset two lines and add the circle at the intersection.

    Offset the left line .35 to the right and the bottom line 1.11 up.

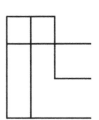

**Lines Offset**

10. Using the Circle tool, snap the center at the intersection of the lines.

    Set the diameter of the circle using the diameter option. Press "D" while in the command to activate. The size is .39.

    Delete the two lines when finished.

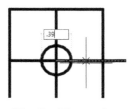

**Circle Placed**

11. The second method will use the FROM command modifier and coordinate key-in to locate the center of the circle.

    Delete the circle to try this second method.

12. Click the circle tool.

    For the first point, type "from" instead of the coordinate.

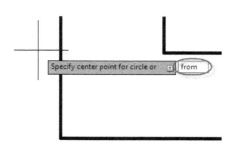

**FROM Key-in**

13. The coordinate display will change to Base Point.

    Snap at the lower left corner of the view.

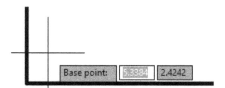

**Change to Base Point**

14. The display will change to Offset.

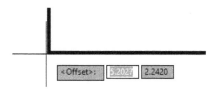

**Offset Display**

15. Drag the mouse up and to the right from the point.

    Type the "@" symbol for relative coordinates and .35, 1.11 for the location of the center of the circle.

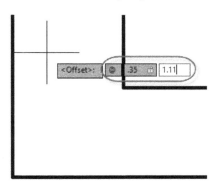

**Coordinates Entered**

16. Press the Enter key.

    The new circle center will be .35 to the right and 1.11 up from the corner of the view.

    Enter the size of the circle as before.

**Circle Placed**

17. This as far as you will go with the front view for now.

    You will use the top and side views to locate the remaining lines.

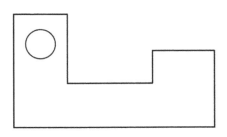

**Front View Progress**

Projecting the Top and Side Views

Next you will project vertical and horizontal lines from the edge of the front view.

This is similar to the process you would use if you were drawing the elements using traditional methods (pencil and paper).

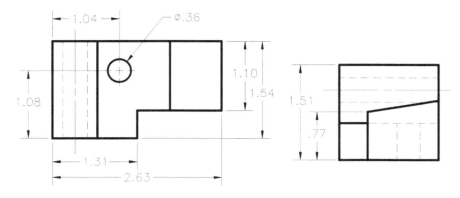

**Completed Top and Side Views**

1. Draw lines from the vertical lines in the front view as shown.

   Make sure to snap on the ends of the lines and the edges of the circle when drawing.

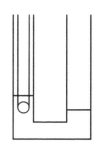

**Lines Projected**

2. Draw two lines 1.54 apart above the front view.

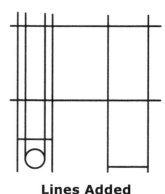

**Lines Added**

3. Use the Trim tool update the view as shown.

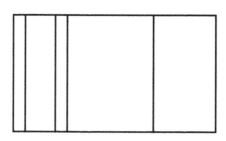

**Lines Trimmed**

4.  Use the Offset and Trim tools to draw the corner notch at the lower right corner of the view.

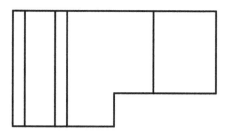

**Notch Drawn**

5.  Place the circle using either technique discussed in the previous section.

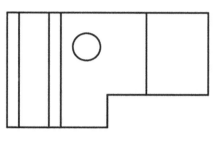

**Circle Placed**

6.  Two of the lines will need to be changed to the Hidden linetype.

    This will be done by changing the layer that the lines are on.

    Select the two lines for the edge of the circle and select the Hidden layer in the Layers panel. (See examples on next page.)

    **Note:** This will only change the lines to the new layer. The current layer will remain Object Lines.

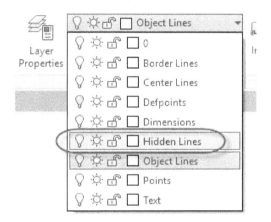

**Hidden Layer Selected**

7.  Project lines from the edges of the front view to the right side.

**Lines Projected to Right**

8. For the vertical lines, you will use the Miter Line Technique.

   Draw lines from the bottom of the top view to the right and up from where the left side of the right view will be.

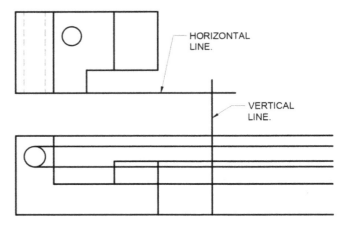

**Horizontal and Vertical Lines Added**

9. Draw a 45 degree line from the intersection of the two lines.

   Make the line long enough to extend above the top edge of the top view.

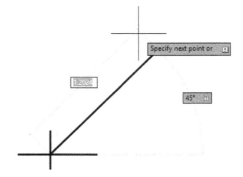

**45 Degree Line**

10. Draw horizontal lines from the top view to the miter line.

    Using Object Tracking and the Intersection Snap to end the lines at the miter line.

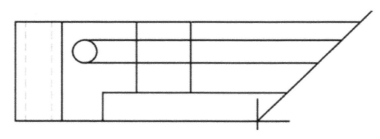

**Lines Projected to Miter Line**

11. Draw vertical lines down to the right side view.

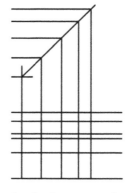

**Vertical Lines Projected**

12. Trim the lines as shown.

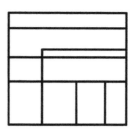

**Lines Trimmed**

13. Offset the bottom line up .77 inches.

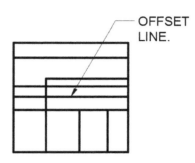

OFFSET
LINE.

**Offset Line.**

14. Snap a line from the lower left intersection to the upper right intersection as shown.

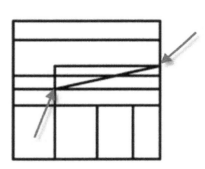

**Line Snapped to Intersections**

15. Trim and delete the lines to complete the object lines for the view.

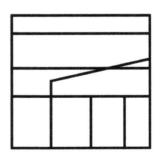

**Lines Trimmed and Deleted**

16. Change the edges of the circle to hidden lines.

    You will need to break the horizontal line to make a portion of it hidden. Use the Break tool in the Modify panel to do this.

    The tool is located in the extra tools below the panel. Click the down arrow next to Modify at the bottom of the panel to see these tools.

**Down Arrow**

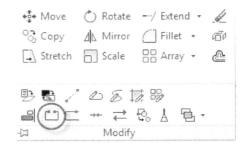

**Break Tool**

17. Click Break tool and then the horizontal line. You will see the line change into two parts.

    Click again to end the command.

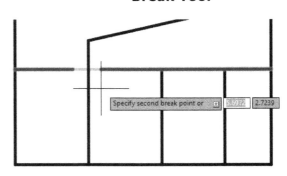

**Breaking the Line into Two Parts**

18. Change the lines to the Hidden layer and extend the lines to meet the vertical line.

    Use the Extend tool under the Trim tool to do this.

    This tool works the same way as the Trim tool except lines are extended to meet with the other lines.

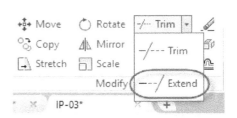

**Extend Tool**

19. This will complete the right side view.

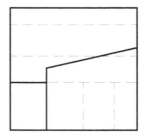

**Right Side View Completed**

20. Project the remaining lines from the top and side views back to the front view to completed the views.

    Trim and change the layers of the lines.

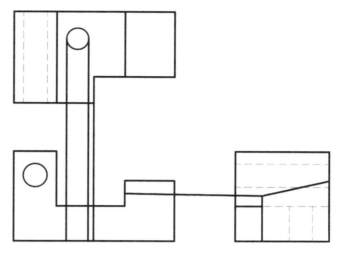

**Lines Projected**

21. At this point the object lines and hidden lines are completed for the three views.

    Next you will add center lines and dimensions.

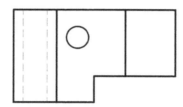

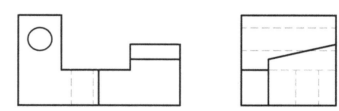

**Objects Lines and Hidden Lines Completed**

Setting Up the Dimension Styles for the Drawing

You will begin this section by setting up dimension styles for your drawing. These styles will continue to be used in later projects and will be modified depending on the dimensioning requirements.

1. Click on the Annotate tab at the top of the screen.

   These tools are used to add text, dimensions, leaders, tables, and markups to the drawing.

**Annotate Tab**

2. Click on the small arrow at the bottom right corner of the Dimensions panel.

   This will open the Dimension Style dialog box.

**Dimensions Panel**

3. The dialog box opens.

   This dialog box will be used to setup the various setting for the dimensioning used on this project.

   You will begin with the Standard style as a base style and create a new style from it.

   Click the New... button on the right to create a new style.

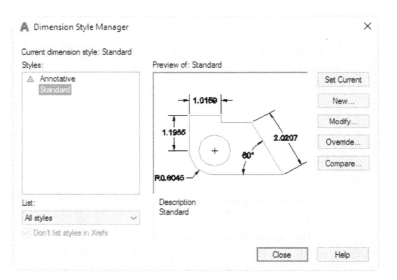

**Dimension Style Manager**

4. The Create New Dimension Style dialog box opens.

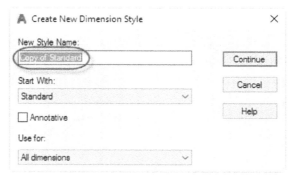

**Create New Dimension Style Dialog Box**

5.  Rename the style "Mech 1-1".

    This means: Mechanical Style and Full
    Scale (1:1).

    Press the Continue button to move to
    the next step.

**Style Renamed**

6.  The New Dimension
    Style: Mech 1-1 dialog
    box opens.

    As you change the
    setting for the style,
    you will press on the
    tabs at the top.

    Each tab controls
    different parts of the
    style.

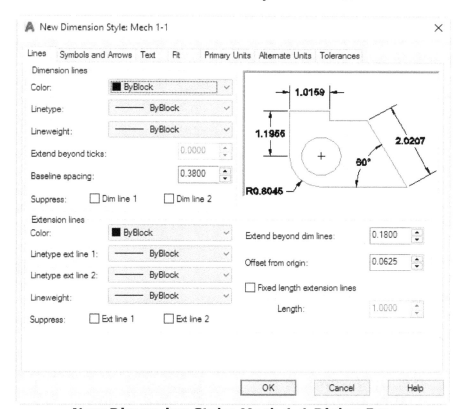

**New Dimension Style: Mech 1-1 Dialog Box**

7. Click on the Lines tab and make the following changes:

   Set the Extend beyond dim lines setting to 0.125.

   Set the Baseline spacing setting to .2500

   **Note:** As you make changes you will see the preview of the dimension style update.

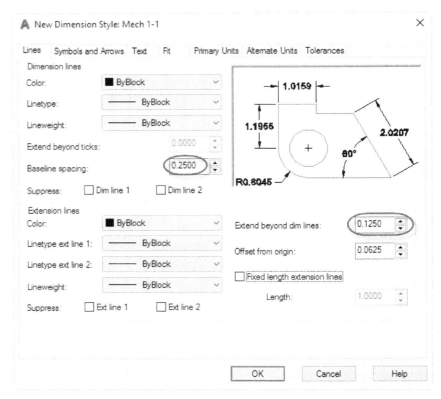

**Lines Tab Settings Changed**

8. Click on the Symbols and Arrows tab and make the following changes:

   Set the Arrow size setting to 0.125.

   Set the Center marks setting to None.

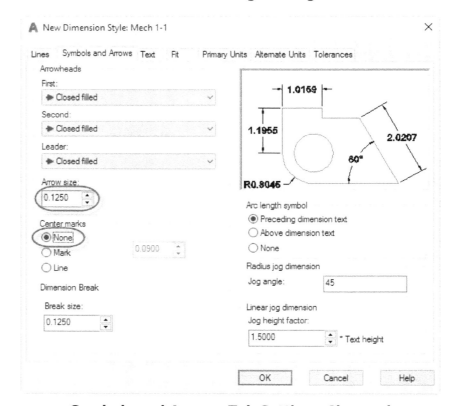

**Symbols and Arrows Tab Settings Changed**

9.  Click on the Text tab and make the following changes:

    Change the Text Style setting to MECHANICAL. (This style was added to the drawing when the title block file was pasted into the drawing.)

    Change the Text height to 0.125.

    Change the Offset from dim line setting to .0625.
    (This controls the gap between the start and end of the dimension text and the dimension line.)

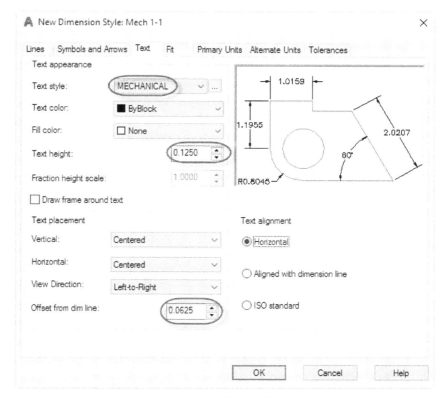

**Text Tab Settings Changed**

10. Click on the Fit tab and make the following change:

    Click the checkbox for Place text manually. This will allow you to move the text after the dimension has been placed.

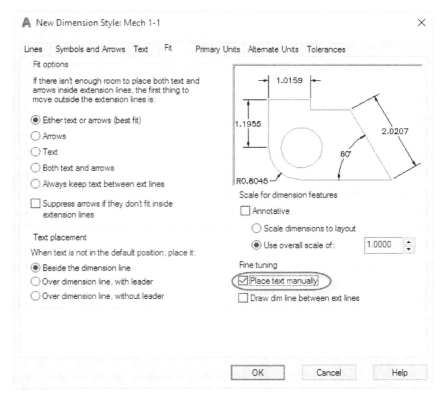

**Fit Tab Settings Changed**

11. Click on the Primary Units tab and make the following changes:

    Change the Precision setting to 0.00.

    Click the checkbox for Leading zero suppression.

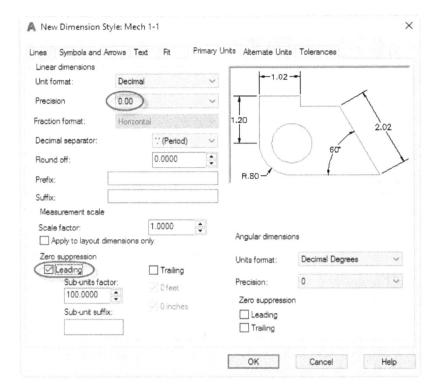

**Primary Units Tab Settings Changed**

12. The two remaining tabs will remain the same.

    Press the OK button to close the dialog box.

    The dimension style is now set up.

13. Create another style called Center Marks.

    Use the Mech 1-1 style as the beginning style.

    **Note:** This style will be used if adding center marks as part of a radial dimension.

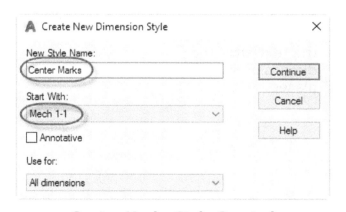

**Center Marks Style Created**

14. Make one change to the style.

    In the Symbols and Arrows tab, click the button for Line in the Center Marks area.

**Center Marks Set to Line**

15. The two dimension styles are now set up.

## Adding the Center Lines and Center Marks

When adding center marks, you have two options: The first is to add the marks as separate elements. The second is to add the center mark as part of a radial dimension. The first method is preferable because this way it will allow you to modify the center mark and have it separate from the dimension.

1. Set your current layer to the Center Lines level.

**Current Layer Set to Center Lines**

2. Before adding the center mark, you will need to modify the size of the gaps and the line style.

   Type CENTERCROSSSIZE to access the system variable.

   Set the size of the cross to .125.

   **Note:** You may also set the cross size relative to the size of the circle by adding an "x" after the value.

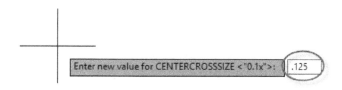

**CENTERCROSSSIZE Set to .125**

3. To change the gap size, type CENTERCROSSGAP.

   Set the size of the gap to .0625.

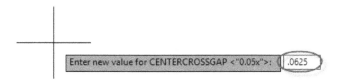

**CENTERCROSSGAP Set to .0625**

4. To change the default line type, type CENTERLTYPE.

   Set the value to "." (period) to use the current line type.

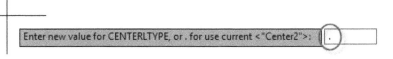

**CENTERLTYPE Set to "." (Period)**

5. Click on the Center Mark tool.

   This is located in the Annotate tab, Centerlines panel.

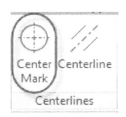

**Center Mark Tool**

6.  Click on the edges of the two circles to add the center marks.

    You may adjust the lengths of the lines by selected and then stretching with the handles.

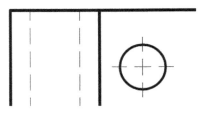

**Center Mark Added**

7.  Click on the Centerline tool to add the center lines. This tool will automatically place the center line halfway and parallel between two picked lines.

    The lines should extend between .25 and .50 inches beyond the edge of the view. Use the grids to help do this.

    You may notice that the two shorter center lines are not showing the dashes.

    Select the CENTER-Short or CENTER-X-Short linetype for the linetype.

    This is done in the Home tab, Properties panel.

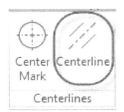

**Centerline Tool**

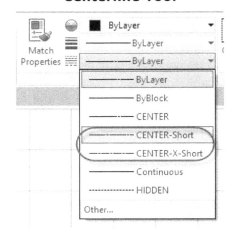

**CENTER-Short and
CENTER-X-Short Linetypes**

8.  The center lines and center marks are now added.

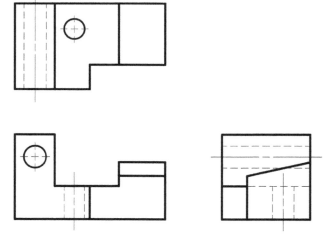

**Center Lines and Center Marks Added**

## Dimensioning the Drawing

1.  Before adding the dimensions you may need to move the views farther away from one another.

    Change the active style of the dimensions to Mech 1-1. This is done in the Home tab, Annotation panel.

    Click on the down arrow next to the word Annotation to do this.

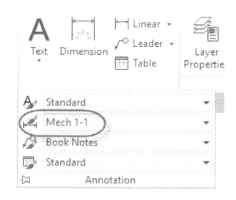

**Change Dimension Style to Mech 1-1**

2.  Begin by clicking on the Linear tool in the Annotation panel.

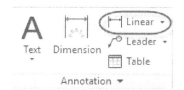

**Linear Tool**

3.  Add the vertical dimensions in the right side view first.

    Snap on the lower left corner of the view then the corner.

    Drag the dimension line approximately 1 1/2 grid squares away from the view for the third point. You may also move the text up and point during this step.

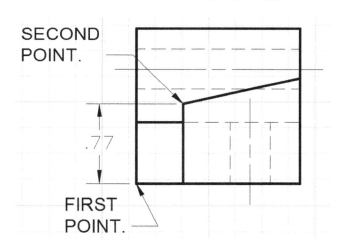

**Dimension Endpoints**

4.  For the next dimension, click on the Dimension tool in the panel.

    Right-click in the drawing area and select the Baseline option.

    Click the first dimension and then snap on the upper left corner of the view.

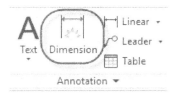

**Dimension Tool**

5.  After placing the dimension, select it and drag the text
    to the correct location.

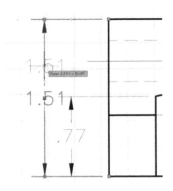

**Moving the Dimension Text**

6.  When placing the chain dimensions
    use the Continue option.

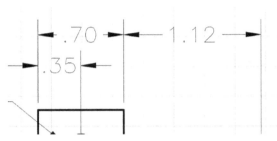

**Chain Dimension**

7.  Repeat the process for the other linear
    dimensions.

    When dimensioning the hole centers,
    snap to the edge of the circle so that
    you do not cover the gap in the center
    mark.

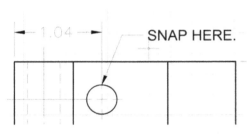

**Snap Point for Dimensioning Hole Centers**

8.  Your views should look
    like this when finished.

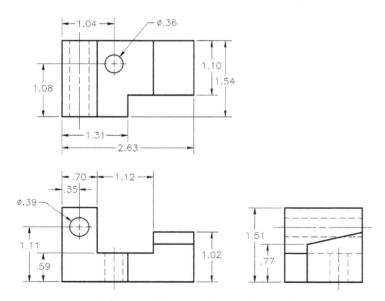

**Linear Dimensions Placed**

9.  Next you will place the radial dimensions.

    Click the down arrow next to the Linear dimension
    tool to expose the other tools.

    Select the Diameter dimension tool.

    Click on the edge of the circle to place the
    dimension.

    The angle of the leader line should be between 30
    and 60 degrees.

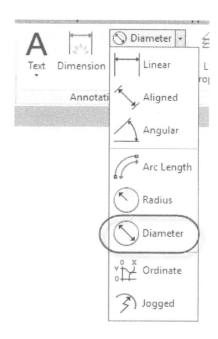

**Diameter Dimension Tool**

10. The diameter symbol with be automatically placed
    in front of the value.

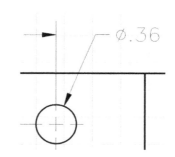

**Diameter Dimension Placed**

Filling Out the Title Block and the Drawing Notes

1.  Zoom in on the title block.

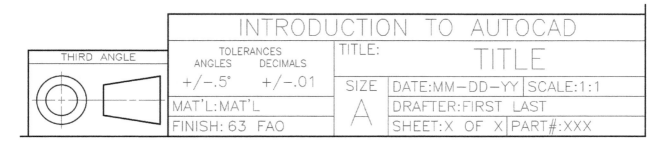

**Title Block for Project #3**

When the title block was created, the text fields were set up as part of a block
attribute.

This was done to make the title block easier to fill out.

2. Double-click on the word TITLE in the title block.

   The Enhanced Attribute Editor dialog box opens.

**Enhanced Attribute Editor Dialog Box**

3. To fill out the title block, click on the tag and update the Value field.

   Some of the fields have been filled out partially. Refer to the Prompt for the meaning of the information in each field.

   When finished, click the OK button.

**Dialog Box with Fields Filled Out**

4. In the upper left corner of the border text has been provided for drawing notes.

   Double-click on the text to enter the appropriate information.

**Drawing Note Filled Out**

   If entering multiple notes, the lines will automatically number themselves.

5. Save the project. This concludes the tutorial.

   In the next tutorial you will plot the drawing to paper and as a PDF file.

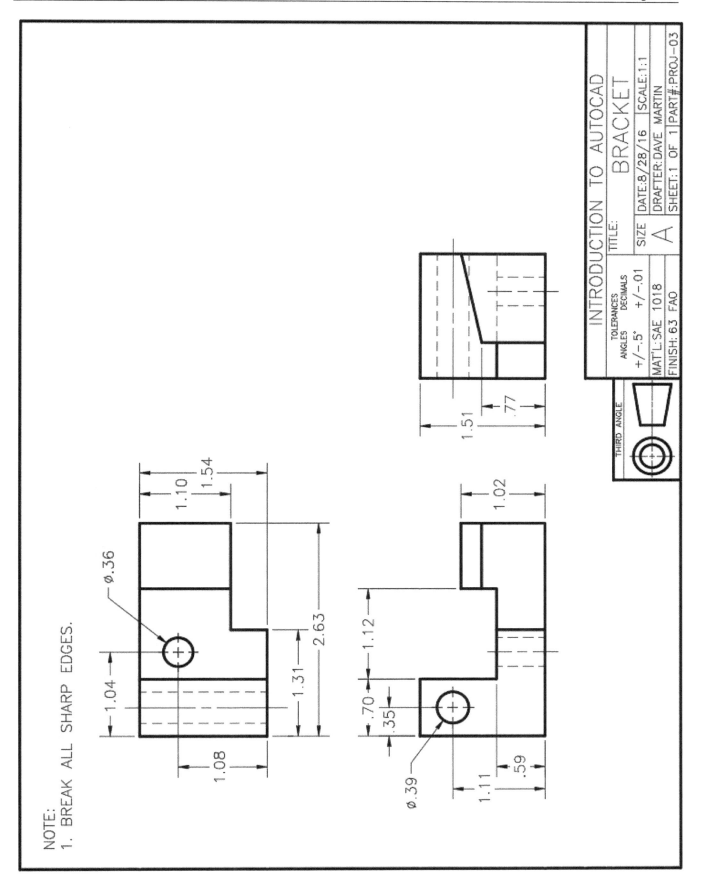

NOTE:
1. BREAK ALL SHARP EDGES.

INTRODUCTION TO AUTOCAD

TITLE:

BRACKET

SIZE | DATE:8/28/16 | SCALE:1:1
A | DRAFTER:DAVE MARTIN
| SHEET:1 OF 1 | PART#:PROJ-03

TOLERANCES
ANGLES      DECIMALS
+/-.5°      +/-.01

MAT'L:SAE 1018
FINISH: 63 FAO

THIRD ANGLE

# Printing Your Drawing

Note: All screenshots are from the Autodesk® AutoCAD® software.

**Description:** The procedure will introduce you to the process of printing your drawings. Two methods will be discussed; printing to a printer and to a PDF file.

## Printing the Drawing to a Printer

In this procedure you will use Project #3 as the example for printing.

1.  Open the PROJ-03.dwg file and fit the drawing to the view. At this point the drawing should be finished and ready for printing.

    This first procedure will cover printing the drawing to an actual printer.

2.  Click on the Print tool in the Quick Access Toolbar at the top left of the screen.

    You may also select the Print tool in the Application menu.

**Print Tool Locations**

4.  The Plot - Model dialog box opens.

    **Note:** Your settings will most likely be different than these. Depending of which type of printer is installed, the settings will change.

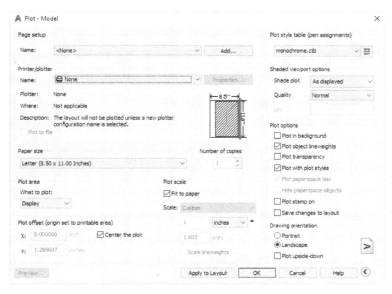

**Print Dialog Box**

5. Click on the down arrow for the Name: field under Printer/plotter.

   If you have a printer connected to your computer, choose it from the list.

   In this example a Canon MP495 series printer will be used.

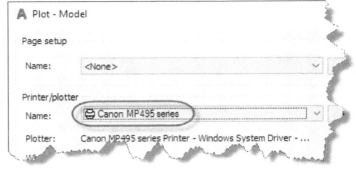

**Printer Name**

6. Set the paper size to letter size or ANSI A.

   Your choices may be different depending on the printer configuration.

**Paper Size**

7. Confirm the setting or set the drawing orientation to Landscape.

**Drawing Orientation**

8. Set the Plot scale to 1:1 (Full scale).

   **Note:** This setting will change depending on the plot scale of the drawing.

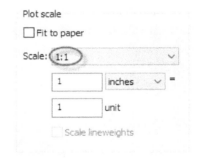

**Plot Scale**

9. Set the Plot style table (pen assignments) to Monochrome.

   Answer "Yes" when asked to Assign this plot style table to all layouts.

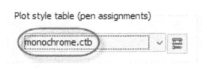

**Plot Style Table**

10. Click the checkbox for the Plot offset (origin set to printable area) next to "Center the plot".

    Your X and Y values will be different.

**Plot Offset**

11. Click the Apply to Layout button at the bottom to save the settings and then close the Plot dialog box.

**Apply to Layout Button**

12. Now that the settings are entered, the next thing is to set the Window for the plot.

    The title block file is provided with small points at the upper left and lower right corners of the border.

    The reason for these points is to insure that the full width of the border lines is printed.

    You will use these points to set the size of the window.

    To see the points, type in the key-in PTYPE and set the Point Style as shown.

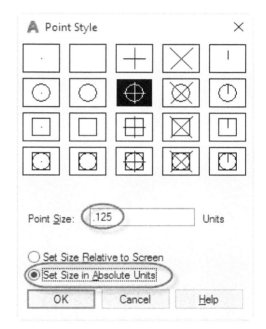

**Point Style Dialog Box**

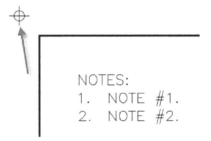

**Point at Upper Left Corner
of Border**

13. Re-open the Plot dialog box.

    Set the "What to plot" setting to Window.

    Click on the Window< button to the right.

    Snap to the upper left point and then the lower right point. The Node snap mode will be used when snapping to the points.

**Plot Area Set to Window and Window< Button**

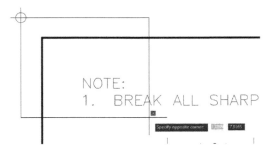

**Snapping the Upper Left Corner of the Window**

14. After snapping the second point, the Plot dialog box will re-open.

    You will see red lines in the preview area. This is normal.

    As long as the entire border is visible when the plot is previewed, the drawing will print correctly.

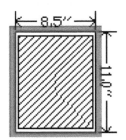

**Preview Area**

15. To see a full preview of the drawing before plotting, click the Preview... button at the lower left corner of the dialog box.

    To close the Preview window, click the "X" icon at the top left of the screen.

    **Note:** Some printers will not be able to fit the entire border on the sheet. If this is the case with your printer, change the scale to Fit to Paper. You may also get a better result if you first print the drawing as a PDF and then print the file.

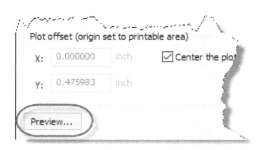

**Preview Button**

**Close Preview Window Button**

16. Click the Apply to Layout button to once again to save the plot settings.

    Press the OK button to send the drawing to the printer.

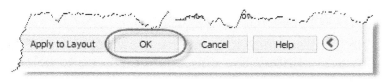

**OK Button**

17. To print Projects #1 and #2, use the same settings as before with the exception of the scale.

    For these two drawings you will use 1:2 scale (Half scale).

    These two drawing will not have points to snap to at the corners. You may estimate the window corners instead.

Saving the Print Settings

Before creating the PDF file, you will save the print settings from the previous section.

1.  Open the Plot dialog box.

2.  Create a Page setup name for the file.

    Click the Add... button next to the Page setup name.

**Add... Button**

3.  The Add Page Setup dialog box opens.

    Enter the name of your printer as the new page setup name.

    Click OK to close the dialog box.

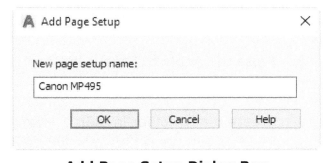

**Add Page Setup Dialog Box**

4.  By saving the page setup, you may switch from one setup to another without having to change the settings for the plot.

    These settings will be saved to the next file when you save the drawing again.

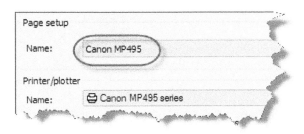

**New Page Setup**

Printing to a PDF File

The print settings to print the drawing as a PDF file will be similar to printing to a physical printer. The only change will be to select a different Print Driver.

1.  Open the Plot dialog box.

2.  Select the AutoCAD PDF (High Quality Print) printer configuration file.

    Confirm the other settings are the same as with the physical printer setup.

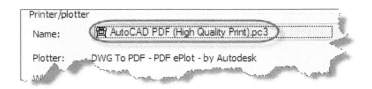

**PDF Printer Configuration**

3.  Set the paper size to ANSI full bleed A (8.50 x 11.00 Inches).

**Paper Size Setting**

4.  Press the Preview... button to preview the drawing.

5.  Save the Page setup as PDF

**Page Setup**

6.  Press the Apply to Layout button.

7.  Press OK to create the PDF file.

    Create a new folder in your 1 – Projects – 2D folder called: PDF Files. The default name of the file is PROJ-03-Model.pdf. Modify the name of the file to PROJ-03.pdf

**PDF File Name**

8.  This concludes the tutorial.

    From here on, create PDFs of your files as they are completed.

# Project #4 – Plate

**Filename:** PROJ-04.dwg
Note: All screenshots are from the Autodesk® AutoCAD® software.

**Description:** This project will introduce you to the use of the Arc tool, angular dimensioning, and constructing fillets.

> **Note:** At this point in the book you may choose to move to Part Two – 3D Projects. This part of the book contains tutorials about creating 3D versions of the Projects. After the third 3D project, there is a procedure to create 2D views from the 3D solid. You may wish to use this method to create your views instead on drawing the views using 2D methods. Some procedures in Part Two will utilize elements created in Part One.

## Beginning the Project

1.  Open PROJ-03.dwg and save the drawing as PROJ-04.dwg.

2.  Delete the objects left over from PROJ-03. Leave the title block and general notes.

3.  Edit the text in the title block and the notes in the upper left corner of the border.

## Drawing the Object (Outside Shape and Circle)

1.  When beginning the drawing, it may help to draw the view outside of the border. After you are finished you may move the view into the border.

    Begin at the lower left corner of the view.

    Draw a 1.73 vertical line and a 1.33 horizontal line.

**Lines Drawn**

2.  Draw the .58 diameter circle from the corner.

    Use the FROM variable to help locate the center.

    The circle is .56 to the right and .55 up from the corner.

**Circle Placed**

3.  Draw a 12 degree line from the left end of the 1.33 line.

    The length will be approximately 3.00 inches.

    Use the dynamic input to lock the line at 12 degrees.

**Angled Line Drawn**

4.  Offset the vertical line 5.62 from the left to right.

    Trim the corner above the new vertical line using the Fillet command set to 0.00 radius. You will round the corner later.

**Line Offset Horizontal and Trimmed**

5.  Offset the bottom horizontal line 3.02 upward.

    Trim the right vertical line to the corner of the two lines.

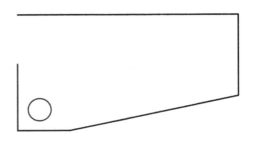

**Line Offset Vertical and Trimmed**

6.  Offset the bottom line 4.48 upward and the far right line 1.01 to the left.

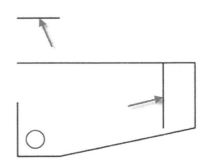

**Lines Offset**

7.  Fillet the lines together as shown.

    Do not create the rounded corners yet.

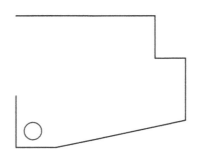

**Lines Filleted Together**

8.  Draw a 36 degree angle line from the top endpoint of the left vertical line.

    Draw the line approximately 1.30 inches.

    Since the angle is given from vertical, the line will be drawn at 54 degrees (90 – 36 = 54).

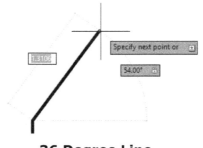

**36 Degree Line**

9.  To create the 3.50 radius at the top left of the view, you will use the Fillet tool.

    This tool will automatically create a tangent arc from both lines.

    Click the fillet tool and set the radius to 3.50.

    To set the radius, type R after clicking the tool.

    Click near the bottom of the 36 degree angle line and near the right end of the top horizontal line.

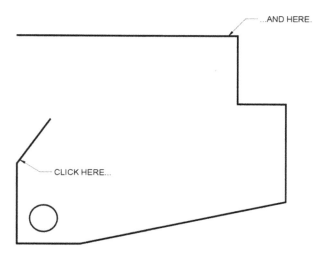

**Points to Click for Rounded Corner**

10. The corner is rounded.

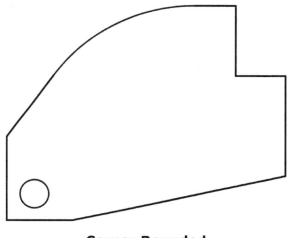

**Corner Rounded**

Drawing the Two Slots and Second Circle

1.  Draw an arc at 2.87 radius from the center
    of the .58 diameter circle.

    Use the Center, Start, End option for the arc.

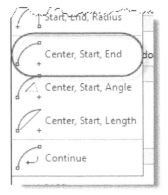

**Center, Start, End Option**

2.  Snap to the center of the circle first and then
    click to the right and then up.

    Enter the radius before clicking the first
    endpoint.

    The arc is draw in a counter-clockwise
    direction.

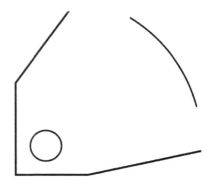

**2.87 Arc Drawn**

3.  Draw two angled lines from the center of the
    circle.

    The first line is drawn 30 degrees from
    horizontal and the second is drawn 61
    degrees (30 + 31 = 61).

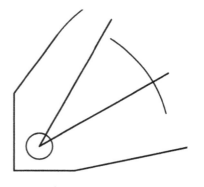

**Angled Lines Drawn**

4.  Offset the arc .30 inches in both directions.

    This will create a slot .60 inches wide.

**Arc Offset**

5. Trim the lines together using the Fillet tool set to 0.00 radius.

   Delete the original 2.87 arc.

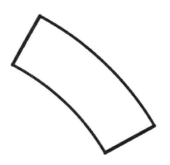

**Lines Trimmed Together**

6. Using the Arc tool, create the two .30 radius arcs at the ends of the shape.

   Use the Center, Start, End option.

   For the top arc, snap to the midpoint of the line, then the top corner, and then the bottom corner.

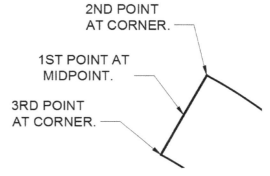

**Points for Arc**

7. The arc is placed.

   Repeat the process for the lower arc.

   Delete the straight lines.

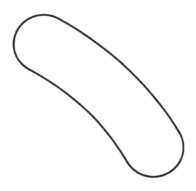

**Slot Completed**

8. To draw the second slot, begin by offsetting the right vertical line 1.57 to the left.

   Offset this line .25 in both directions for a width of .50.

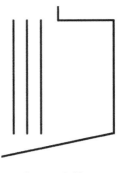

**Lines Offset**

9.  Offset the bottom horizontal line 1.56 upward.

    Offset this line another 2.49 upward.

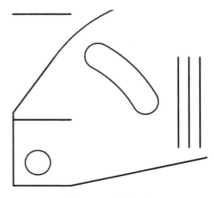

**Lines Offset**

10. Trim the lines with the two outside vertical lines on the left together to form a rectangular shape.

    Delete the original middle line of the slot.

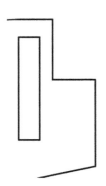

**Rectangle Drawn**

11. Draw the arc at the bottom edge using the same method as in the previous slot.

    Round the two upper corners using the Fillet tool set to .13 radius.

    Delete the horizontal line at the bottom of the slot.

    **Note:** You could have also used the Fillet tool set to 0.00 radius for the bottom arc. This only works with straight, parallel lines.

**Slot Completed**

For the second circle, you will use the FROM variable and Object Snap Tracking to place the center without using construction lines.

12. Make sure that the Object Snap Tracking is turned on.

OBJECT SNAP TRACKING.

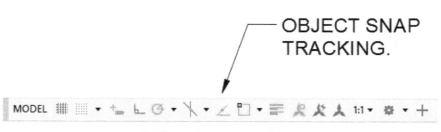

**Object Snap Tracking**

13. Click the Circle tool.

Mouse over and snap (do not click) on the left side of the bottom line.

Drag the mouse to the right. You will see a horizontal, dashed green line appear.

Mouse over and snap (do not click) on the bottom end of the far right vertical line.

The intersection of these two lines is the origin of the dimensions for the center of the circle.

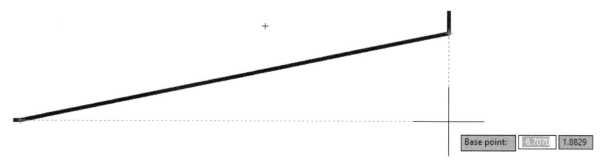

**Origin of the Circle Center Dimensions**

14. Type in @-.65, 2.08 for the offset from the base point.

**Offset from Basepoint**

15. Enter the size for the circle at .58 diameter.

**Circle Added**

16. Fillet and round the remaining corners at R .13.

The object lines are completed for the drawing.

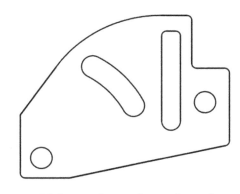

**Object Lines Completed**

Adding the Center Lines and Center Marks

1.  Use the Center Mark tool in the Annotate tab, Centerlines panel to add the center marks to the circles and slots.

    For the curved slot, use the center linetype for the lines and arc.

    **Note:** After placing the lines and arc for the slot, you may need to lengthen the line. Select the line and mouse over the handle on the end. You will see a menu popup, select Lengthen to make the line longer.

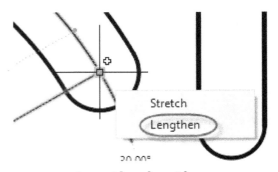

**Lengthening Lines**

2.  When finished, your drawing will look like this...

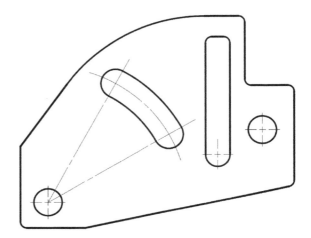

**Center Marks and Center Lines Added**

Dimensioning the Drawing (Linear Dimensions)

1.  Add the linear dimensions first.

    Use the Mech 1-1 style that you created in the previous project.

    As before, spacing the dimensions 1 1/2 grid squares (.375) for the first dimension line and 1 square (.25) for the next ones.

2. You may notice that the 2.49 dimension on the left is crossing over the extension lines of two other dimensions.

   You will use the Break tool in the Dimensions panel to break the extension lines so that the dimension line does not cross other lines.

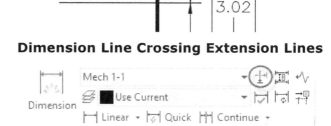

**Dimension Line Crossing Extension Lines**

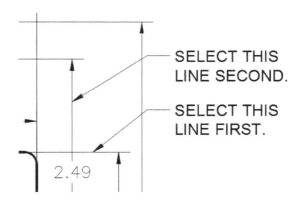

**Break Tool**

3. Click the Break tool.

   Select the extension line and then the dimension line.

   Repeat for the other intersection.

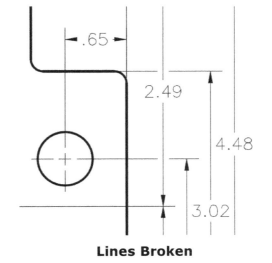

**Lines to Select for Break**

4. The extension lines are now broken.

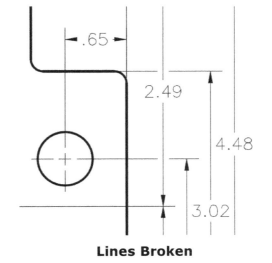

**Lines Broken**

5.  To add the .60 dimension that shows the width of the slot, you will use the Aligned dimension tool.

    When placing the dimension snap to the midpoints of the two arcs.

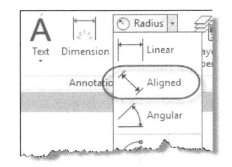

**Aligned Dimension Tool**

6.  The aligned dimension is placed.

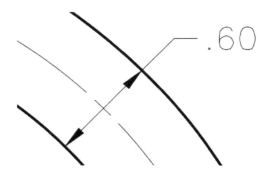

**Aligned Dimension Placed**

7.  This completes the linear dimensions.

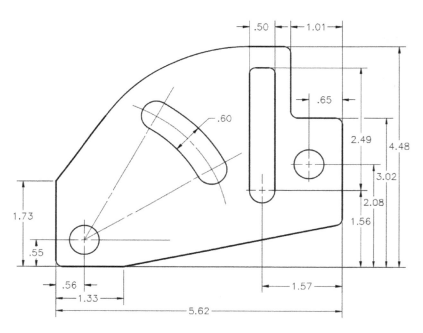

**Linear Dimensions Completed**

## Dimensioning the Drawing (Angular Dimensions)

1.  Next you will add the four angular dimensions.

    Click on the Angular dimension tool in the
    Annotation panel.

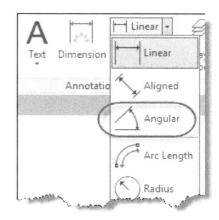

**Angular Dimension Tool**

2.  This tool works by selecting the
    two lines that will make up the
    dimensioned feature.

    Begin with the 12 degree
    dimension.

    Select the two lines as shown
    then stretch the dimension text
    to the correct location.

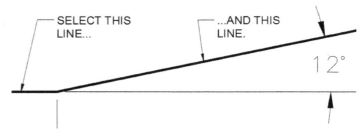

**Lines to Select for Angled Dimension**

3.  Repeat the process for the 36 degree
    dimension...

**36 Degree Dimension**

4.  ...and for the 30 and 31 degree dimensions.

    Line up the dimensions so that they are
    chained together.

    Add an extra line to cover the gap as
    shown.

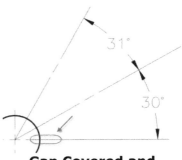

**Gap Covered and
Dimensions Lined Up**

Dimensioning the Drawing (Radial Dimensions)

1. Click on the Radius dimension option in the Annotation panel.

   There are a variety of ways to dimension a radius. Pick the method that works best for your style of drafting.

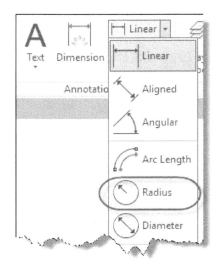

**Radius Dimension Tool**

2. Select the 2.87 radius.

   Normally you will try to place all dimensions outside of the object, but in this case this is the best option.

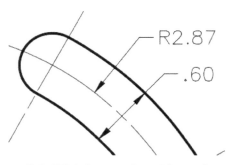

**R2.87 Dimension Placed**

3. Add the 3.50 radius and the two radius dimensions for the slots.

   For the radius dimensions on the slots, it is correct drafting practice to remove the numerical value and just show the R. This is because the width of the slot will control the size of the radius.

4.  Click the Diameter dimension tool.

    Select the lower left circle to add the dimension.

    Edit the text by double-clicking on the numerical value and add the 2X to indicate there are two of the same feature on the part.

    Leave a space between the 2X and the value.

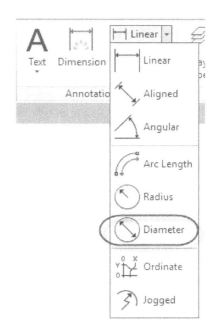

**Diameter Dimension Tool**

5.  The radial dimensions are now placed.

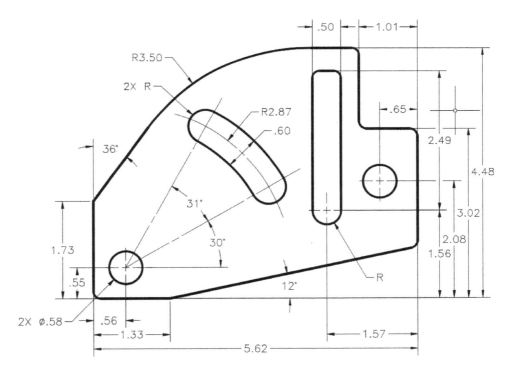

**Radial Dimensions Placed**

<u>Dimensioning the Drawing (Adding the Local Notes)</u>

The last thing you will need to add are the local notes.

These are used to reference a note in the general notes that only affects a portion of the drawing.

You will use the Leader and Polygon tools to add these.

1.  First you will need to set up a new leader style.

    Click on Multileader Style tool under the Annotation panel.

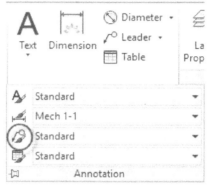

**Multileader Style Tool**

2.  The Multileader Style Manager dialog box opens.

    Click on the New... button to create a new style.

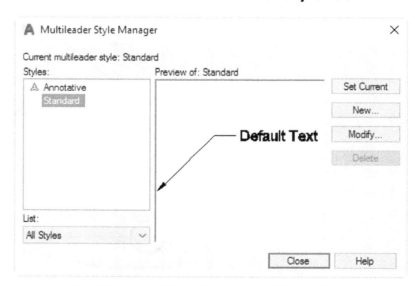

**Multileader Style Manager Dialog Box**

3.  Name the style Mech 1-1 and click the Continue button.

**Create New Multileader Style Dialog Box**

4. In the Leader Format tab, make the following change:

    Set the size of the arrowhead to 0.1250.

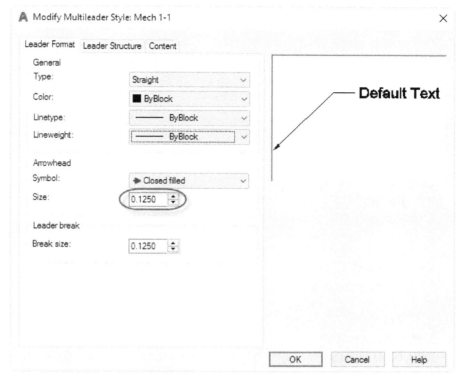

**Arrow Size Set to 0.125**

5. In the Leader Structure tab, make the following change:

    Set the size of the landing distance to 0.2500.

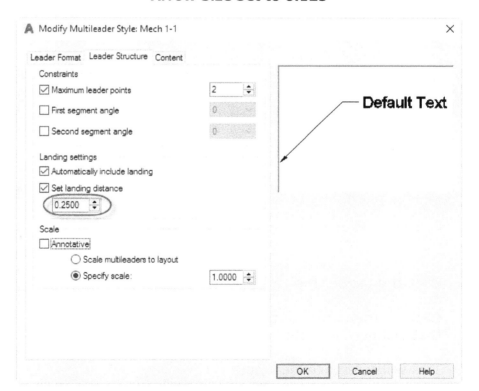

**Landing Distance Set to 0.2500**

6.  In the Content tab, make the following changes:

    Set the Text style to Mechanical.

    Set the Text height to 0.1250.

    Check the "Always left justify" checkbox.

    Set the Right attachment to Middle of bottom line.

    Set the Landing gap to 0.0625

    Check the "Extend leader to text" checkbox.

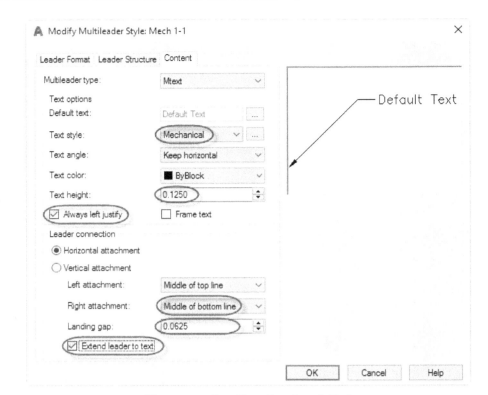

**Changes for the Content Tab**

7.  Click OK and then Close to save the style and close the dialog box.

8.  Set the Leader style to Mech 1-1.

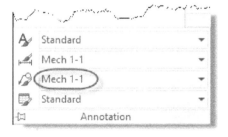

**Leader Style set to Mech 1-1**

9.  Click the Leader tool.

    Click on the corner of the view to indicate the corner that will not be filleted.

    This will reference local note #4.

    Type in 4 for the note text.

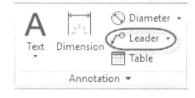

**Leader Tool**

10. Add the text note for one of the corners.

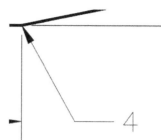

**Note Added**

11. Click on the Polygon tool in the Draw panel.

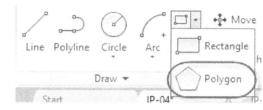

**Polygon**

12. Set the number of sides to 3.

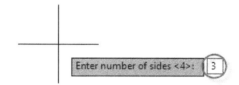

**Number of Side set to 3**

13. Click a point near the text for the center of the polygon.

    Chose "Inscribed in circle" for the method.

    Use .2000 for the radius of the polygon.

    Positon the polygon around the text and touching the leader line.

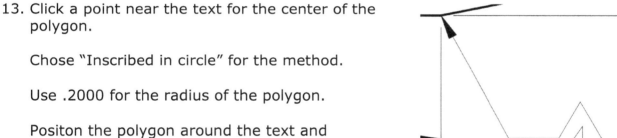

**Polygon Placed**

14. Copy the note and the polygon to the other position.

    Drag the arrowhead to the corner.

    Reposition the polygon if needed.

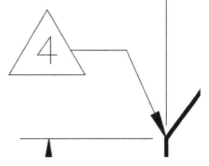

**Note Copied**

15. Add a triangle around the number in Note #4.

    You will need to remove the automatic numbering for this line only.

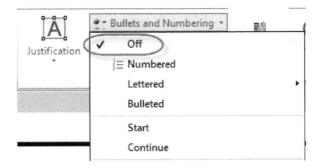

**Numbering Turned Off**

16. You will need to make a smaller triangle for the note.

NOTES:
1.  BREAK ALL SHARP EDGES.
2.  PART IS .375 THICK.
3.  ROUNDS AND FILLETS R.13.
4.  DO NOT ROUND THESE CORNERS.

17. The drawing is now fully dimensioned.

    **Note:**
    Some dimensions may need to be moved when placing the drawing into the border.

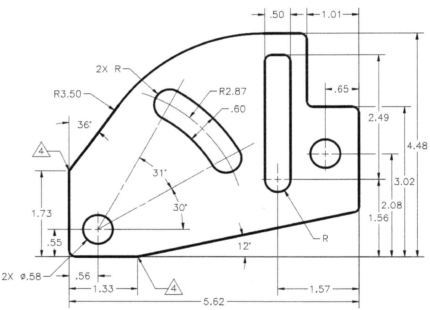

18. Save the project. This concludes the tutorial.

    Create a PDF of the project and print if desired.

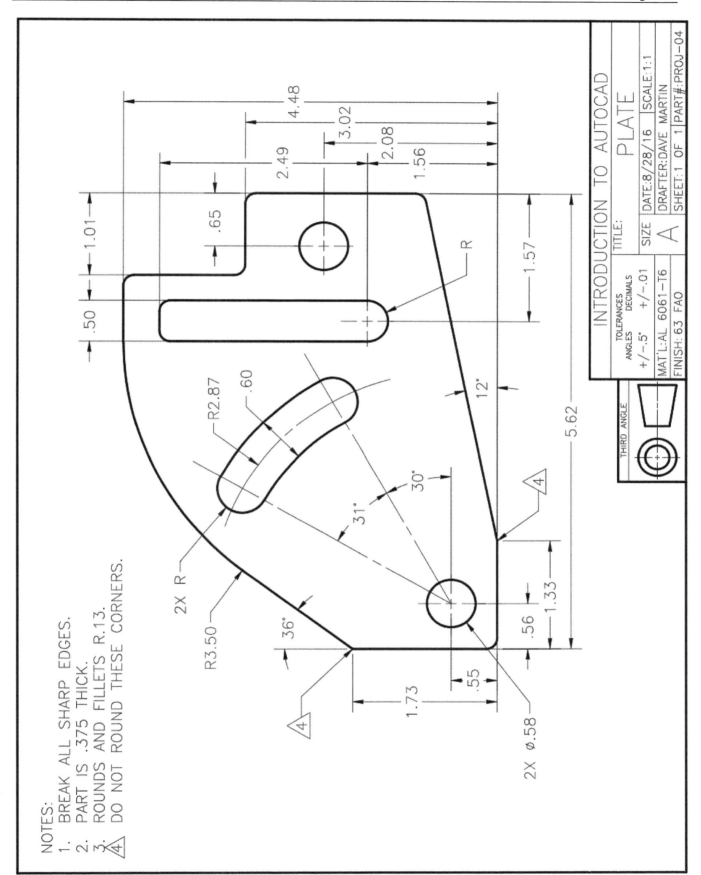

NOTES:
1. BREAK ALL SHARP EDGES.
2. PART IS .375 THICK.
3. ROUNDS AND FILLETS R.13.
4. DO NOT ROUND THESE CORNERS.

INTRODUCTION TO AUTOCAD

TITLE: PLATE

SIZE A

DATE:8/28/16   SCALE:1:1
DRAFTER:DAVE MARTIN
SHEET:1 OF 1  PART#:PROJ-04

TOLERANCES
ANGLES  DECIMALS
+/-.5°   +/-.01

MAT'L:AL 6061-T6
FINISH: 63 FAO

THIRD ANGLE

# Project #5 – Saw Handle

**Filename:** PROJ-05.dwg
Note: All screenshots are from the Autodesk® AutoCAD® software.

**Description:** This is the first project where you will use the B-Size Border for the project. Many of the commands that you have learned up to this point will continue to be used and their use reinforced.

Beginning the Project

1.  Open PROJ-04.dwg and save the drawing as PROJ-05.dwg.

2.  Delete the objects left over from PROJ-04.

    Also delete the title block and general notes.

3.  Copy and paste the information from the B-Size Border.dwg.

    As with the beginning of PROJ-03, use the Paste to Original Coordinates option. The lower left corner of the border will be at the 0,0 location.

4.  Edit the text in the title block and the notes in the upper left corner of the border.

    Draw a diagonal line through the Finish box in the title block.

Drawing the Object

1.  Begin by locating the slot on the right side of the front view. Use the Center, Start, Angle option in the Arc tool to place a R4.19 arc.

    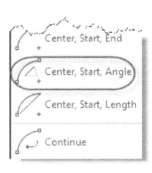

    After clicking the center point, set the distance at 4.19 then use the tab key to set the start angle at 0 degrees. When sweeping the arc up, lock the sweep of the arc at 38 degrees.

    **Center, Start, Angle Option**

2.  Use the Offset tool to copy the arc .59 inches in each direction.

    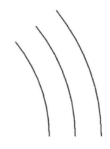

    **Arcs Placed**

3.  Place two arcs to create the ends of the slot.

    Use the snap tool as in the previous project.

**Slot Completed**

4.  Add a R5.49 arc concentric with the other arcs.

    The start and end points are approximated.

**R5.47 Arc Added**

5.  Draw the upper and lower edges of the view.

    The lower line will be 1.51 from the center of the arcs and the upper line will be 5.35 from the lower line.

    Use Object Tracking for the first line and the Offset tool for the second line.

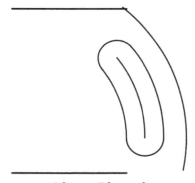

**Lines Placed**

6.  Fillet the corners.

    Use .25 for the fillet radius.

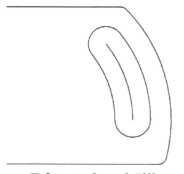

**Lines Trimmed and Filleted**

7.  Draw a line from the center of the arcs at 110 degrees. (This measurement came from subtracting 70 degrees from 180.)

8.  Using the Offset tool, create three parallel lines at .75, 1.50, and 2.25 from the original line.

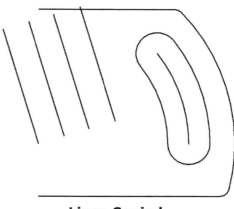

**Lines Copied**

9.  Change the far right line that was copied to the Hidden Line layer.

    Change the third line and the 4.19 arc to the Center Line layer.

10. Offset the bottom line twice, .59 up and 4.35 up.

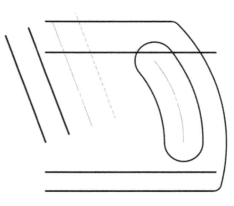

**Lines Copied**

11. Use the Fillet tool to round the corners, trim, and extend the lines.

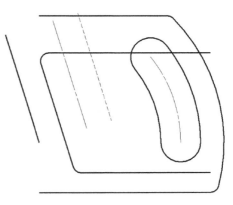

**Lines Filleted and Trimmed**

12. Next you will add the 120 and 30 degree lines.

    Locate the 120 degree line by placing a parallel line 1.00 from the left edge of the object.

    You may need to lengthen the line after drawing it. Select the line and mouse over the endpoint and select Lengthen.

    Locate the 30 degree line 3.08 from the center of the arcs.

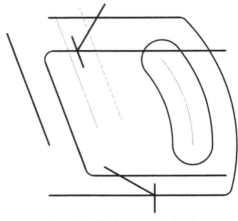

**Angled Lines Added**

13. Fillet and trim the angled lines to the corners of the object.

    Delete the construction lines.

    Trim and extend the hidden line to the top and bottom intersections of the view.

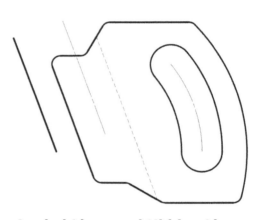

**Angled Lines and Hidden Lines Filleted and Trimmed**

14. Add the first .50 diameter circle.

    Locate it by drawing an intersecting line 1.25 to the right of the center of the arcs.

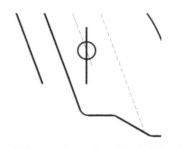

**.50 Diameter Circle Added**

15. To create the other two circles, use the Copy tool.

    When placing the copy lock the distance at 1 inch and the angle at 110 degrees.

    Repeat for the other circle. Use the same distance but 290 degrees for the angle.

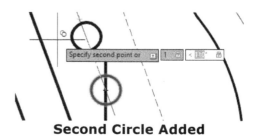

**Second Circle Added**

16. Delete the construction lines and the center line.

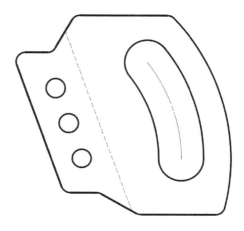

**View Completed**

17. Extend the edges of the view to the left side of the drawing to begin the left side view.

    Draw the first horizontal line from the top edge of the view.

    Use the Copy tool to add the remaining lines.

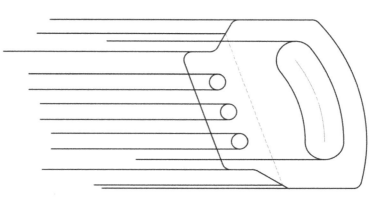

**Lines Projected**

18. Change the appropriate lines to the Hidden Lines layer.

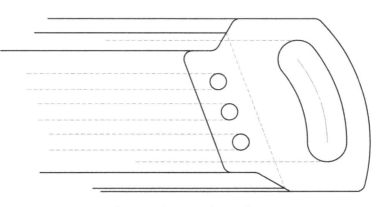

**Lines Changed to the Hidden Lines Layer**

19. Draw a vertical line in the left side view and use the Offset tool to add the other lines.

20. Trims the lines for the two middle vertical lines using a zero radius fillet.

21. Use the Fillet tool for the outside rounds. The radius is .25.

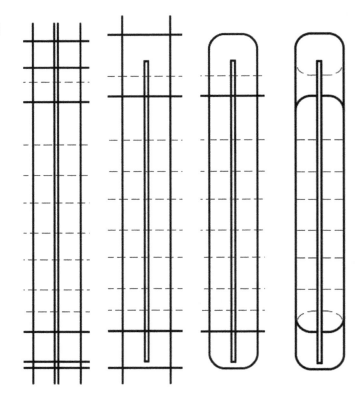

**Step #19     Step #20     Step #21     Step #22**

22. Change trim option for the Fillet tool to No Trim.
Change the layer to hidden lines for the hidden fillets and rounds.

    After filleting, trim the excess lines and the hidden lines to the edges of the view with the Trim tool.

    Be sure to trim down the middle of the two inner parallel lines.

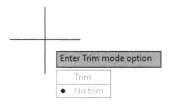

**No Trim Option**

23. Add the center lines for the holes in the left side view.

    Use the CENTER-Short linetype.

24. Both views are completed.

    The center lines for the slot centers are omitted from the left side view.

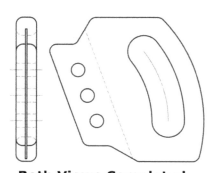

**Both Views Completed**

## Dimensioning the Views (Center Marks, Linear, and Angular Dimensions)

1.  Add the center marks to one of the three holes.

    After adding the first center mark, rotate the mark to align with the angle of the hole centers.

    Use the Rotate tool and the center of one of the other holes when rotating.

**Rotating the Center Mark**

2.  Copy the center marks to the other three holes.

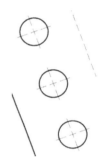

**Center Marks Copied**

3.  Add a center line between the holes.

    You will need to use the CENTER-X-Short linetype.

    Snap on the inside end of the center mark to make the line long enough to show the dash.

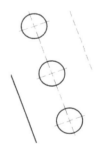

**Center Lines Added**

4.  Add the 1.00 dimensions for the hole centers.

    Use the Aligned dimension tool and then the Continue option for the second dimension.

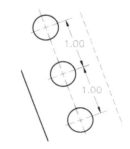

**1.00 Dimensions Added**

5. Add a small center mark for the center of the right side arc and the slot.

   After adding the center mark delete the four long lines leaving the mark in the center.

   To delete the four lines you will need to use the Explode tool. This will break the center mark up into individual elements. The Explode tool is located in the Home tab, Modify panel.

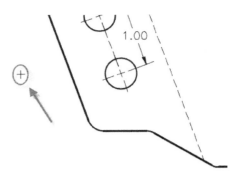

**Center Mark Added**

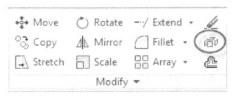

**Explode Tool**

6. Add the remaining linear dimensions for the front view.

   When dimensioning the 3.08 dimension, you will need to add two short lines intersecting at the corner. This is used to locate the corner prior to filleting.

   Make the lines approximately .38 inches long.

   When adding the angled line, used the Extension Snap mode. This can be turned on temporarily by holding the CTRL key on the keyboard and right-clicking the mouse. Select the Extension snap mode from the choices.

   By holding the mouse over the angled line and then dragging the cursor, you can add a new line with the same angle as the original line.

**Intersecting Lines**

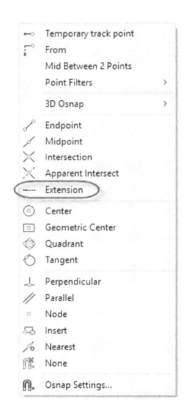

**Temporary Snap Modes**

7.  When adding the angled 1.50 dimension, you will need and add another angled dimension first.

Use the Perpendicular snap mode for the second endpoint of the first dimension.

The location of this dimension is not important since you will be deleting it after adding the 1.50 dimension.

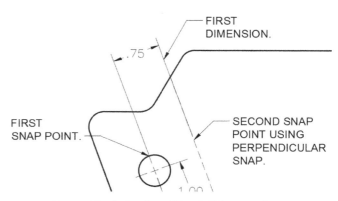

**Snap Points for First Dimension**

8.  Use the Continue option to add the 1.50 dimension.

This dimension will be at the same angle regardless of the location of the endpoint.

Delete the .75 dimension when finished.

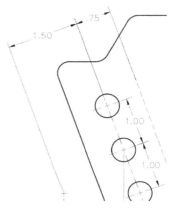

**1.50 Dimension Continued
from .75 Dimension**

9.  Add the intersecting lines for the 120 degree corner.

Add two dimensions, one for the corner and the other for the distance from the left edge to the center of the arcs.

You can use the Continue option from the 1.50 dimension and then adjust the location of the dimension line by stretching the handles.

When moving the 1.00 text to the left, you will use the Move with Dim Line option. This will appear by selecting the dimension and then holding the mouse over the handle for the text.

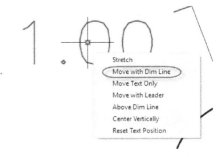

**Move With Dim Line Option**

10. Break the extension line for the 1.50 dimension where it intersects with the 1.00 dimension line.

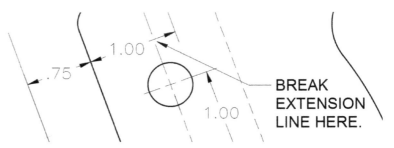

**Extension Line Break**

11. When adding the 120 degree dimension, break the extension line for the 1.50 dimension.

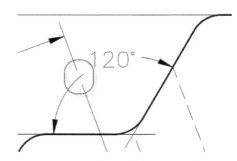

**Extension Line Break**

12. Add the linear dimension for the width of the slot.

    Use Midpoint snap to add the dimension at the correct angle.

**Slot Width Dimension Added**

13. Add the bottom 1.50 dimension using the Continue option from one of the other angled linear dimensions.

    You will need to stretch the 1.25 and 3.08 dimensions further away from the edge of the view.

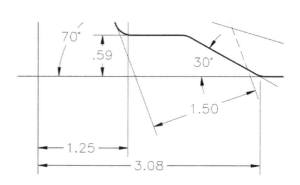

**1.50 Dimension Added**

14. The Linear and Angular dimensions are completed for the front view.

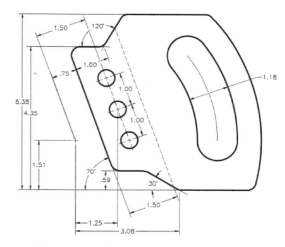

**Linear and Angular Dimensions Completed**

## Dimensioning the Views (Radial and Remaining Angular Dimensions)

1. For some of the radius dimensions, you will need to create a new dimension style.

   The name of the style will be "Mech 1-1 (Radius Extended)".

   Start with the Mech 1-1 style.

   The only change will be to change the Fit options to Text.

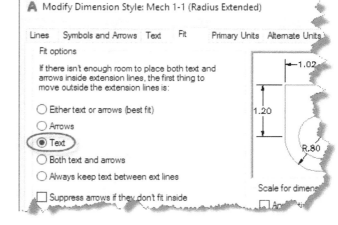

**Fit Options Changed to Text**

2. Place the R5.47, R4.19, and slot radius dimensions using this new style.

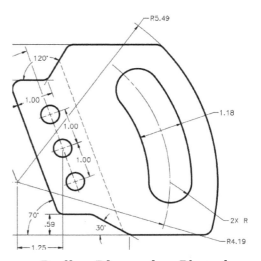

**Radius Dimension Placed**

3. Draw two center lines for the 38 degree angular dimension.

   Add the angular dimension and draw two short lines to cover the gaps.

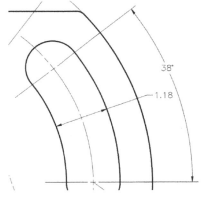

**38 Degree Dimension Added**

4. Add the diameter dimension for the three holes.

   Use the Mech 1-1 dimension style so that the arrow goes to the outside of the circle.

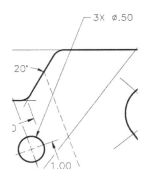

**Diameter Dimension Added**

5. Add the three linear dimensions to the left side view.

   At the top of the view, show the location and width of the slot using the method shown.

   Add the overall width at the bottom of the view.

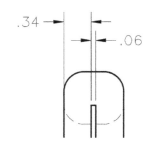

**Slot Location and Size
Dimensions**

6. The views are fully dimensioned.

7. When plotting this drawing the settings will remain the same with the exception of the paper size.

**Paper Size for B-Size Drawings**

   Use the "ANSI full bleed B (11.00 x 17.00 Inches)" paper size.

   Snap to the points when setting the window boundary for the plot.

8. Save the project. This concludes the tutorial.

   Create a PDF of the project and print if desired.

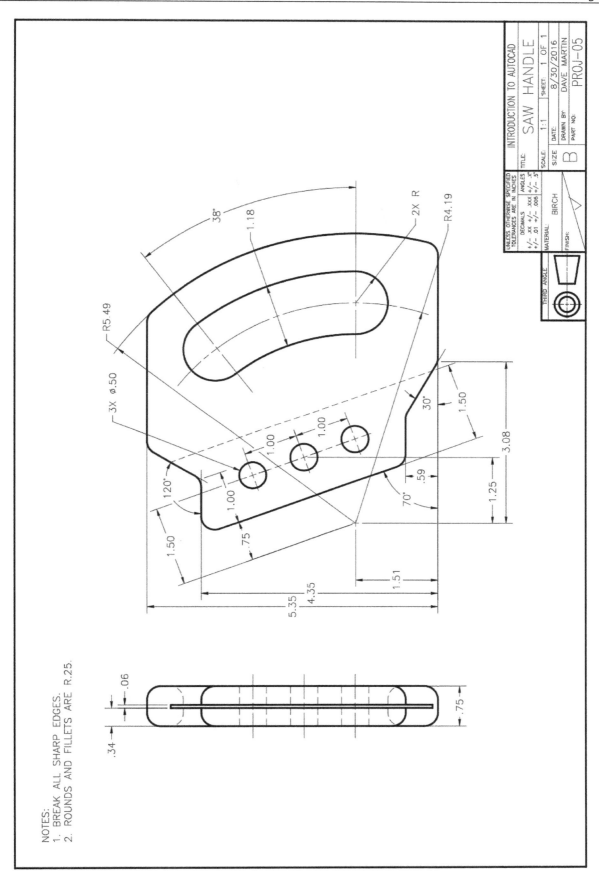

# Project #6 – Guide

**Filename:** PROJ-06.dwg
Note: All screenshots are from the Autodesk® AutoCAD® software.

**Description:** This project will introduce you to creating section views. In this case the type of section will be a full section. This drawing is considered a machining drawing but will also show information for the casting operation. The creation and use of symbols used for machining operations will also be covered. Lastly, you will add Geometric Dimensioning and Tolerancing (GDT) Symbols.

Beginning the Project

1. Open PROJ-05.dwg and save the drawing as PROJ-06.dwg.

2. Delete the objects left over from PROJ-05.

   Do not delete the title block and general notes.

3. Edit the text in the title block and the notes in the upper left corner of the border.

   Remove the diagonal line through the Finish box.

   About the Notes...
   - Notes #1 and #2 will remain unchanged.
   - Note #3 refers to the original size of the casting to be machined.
   - Note #4 refers to material called cores that are left in the mold to create spaces for the metal to flow around. This helps to use less material for the casting and cuts down on machining time.
   - Note #5 shows the original boundary of the edge of the casting and helps the machinist to see which surfaces are to be machined. The surface texture symbol is also used to indicate surfaces to be machined. This note is a Local Note; a triangle will be added later around the number 5.

   NOTES:
   1. BREAK ALL SHARP EDGES
   2. ROUNDS AND FILLETS ARE R.25.
   3. DASHED LINES INDICATE EDGE OF ORIGINAL CASTING.
   4. CORE HOLES .125 UNDER DIAMETER.
   5. .12 MACHINING ALLOWANCE.

   **Notes for Project #6**

## Drawing the Object (Top View)

1. Begin with the top view of the project.

   Draw the three groups of circles based off the example.

   The left circles consist of three circles; 1.44, .92, and .54 diameter.

   This is showing a counterbored hole.

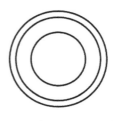

**Circles Placed**

2. Draw lines from the left edge of the left outside circle down and from the bottom of the center circle to the left.

   Using the Fillet tool, round the corners at a radius of .25.

   Repeat for the upper right corner.

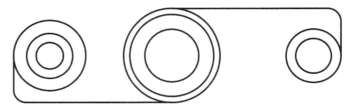

**Lines and Rounds Added**

3. Using the Tangent snap override, add a tangent line from outer edge of the left circle to the outer center circle.

   Repeat for the lower right corner of the view.

   When using the tangent snap, the first point for the line will "stick" at the tangent point on a circle or arc.

   For the second point you may see a Deferred Tangent point.

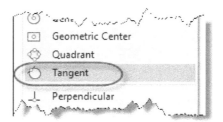

**Tangent Snap Override**

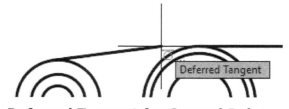

**Deferred Tangent for Second Point**

4. The tangent lines are added.

   The top view is completed.

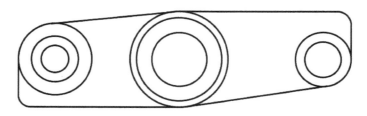

**Tangent Lines Added**

## Drawing the Object (Front View)

1.  Project lines down from the top view for the edges of the front view.

    Estimate the lengths of the lines.

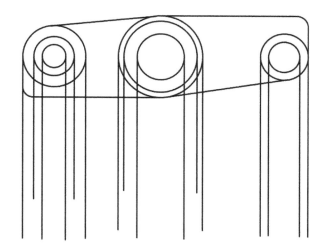

**Lines Projected**

2.  Draw a horizontal line for the bottom of the view.

    Offset the line up to .54, 1.40, 1.98, and 1.72 inches.

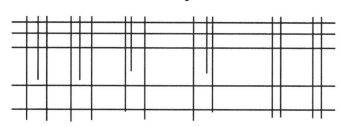

**Lines Offset**

3.  Use the Trim and Fillet tools to trim and extend the corners.

    Set the Fillet tool to 0.00 radius.

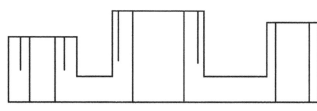

**Lines Trimmed**

4.  Draw the edges of the counterbored hole.

    The counterbored hole has a depth of .31.

    Offset the top line on the left down this distance.

    Dimension is for reference only.

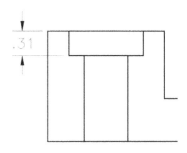

**Counterbored Hole**

5.  Draw the edges of the countersunk hole.

    The countersunk hole has a diameter of 1.68. Draw the angled lines at 45 degrees.

    Dimensions are for reference only.

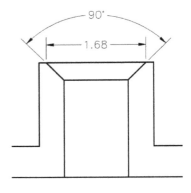

**Countersunk Hole**

6.  Fillet the corners to .25 radius.

    The object lines for the front view are completed.

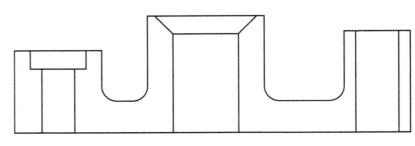

**Object Lines Completed**

## Adding the Section Lines

Now that you are completed with the object lines, you will now add the section lines in the front view.

Section lines show where a simulated cut is located on a drawing. In this case you will be simulating a cut along the horizontal axis of the object through the centers of the circles.

1.  Create a new layer called Section Lines.

    Use the attributes as shown and make the layer current.

**Section Line Attributes**

2.  Find and click on the Hatch tool in the Draw panel.

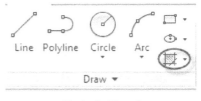

**Hatch Tool**

3.  A new tab will appear called Hatch
    Creation.

    Select the ANSI131 style from the
    Pattern panel.

    **Note:** There are many standard patterns
    available for different uses.

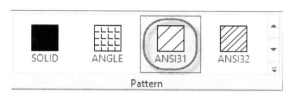

**ANSI131 Pattern**

4.  You will also see that the Associative
    toggle is turned on.

    This will allow you to stretch the
    boundary of the pattern if needed.

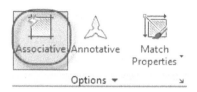

**Associative Toggle**

5.  Pick an internal point inside the area to be
    patterned.

**Internal Point**

6.  The area is hatched (patterned).

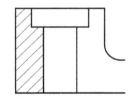

**Area is Hatched**

7.  Repeat the process for the
    other areas.

    The section lines are
    completed.

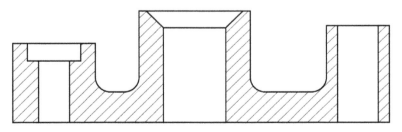

**Section Lines Completed**

8. To modify the pattern after placement, select the hatch pattern and then select the Hatch Settings icon in the Options panel.

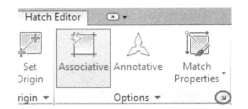

**Hatch Settings Icon**

9. The Hatch Edit dialog box opens.

   You may use this dialog box to adjust the pattren, scale, add additional boundaries, change the associativity, draw order and the level.

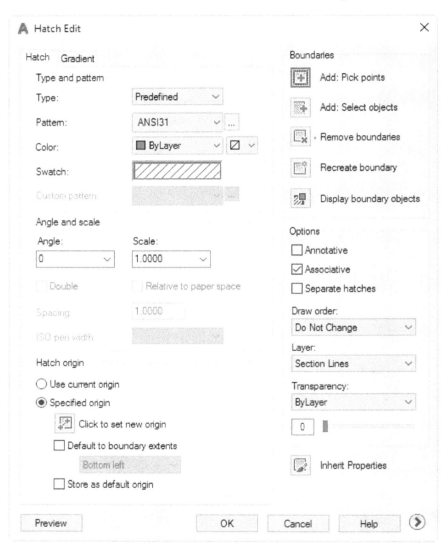

**Hatch Edit Dialog Box**

## Adding the Center Lines, Center Marks, and Dimensioning the Views

1.  Add the center lines and center marks on the Center Lines layer.

    Use the Offset to offset the top and bottom surfaces .12 inches.

    You may need to use the shorter versions of the center linestyle to make the dashes appear.

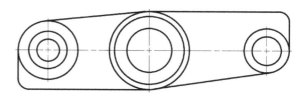

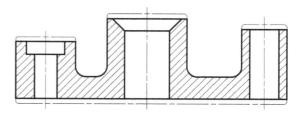

**Center Marks and Center Lines Added**

2.  Add the linear dimensions.

    Add the diameter symbol for the appropriate dimensions.

    Use the Symbol tool in the Text Editor panel and select "Diameter %%c" to add the symbol.

    You may also key-in %%c in front of the dimension text to add the symbol.

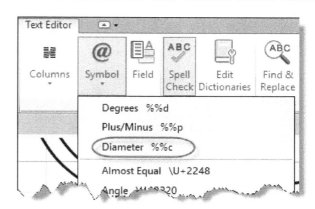

**Choice for Diameter Symbol**

3.  The linear dimensions should be placed like this...

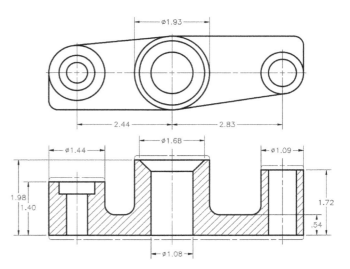

**Linear Dimensions Added**

4.  Place the radial dimensions.

    You will need to use the Mech 1-1 (Radius Extended) style for the diameter dimensions.

    You will also need to edit the text for the .92 diameter dimension on the left.

    When editing the text, change the font to AMGDT. Use the lowercase letter "v" for the Counterbore symbol and the letter "x" for the Depth symbol.

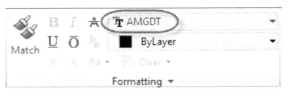

**AMGDT Font**

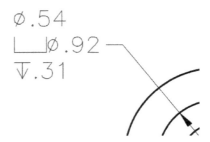

**Dimension Text Edited**

5.  Add the angular dimension for the countersink angle.

    The views are now dimensioned.

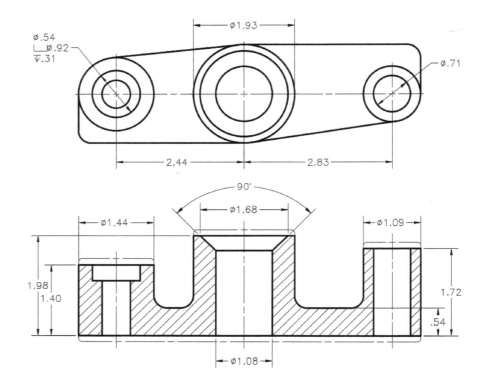

## Adding the Surface Texture Symbol and Local Note

1.  Use the drawing to create the Surface Texture Symbol.

    The height of the symbol is three times the text height.

    When placing the symbol, it may be placed on the extension line or attached to a leader line.

    The lines are placed on the Dimensions layer.

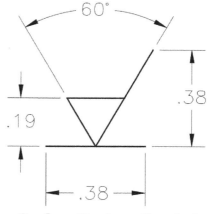

**Surface Texture Symbol**

2.  After creating the symbol use the Group tool to group the lines together.

    Click on the Group tool in the Groups panel in the Home ribbon.

**Group Tool**

3.  To name the group, click on the Group Manager tool to open the Object Grouping dialog box

    The group will be named "Surface" as in Surface Texture.

    Click on one of the elements of the group.

    All of the elements will select.

**Group Manager Tool**

4.  Type in the word Surface in the Group Name field and click the New button.

    The dialog box will close temporarily, pick the group.

5. You will see the group appear in the Group Name box.

   .

   **Note:** If you delete all the groups on the drawing, the group cannot be retrieved.

**Object Grouping Dialog Box**

6. Place the surface texture symbol at the appropriate locations.

   You will need to move the dimensions on the left side of the view to place the surface marks.

   When placing the leader do not add text. Snap the end of the leader line to the bottom line of the surface texture mark group.

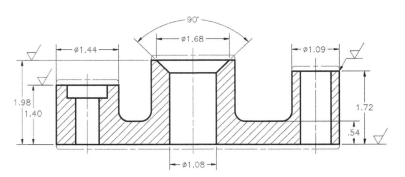

**Surface Texture Marks Added to Front View**

7. To add the local note symbol, open the PROJ-04.dwg drawing and copy to symbol to the clipboard.

   Switch back to the PROJ-06.dwg drawing and paste the symbol.

   Edit the text for the number to "5".

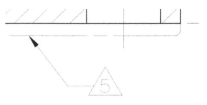

**Local Note Symbol Placed**

8.  Add a triangle around Note #5 in the notes.

    You will need to turn off the Bullets and Numbering for the note.

**Triangle Added on Note #5**

9.  Starting with the MECH 1-1 style, create a new dimension style called: MECH 1-1 – 3PLC.

**MECH 1-1 – 3PLC Style Created**

10. In the Primary Units tab, change the precision to 0.000.

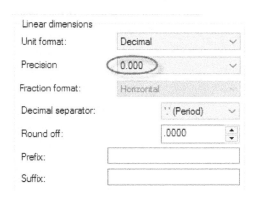

**Precision Changed to 0.000**

11. Change the 3-place decimal dimensions shown in the example on the drawing using the Properties window.

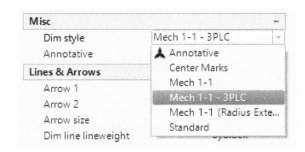

**Properties Setting for Dim Style**

## Adding the Geometric Dimensioning and Tolerancing (GDT) Symbols

The last elements you will add to the drawing will be GDT symbology. These symbols are used to show relationships between different surfaces and features of the part to a datum. Datums are used as base surfaces or feature to locate other elements of the drawing. For this part the bottom surface and the center of the 1.080 diameter hole will be datums.

1. AutoCAD has a tool that is used to place GDT symbols and boxes with symbols, tolerance values, and datums. These are known as feature control frames.

   Click on the Tolerance tool in the Annotate tab, Dimensions panel.

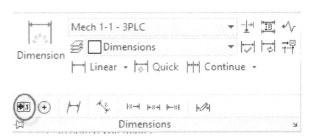

**Tolerance Tool**

2. The Geometric Tolerance dialog box opens.

   This will be used to fill in the feature control frame.

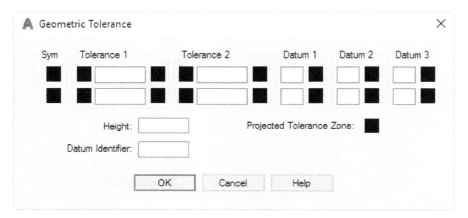

**Geometric Tolerance Dialog Box**

3. Start with the feature control under the .71 diameter hole on the left side of the top view.

   This frame is filled out to indicate that the center of the hole is located within a .01 diameter cylindrical tolerance zone with respect to datum A and B.

   Later you will also update the location dimension for the hole to include a frame around the dimension value.

   This is done to indicate that the dimension is controlled by the feature control frame and not the tolerance in the title block.

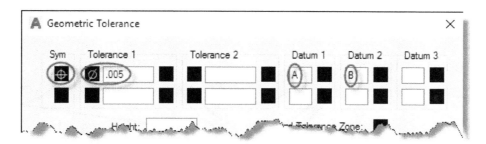

**Geometric Tolerance Dialog Box Filled Out**

4.  Press the OK button.

    The frame will be attached to your cursor.

    Locate the frame below the .71 diameter dimension.

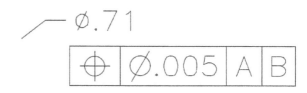

**Feature Control Frame Placed**

5.  Next, you will create a new dimension style with frames around the dimension text.

    Open the Dimension Style Manager dialog box and make the Mech 1-1 – 3PLC style current.

6.  Click the New... button and name the new style: Mech 1-1 – 3PLC – Frame.

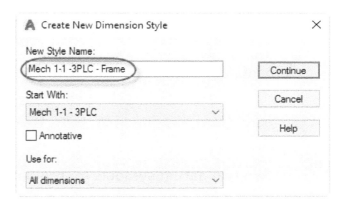

**New Dimension Style**

7.  Click Continue and then click on the Text tab.

    The only change you will make will be to check the "Draw frame around text" checkbox.

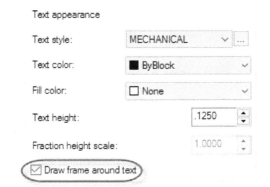

**Draw Frame Around Text Checkbox**

8.  Click Ok and Close to close the dialog boxes and save the dimension style.

9. Select the two length dimensions for the holes in the top view and change them to the new style.

   Use the Properties box to do this.

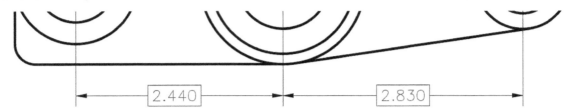

**Dimensions Changed to Frames Style**

10. Add in the other feature control frames.

    The top of the 1.09 diameter cylinder will have a Parallelism control, the bottom of the part will have a Flatness control, and the countersunk portion of the 1.080 hole will have a Concentricity control.

11. Next you will create the Datum Feature Symbol.

    This is used to mark surfaces or features that are datums.

    Use the drawing for the sizes of the elements.

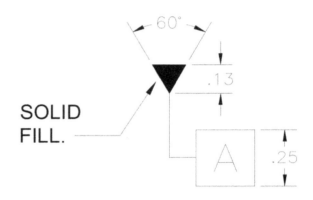

**Datum Symbol Dimensions**

12. Add the two datum symbols for the bottom of the part and the 1.680 diameter hole.

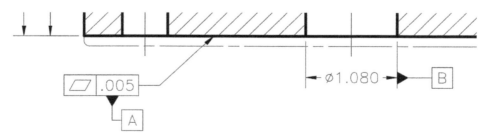

**Datum Symbols Added**

13. Save the project. This concludes the tutorial.

    Create a PDF of the project and print if desired.

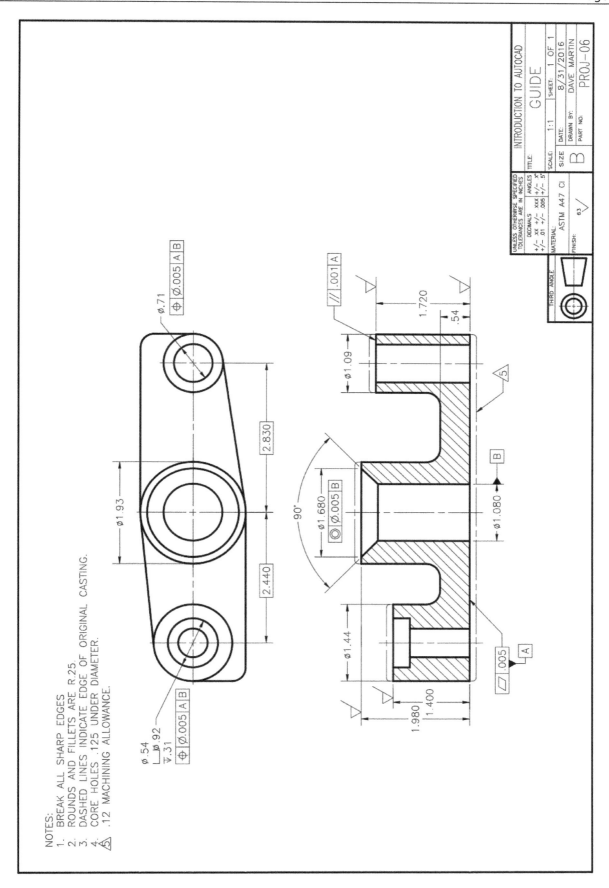

NOTES:
1. BREAK ALL SHARP EDGES
2. ROUNDS AND FILLETS ARE R.25.
3. DASHED LINES INDICATE EDGE OF ORIGINAL CASTING.
4. CORE HOLES .125 UNDER DIAMETER.
5. .12 MACHINING ALLOWANCE.

INTRODUCTION TO AUTOCAD
TITLE: GUIDE
SCALE: 1:1   DATE: 8/31/2016   SHEET: 1 OF 1
SIZE B   DRAWN BY: DAVE MARTIN
PART NO.: PROJ-06
MATERIAL: ASTM A47 CI
FINISH: 63

UNLESS OTHERWISE SPECIFIED
TOLERANCES ARE IN INCHES
DECIMALS          ANGLES
+/- .XX +/- .XXX +/- .X°
+/- .01 +/- .005 +/- .5°

THIRD ANGLE

# Project #7 – Gasket

**Filename:** PROJ-07.dwg
Note: All screenshots are from the Autodesk® AutoCAD® software.

**Description:** This project will introduce you to the use of the Mirror and Array tools. The setup for this project will be the same as the previous project. You will also be adding toleranced dimensions for some of the features.

## Beginning the Project

1. Open PROJ-06.dwg and save the drawing as PROJ-07.dwg.

2. Delete the objects left over from PROJ-06.

   Do not delete the title block and general notes.

3. Fill out the title block and general notes.

## Drawing the Object

1. Begin by laying out the top portion of the exterior shape of the view.

   When drawing the lines use the center of the 3.43 circle as the origin if using the FROM command.

   Also include the .54 diameter hole on the right side of the view.

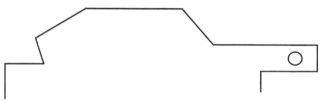

**Completed Top Half of the View**

2. Next you will mirror the top half to the bottom of the view.

   Select the elements in the top half of the view with the exception of the two bottom vertical lines.

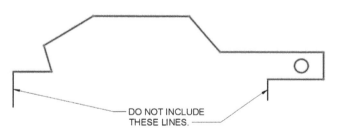

**Lines Selected to Mirror**

3. Click on the Mirror tool in the Manipulate toolbox.

   Set the Mirror About setting to Horizontal and check the Make Copy checkbox.

**Mirror Tool**

4. Click at the midpoint of the left or right vertical line.

   You will see a mirror image of the selected objects appear on the opposite side of the view.

   Press Enter to not erase source objects and to accept the mirrored elements.

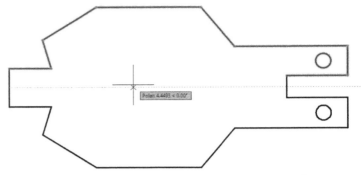

**Midpoint of Line Snapped for Mirroring**

5. Next you will create a polar array of the eight holes surrounding the larger, 3.54 diameter hole.

   Place the larger hole 4.63 from the midpoint of the far left vertical line.

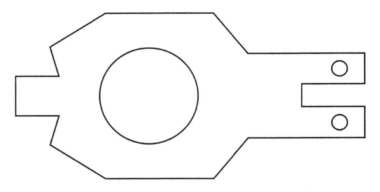

**3.43 Diameter Hole Placed**

6. Place one .51 hole 2.23 from the center of the larger hole.

   The 2.23 distance is half of the 4.46 diameter for the centers of the eight holes.

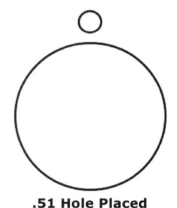

**.51 Hole Placed**

7.  Click on the arrow next to the Array tool in the Modify panel.

    Select the Polar Array option.

    Select the .51 diameter hole and press Enter.

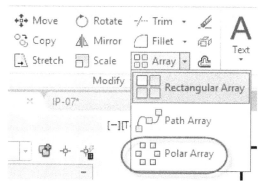

**Array Tool, Polar Array Option**

8.  The first point will be the center of the 3.43 diameter circle.

    By default, there will be six holes created.

    In the Items field in the Items panel, change the value to 8.

    You will also see the number of holes change to eight.

    Press Enter to accept the array.

**Number of Items**

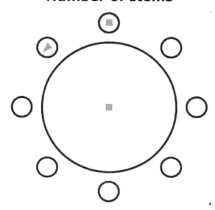

**Eight Holes Arrayed**

9.  Add the .75 circle to the left side of the part.

    The hole center is 3.93 to the left of the center of the 3.43 diameter hole.

    This completes the object lines for the view.

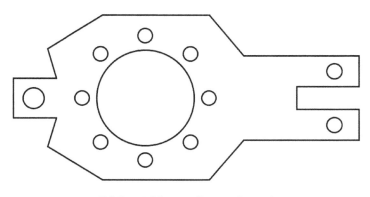

**Object Lines Completed**

Adding the Center Marks, Center Lines and Dimensioning the View

1.  Add the center marks for
    the holes as shown.

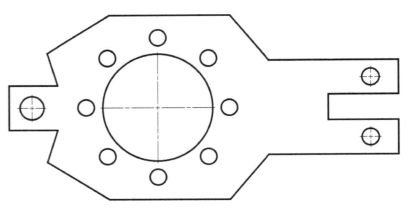

**Center Marks Added**

2.  For the center lines used for the eight holes,
    begin by drawing a short center line through
    the top hole.

    Then draw a center line arc through the hole.
    The angle of the arc will be 45 degrees.

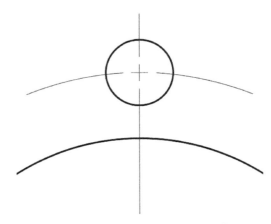

**Center Lines for Top Hole**

3.  Array the two lines around the center
    of the large hole.

    The ends of the arc will touch the other
    lines.

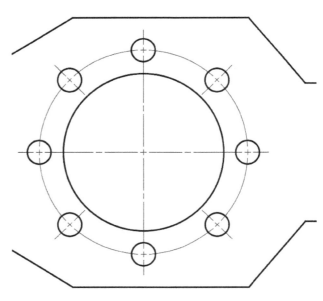

**Center Lines Arrayed**

4.  Add smaller center lines to connect the other center lines.

    Create symmetry marks on both ends of the view.

    Use the symmetry symbol to indicate that features are located at the same relative location on opposite sides of the view.

    The lines are drawn .25 long and .06 apart from each other.

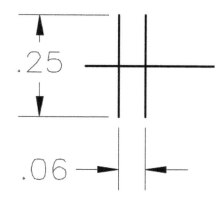

**Symmetry Mark Dimensions**

5.  Use the techniques learned in the previous tutorials to complete the remaining dimensions for the view.

    **Note:** Some of the dimensions have parentheses around the numbers. This is to indicate that these are reference dimensions. This type of dimension is for reference only and are not to be measured/toleranced on the inspected part. The other dimensions fully describe the locations and sizes of all features.

Creating the Toleranced Dimension Styles

In this section you will create two new dimension styles. One will be a Plus/Minus dimension and the other will be a Limit dimension. These types of dimensions are used to indicate that the size/location of a feature is to be inspected with a different tolerance as the rest of the drawing.

1.  Open the Dimension Style Manager.

2.  Select the Mech 1-1 – 3PLC dimension style.

3.  From this style, create a new style called: Mech1-1 – 3PLC - Limit

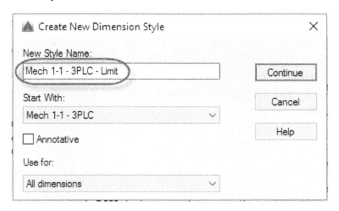

**Mech 1-1 – 3PLC – Limit Style Created**

4. In the Tolerances tab, change the Method setting to Limit and check the Leading checkbox to suppress the leading zero.

   This will add an additional dimension below the original dimension.

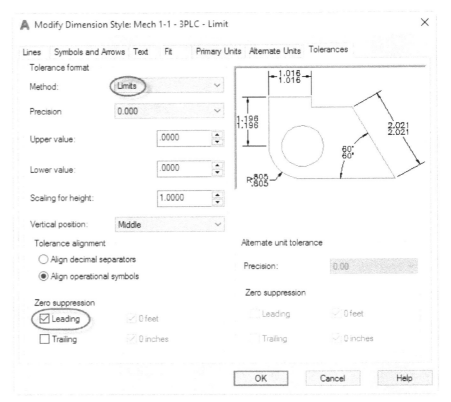

**Method Changed to Limit**

5. Change the .544 diameter dimension to this new style.

   Select the dimension and use the Properties box to change the values. Use .001 for the lower limit and .002 for the upper limit.

   **Note:** The reason for changing the value here and not in the Dimension Styles Manager is that limit dimensions may have different range of values with in the same drawing.

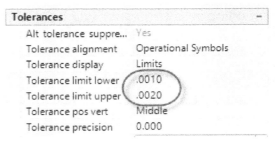

**Values Changed in the Properties Box**

6. The diameter dimension value is now updated.

**Dimension Updated**

7. Create a new style starting from the Limit style.

   Name the new dimension style: Mech 1-1 – 3PLC – Plus-Minus

8. In the Tolerance tab, change the method to Deviation.

   Change the Scaling for height setting to .75.

   This will make the text 3/4 of the dimension text size.

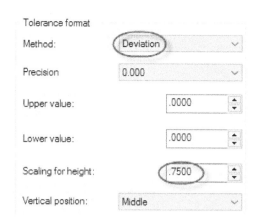

**Tolerance Format Changed**

9. Change the .75 hole diameter dimension on the left side of the view to this new style.

   Select the dimension and use the Properties box to change the values. Use .002 for the lower limit and .001 for the upper limit.

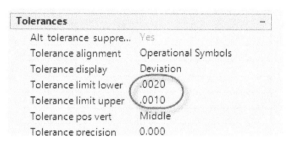

**Values Changed in the Properties Box**

10. The diameter dimension is now updated.

$$\varnothing.750^{+.001}_{-.002}$$

**Dimension Updated**

11. Save the project. This concludes the tutorial.

   Create a PDF of the project and print if desired.

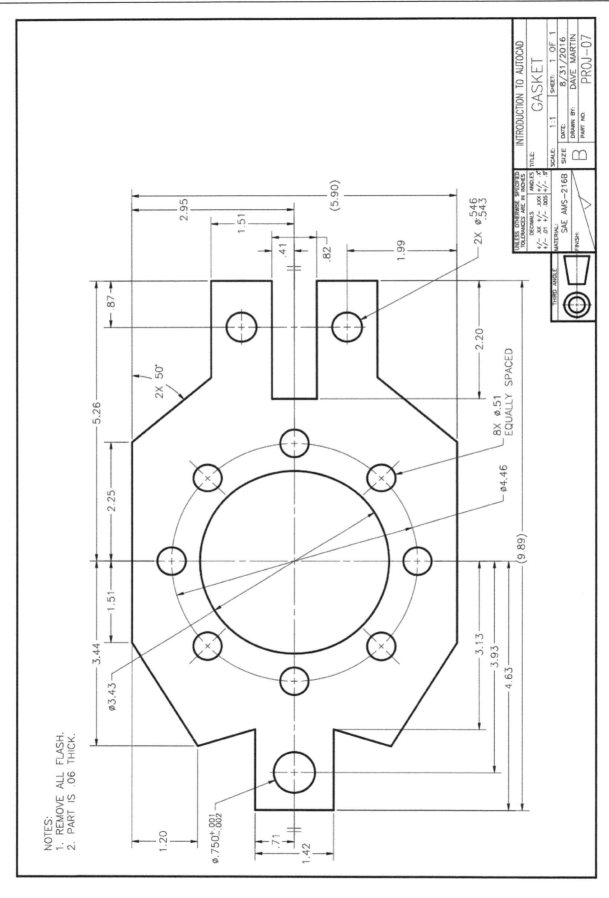

NOTES:
1. REMOVE ALL FLASH.
2. PART IS .06 THICK.

# Project #8 – Geneva Cam

**Filename:** PROJ-08.dwg
Note: All screenshots are from the Autodesk® AutoCAD® software.

**Description:** The object being drawn is of a Geneva Cam. There is an animation of the operation of this mechanism on the book website on the Support Files page. You will draw the Cam as well as the outline of the drive wheel. You will also create a detail view at 2:1 scale which will require an additional dimension style to be created. The Array command will be used to help create the outline of the Cam.

## Beginning the Project

1.  Open PROJ-07.dwg and save the drawing as PROJ-08.dwg.

2.  Delete the objects left over from PROJ-07.

    Do not delete the title block and general notes.

3.  Fill out the title block and general notes.

## Drawing the Object (Creating the Array)

1.  Begin by drawing one portion of the Cam.

    Since the object will be arrayed you will only need to draw one sixth of the object.

    Start with a horizontal line at 4.802 in length.

    Offset the line upward and downward .1405 inches (half of the .281 slot width).

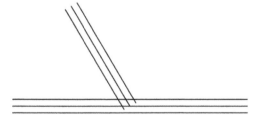

**4.802 Line Offset .1405 in Both Directions**

2.  Draw a construction line at 120 degrees from the midpoint of the middle line.

    The line length is 2.401 (half of the 4.802 outside diameter).

    Offset the line .1405 in both directions.

**Lines Added**

3.  Draw a 4.802 circle from the midpoint.

    Trim and circle to form the arc as shown.

    Use the Fillet tool to create sharp corners at the line intersections.

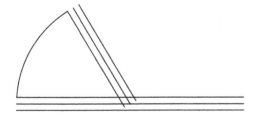

**Circle Drawn and Trimmed**

4.  Draw a construction line from the midpoint at 2.631 in length and at a 30 degree angle.

    Draw a .948 radius circle at the endpoint.

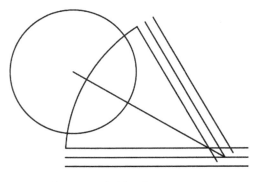

**Line and Circle Drawn**

5.  Delete the construction line and trim the circle and arc as shown.

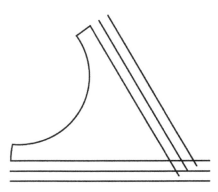

**Circle and Arc Trimmed**

6.  Draw a .281 diameter circle at 1.284 (half of 2.568 diameter locating the rounded ends of the slots) to the left of the midpoint of the 4.802 line.

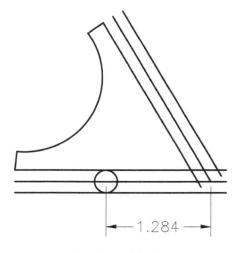

**Circle Added**

7.  At this point you have all the objects needed for the array.

    Trim the lower edge of the slot to make sure that it is the proper length.

    Trim and delete the unneeded lines as shown in the next step.

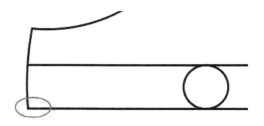

**Use Fillet to Trim Corner**

8.  This is what you will have left to array.

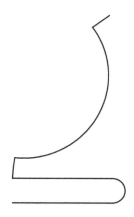

**Remaining Lines and Arcs to Array**

9.  Use the Polar Array tool to create the other five portions of the Cam.

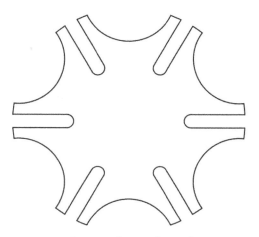

**Array Completed**

Drawing the Object (Center Hole and Keyway, Drive Wheel)

1.  Draw a 1.00 inch circle at the center of the view.

    Draw another .500 diameter circle concentric with the 1.00 circle.

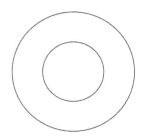

**Circle Drawn**

2.  Draw a horizontal line from the bottom of the .500 circle.

    Approximate the length.

    Offset the line up .600 inches.

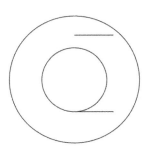

**Line Drawn and Offset**

3.  Draw a vertical line up to the endpoint of the top line from the center of the circle.

    Offset the line .0625 in both directions.

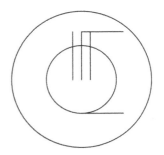

**Line Drawn and Offset**

4.  Use the Fillet and Trim tools to create the keyway.

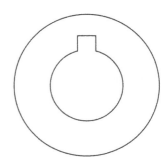

**Keyway Completed**

5.  Before drawing the Drive Wheel, create a new layer named Phantom Lines.

    Set the lineweight to .20mm and the linetype to PHANTOM.

    You will need to load the three Phantom linetypes from the ACAD-MD.lin file found in the support files folder.

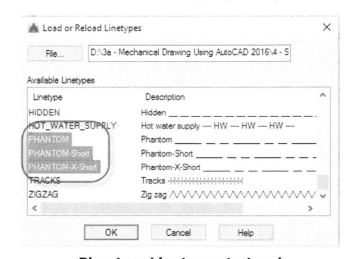

**Phantom Linetypes to Load**

6. Using the Phantom Lines layer, draw 3.366 diameter circle 2.631 inches to the left of the center of the Cam.

   Draw another concentric circle at 1.886 diameter.

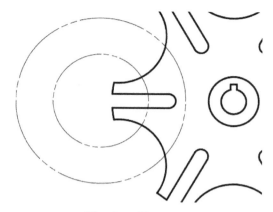

**Circles Drawn**

7. Draw a 2.432 radius circle at the center of the Cam.

   Use the Trim tool to trim the circle and the 3.366 diameter circle.

   When using the Trim tool, instead of pressing the Enter key to select the entire drawing, select only the two arcs.

   This will make the trimming easier.

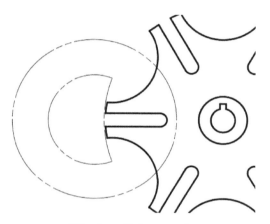

**Circles Trimmed**

8. Add the inner .25 diameter circle and the .25 circle for the pin.

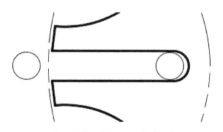

**.25 Circles Added**

<u>Drawing the Object (Projecting the Front View)</u>

1.  Project the edges of the Drive Wheel first
    down from the top view.

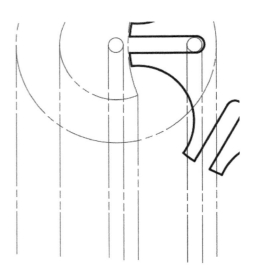

**Lines for Drive Wheel Projected**

2.  Draw and Offset the horizontal lines.

    Trim the lines to create the front
    view of the Drive Wheel.

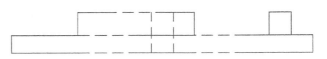

**Completed Front View of Drive Wheel**

    Change the two lines for the .25 hole
    to the Hidden Lines layer.

3.  Set the Object Lines layer to the current layer.

    To make the projection for the Cam easier, temporarily turn off the Phantom Lines
    and the Hidden Lines layers.

    Open the Layer Properties Manager dialog box and click the lightbulbs next to the
    layers to do this.

**Phantom Lines and Hidden Lines Layers Turned Off**

4. Project the visible edges of the Cam down from the top view.

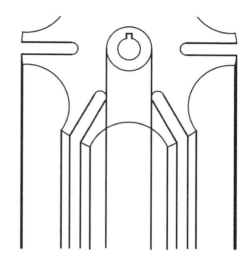

**Lines for Cam Projected**

5. Draw and Offset the horizontal lines.

   Trim the lines to create the front view of the Cam.

**Cam Object Lines Completed**

6. Turn on the Hidden Lines layer and project the hidden edges down from the top view of the Cam.

   You will not project the edges of the slots down to the front view.

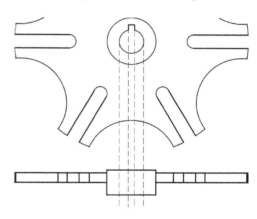

**Hidden Edges Projected**

7. Trim the hidden edges.

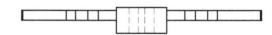

**Hidden Edges Trimmed**

8. Turn on the Phantom Lines layer and line up the two parts.

   It may help to group the lines for each part separately.

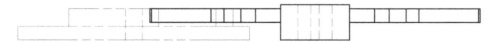

**Drive Wheel and Cam Parts Lined Up**

Adding the Center Marks, Center Lines and Dimensioning the View

1.  Add the center marks
    and center lines for the
    circular features in the
    top view.

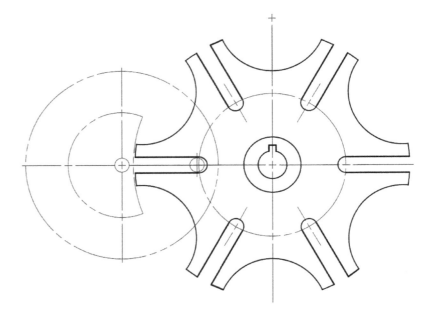

**Center Marks and Center Lines Added for Top View**

2.  Add the center lines
    for the front view.

    Some center lines will
    not be projected.

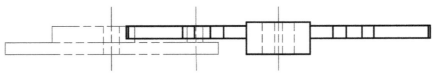

**Center Lines Added for Front View**

3.  Use the Mech 1-1 –
    3PLC style that was
    created in the previous
    project.

    The dimensions for the
    Drive Wheel are
    reference.

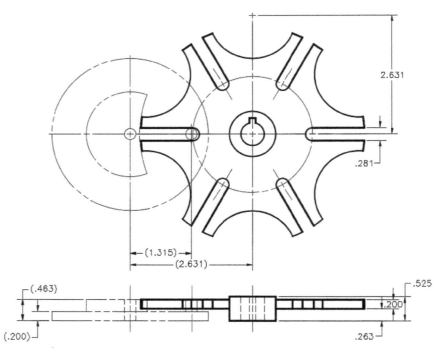

**Linear Dimensions Added**

4.  Add the radial
    dimensions.

    Some dimensions will
    use the Radius
    Extended style. This
    style will also need to
    be modified to 3 plc
    decimal.

    Use the Radius
    dimension tool for the
    two notes.

    The two views are fully
    dimensioned.

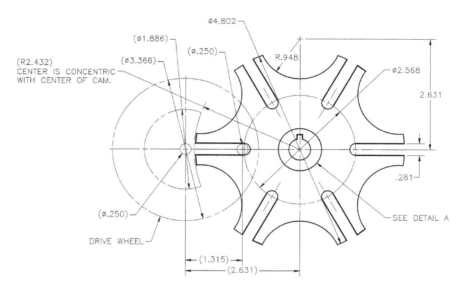

**Radial Dimensions Added**

## Drawing the Detail View

Details Views are used to show a maginified view of a portion of another view. In this case you will draw a 2:1 scale view of the keyway area of the Cam. This will keep from having to add too many dimensions in the top view.

1.  Copy the two center
    circles and the keyway
    to the right of the top
    view.

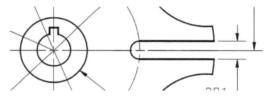

**Elements Copied**

2.  Click on the Scale tool in the Modify Panel.

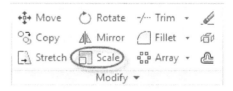

**Scale Tool**

3.  Select the objects and then snap
    to the center for the base point.

    Type 2 for the scale factor.

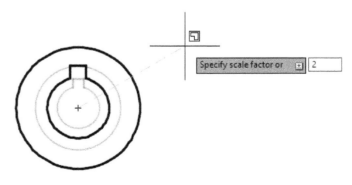

**Scale Factor Set to 2**

4.  The objects are now twice their original size.

5.  To dimension the detail view, you will need to create a new dimension style from the Mech 1-1 - 3PLC style.

    Name the new style: Mech 1-1 – 3PLC - 2-1 Scale.

**Mech 1-1 - 3PLC 2-1 Scale Dimension Style Created**

6.  The only change you will make is to set the measurement scale factor to .5000.

    This will divide the measured values of the dimension in half.

    This setting is located in the Primary Units tab.

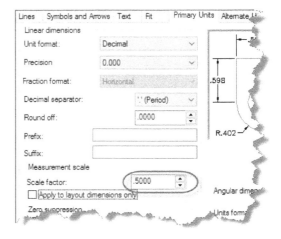

**Scale Factor Changed to .5000**

7.  Add the center mark and dimension the detail view using this new style.

    Add text below the view to label it.

    Use .125 high text.

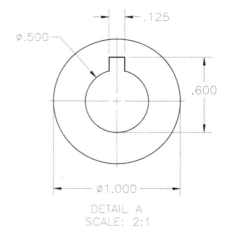

**Detail View Dimensioned and Labeled**

8.  Save the project. This concludes the tutorial.

    Create a PDF of the project and print if desired.

Project #8 — Geneva Cam

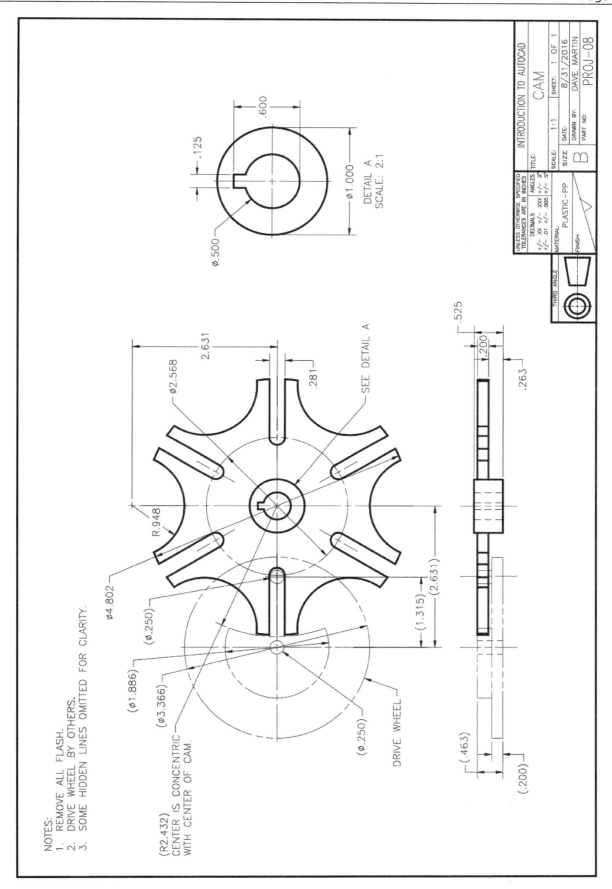

NOTES:
1. REMOVE ALL FLASH.
2. DRIVE WHEEL BY OTHERS.
3. SOME HIDDEN LINES OMITTED FOR CLARITY.

DETAIL A
SCALE: 2:1

SEE DETAIL A

DRIVE WHEEL

CENTER IS CONCENTRIC
WITH CENTER OF CAM.

INTRODUCTION TO AUTOCAD

| | | | |
|---|---|---|---|
| UNLESS OTHERWISE SPECIFIED TOLERANCES ARE IN INCHES | TITLE: | CAM | |
| DECIMALS / ANGLES | | | |
| +/- .XX / +/- .XXX / +/- X° | | | |
| +/- .01 / +/- .005 / +/- .5° | SCALE: 1:1 | DATE: 8/31/2016 | SHEET: 1 OF 1 |
| MATERIAL: PLASTIC–PP | SIZE B | DRAWN BY: DAVE MARTIN | |
| FINISH: | | PART NO: PROJ–08 | |

THIRD ANGLE

# Project #9 – Hole Guide

**Filename:** PROJ-09.dwg
Note: All screenshots are from the Autodesk® AutoCAD® software.

**Description:** This project will be the first to have you draw an auxiliary view. The object will also be drawn using metric units with millimeters as the base unit. This will also require the creation of a new set of dimension styles.

Since the part is in Metric units, it will be drawn to ISO (International Organization for Standardization) standards. Some of the changes will include: different title block size and different projection methods. These will be covered as you work through the tutorial.

Beginning the Project

1.  Open PROJ-08.dwg and save the drawing as PROJ-09.dwg.

2.  Delete all objects left over from PROJ-08 including the title block, border, and general notes.

3.  From the downloaded support files on the website, open the file: A3-Size Border (Metric).dwg.

4.  Select all of the elements in the file and copy to clipboard.

5.  Switch back to PROJ-09 and paste the elements to original coordinates.

You may notice the pasted elements are much larger than before. This is due to the new elements being in millimeters instead of inches.

To see the points at the upper left and lower right corners, change the size of the points to 3.7mm. Use the PTYPE key-in to open the Point Style dialog box.

6.  Fit the elements to the screen.

**Note:** For this project you will be using the A3 Border Size. This is based on the A3 size used for metric drawings. The paper size for A3 vellum is 420mm x 297mm. This is the equivalent metric size to the "B" Size Vellum (17" x 11")

7.  Fill out the title block and general notes.

**Note:** The 1.6 surface finish is in micrometers. This is the equivalent to a 63 micro inch surface finish.

Setting up the File for Metric Units

Even though AutoCAD does not distinguish between Millimeters and Inches in the Drawing Units setup, other changes will need to be made to the drawing. Since you will not be inserting blocks into this drawing using ones that were created using inches as the units, you will not need to change the insertion scale.

1. To verify the Drawing Units, open the Drawing Units dialog box by using the UNITS key-in command.

**Drawing Units for Metric Drawings**

2. Type DS to open the Drafting Settings dialog box.

   In the Snap and Grid tab, make the following changes:

   Change the Snap spacing to 12.7 (millimeter equivalent to .500 inches.)

   Change the Grid spacing to 6.35 (millimeter equivalent to .250 inches.)

**Drafting Settings for Metric Drawing**

## Drawing the Object (Front and Upper Views)

Before beginning the drawing, you will be using First Angle Projection as the method to projects the three views of the project. If you have no experience with this projection you may decide to draw the views in Third Angle Projection instead.

In this tutorial the method will be First Angle but there will also be a Third Angle version available on the website in the Support Files area. If using the Third Angle method, make sure to change the title block projection symbol.

To help with the visualization of the project, a three dimensional view of the object is provided.

**Note:** Later, in Part Two of the book you will draw your own three-dimension solid of this project.

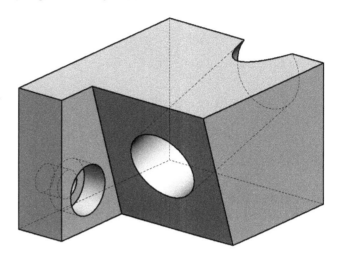

**Three-Dimensional View of Project #9**

1. Begin with the front view.

   Draw the outline of the part, then the holes for the counterbore, and lastly the angled line. The angle for the line will be 73 degrees down.

   This view will be drawn that same way regardless of the projection used.

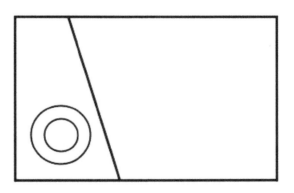

**Object Lines for Front View**

2.  In First Angle Projection, you project through the view instead of projecting from the view.

    Project the edges up to create what would be considered the bottom view.

    Offset the lines from the bottom up for the horizontal surfaces.

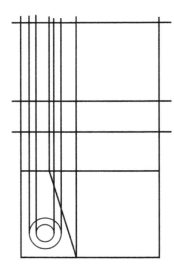

**Lines for Bottom View Projected**

3.  Trim and extend the lines to form the lines for the view.

    Offset the middle horizontal line downward 8.50 for the depth of the counter bore.

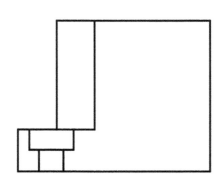

**Lines Trimmed and Extended for View**

4.  Change the lines for the counter bore to hidden.

    You may notice that the dashes do not show up. This is due to the Linetype Scale setting.

    Type LTS for the key-in command to change this setting.

    Set the Linetype Scale to 25.4.

    This will affect all new dashed lines added to the drawing from here on.

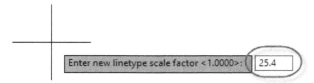

Enter new linetype scale factor <1.0000>: | 25.4 |

**Linetype Scale Set to 25.4**

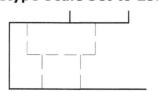

**Counterbore Hole Lines Changed to Hidden**

5.  In the front view, draw the edges of the 25.4 thru hole and the center line.

    The hole center is 25.2mm up from the bottom of the view on the angled surface.

    The hole is perpendicular to the surface.

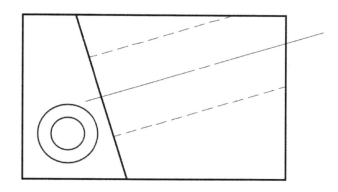

**Hidden Lines and Center Lines Added**

6.  Project the left edge, right edge, and center of the hole up to the upper view.

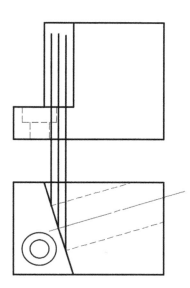

**Lines Projected for Hole**

7.  In the upper view offset the bottom horizontal line up 40.39mm for the center of the hole.

    Offset the new line another 12.7mm for the top of the hole.

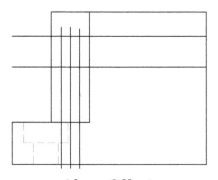

**Lines Offset**

8.  Click on the Ellipse tool in the Draw Panel.

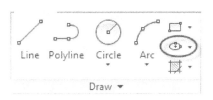

**Ellipse Tool**

9.  Snap to the intersection of the lines
    for the center of the hole.

    Then the first Axis Endpoint.

    Then the second Axis Endpoint.

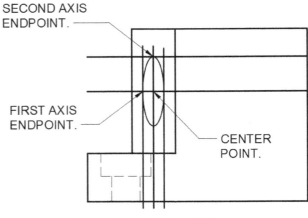

**Snap Points for Ellipse**

10. Delete the construction lines and add
    the hidden lines and center line.

    Also add the center line for the
    counterbored hole.

    You will add the center mark later
    when dimensioning the views.

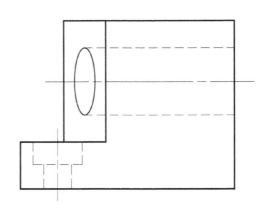

**Hidden Lines and Center Lines Added**

Drawing the Object (Auxiliary View)

When drawing the Auxiliary view, you will project the lines the same way as with the
upper view. The only difference is that you will project the lines parallel to the angle of
the 17 degree hole.

You will also use a field of drafting called Descriptive Geometry to place the elliptical
portion of the hole in the upper view.

1.  Begin by projecting the edges of the
    front view at a 17 degree angle to the
    right.

    You will not need to project the edges
    of the counterbored hole or the 25.4
    thru hole.

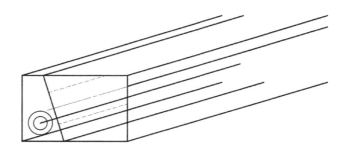

**Edges Projected at 17 Degrees**

2. Draw a perpendicular line through the projection lines to the right of the front view.

   Offset the line 17.61mm, 40.39mm, and 63.17mm.

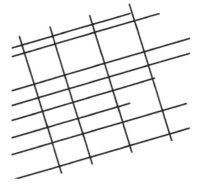

**Lines Offset**

3. Trim the lines as shown to the corners of the view.

   Look carefully to match the corner in the front view to the same corner in the auxiliary view.

   **Note:** Remember, you are projecting through the front view.

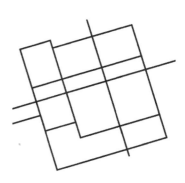

**Lines Trimmed**

4. Change the hidden edge to a hidden line.

   Add the 25.4mm diameter circle at the intersection of the two lines.

   Trim the hidden line where it intersects the circle.

   Delete the construction lines except for the one that is marking the bottom center of the counterbored hole.

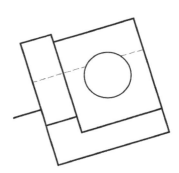

**Lines Deleted**

5. Copy the hidden lines for the counterbored hole from the upper view to the intersection of the construction line at the bottom of the auxiliary view.

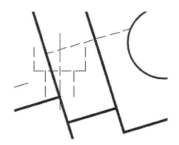

**Counterbore Hidden Lines Copied**

6.  Rotate the hidden lines and the center lines 73 degrees clockwise to align them with the auxiliary view.

    Delete the construction line.

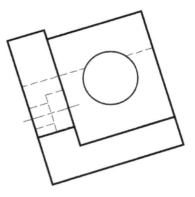

**Auxiliary View Complete**

7.  To construct the ellipse in the upper view, you will utilize Descriptive Geometry techniques to transfer distances from the auxiliary view.

    Project the edge of the hole in the front view to the upper view.

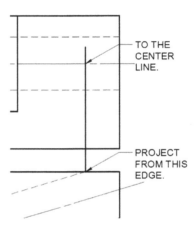

TO THE CENTER LINE.

PROJECT FROM THIS EDGE.

**Line Projected from Edge of Hole**

8.  Extend a line from the top of the front view to the right into the auxiliary view.

    Draw another line from the center of the 25.4mm hole in the auxiliary view to the new line.

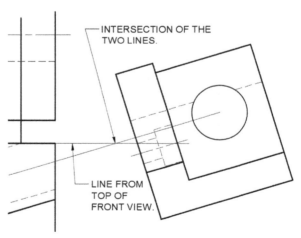

INTERSECTION OF THE TWO LINES.

LINE FROM TOP OF FRONT VIEW.

**Lines Drawn**

9.  Project a line up from the intersection to the upper view.

    Where this line intersects with the center line in the upper view will be the center of the ellipse.

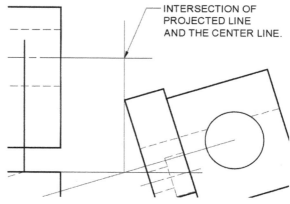

INTERSECTION OF PROJECTED LINE AND THE CENTER LINE.

**Line Drawn from Intersection to Center Line in Upper View**

10. Project a line from the top hidden line in the upper view to the projected line.

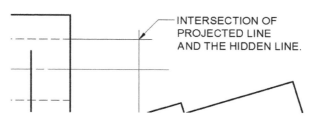

INTERSECTION OF PROJECTED LINE AND THE HIDDEN LINE.

**Line Drawn from Hidden Line to Projected Line**

11. Draw an ellipse from this intersection to the edge of the hole in the upper view.

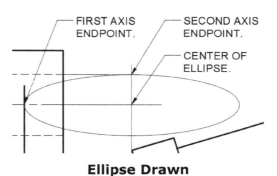

FIRST AXIS ENDPOINT.

SECOND AXIS ENDPOINT.

CENTER OF ELLIPSE.

**Ellipse Drawn**

12. Change the ellipse to hidden linetype and delete the construction lines.

    Trim the ellipse to the edge of the upper view.

    The three views are now complete.

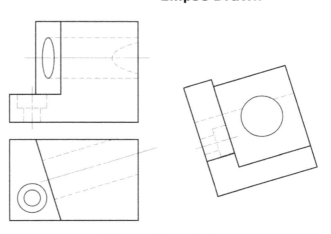

**Views Complete**

Dimensioning the Views (Setting up the Dimension Style)

Dimensioning first angle projection drawings will use the same methods as with third angle projection. What is different will be the style of dimensioning. You will begin by modifying the Mech 1-1 dimension style to conform to the ISO style. This is typically used with first angle projection drawings.

1. Open the Dimension style Manager dialog box.

   Click on the Mech 1-1 style and then the New... button to the right.

   Name the new dimension style, Metric 1-1.

**New Dimension Style: Metric 1-1**

2. Click Continue to modify the new style.

   Make the following changes:

   In the Text tab, change the Text alignment to ISO standard. Also, change the Text placement Vertical setting to Above and the Offset from dim line setting to 0.0625.

   In the Fit tab, change the "Use overall scale of:" setting to 25.4.

   This will multiply the text size and other settings by 25.4.

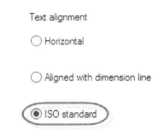

**Text Alignment set to ISO Standard**

**Text Place Vertical Setting set to Above**

**Use Overall Scale set to 25.4000**

3. In the Primary Units tab, set the Precision setting to 0.00.

**Precision set to 0.00**

Even though all dimensions are above 1mm, you will also uncheck the Leading Zero suppression.

**Note:** You may also choose to set the Decimal separator to comma.

**Leading Zero Suppression Unchecked**

4. Click OK to save the new dimension style and close the dialog box.

5. Modify the Center Mark style.

   Set the center cross size to 3.18 and the center cross gap to 1.59.

Dimensioning the Views

1. Separate the views from one another if needed to allow for the dimensions to be placed.

2. Add the missing center marks to the 25.4mm hole.

   Rotate the center mark so that it is aligned with the view.

   When adding the center mark for the elliptical hole in the upper view, you will need to copy the center mark from the other hole and modify the mark.

   The Center Mark tool does not work with ellipses.

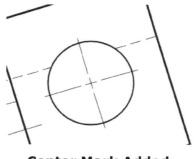

**Center Mark Added**

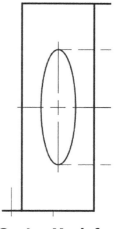

**Center Mark for Elliptical Hole**

3.  Add the linear dimensions.

    Use 9.50mm spacing for the first dimension line and then 6.35 for the second line and beyond.

    **Note:** Since the Grid Dot spacing was changed at the beginning of the tutorial, you may also use the dot spacing to aid in the dimensioning.

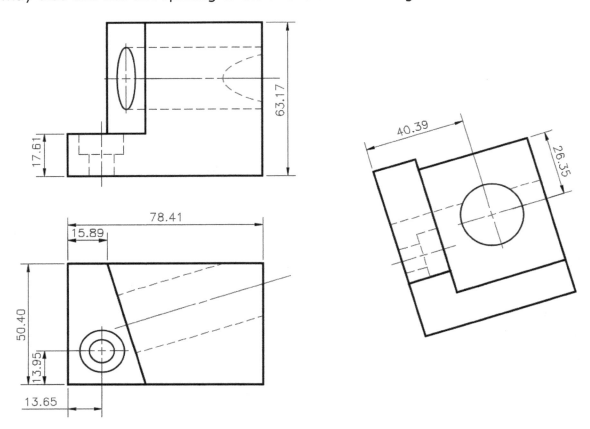

**Linear Dimensions Placed**

4.  Add the radial dimension for the 25.40mm hole in the auxiliary view.

    You will need to create a new style from the Metric 1-1 style so that the text is not above the leader line.

    The name of the new style will be:
    Metric 1-1 (Radial).

    In the Text tab, change the Text alignment setting to ISO Standard.

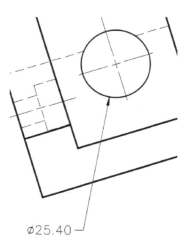

**Diameter Dimension Added**

5. Add the callout for the counter bored hole.

   When editing the text, you will need to use the font containing the GDT symbols.

   Unlike in Project #6, you will use the shx version of the GDT font (gdt.shx).

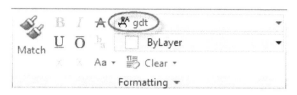

**gdt.shx Font**

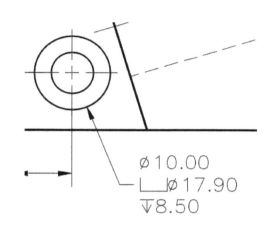

**Callout Added**

6. Add the angular dimension for the angle of the hole in the front view.

   Use the Metric 1-1 style for this dimension.

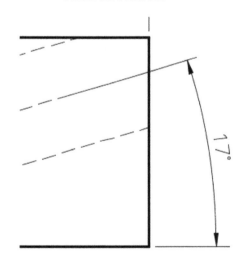

**Angular Dimension Added**

7. Save the project. This concludes the tutorial.

   Create a PDF of the project and print if desired.

   **Note:** You may use the same print settings except the scale will need to change to 25.4. You may also change the paper size to ISO full bleed A3 (420.00 x 297.00 MM) and plot the drawing at 1:1 scale.

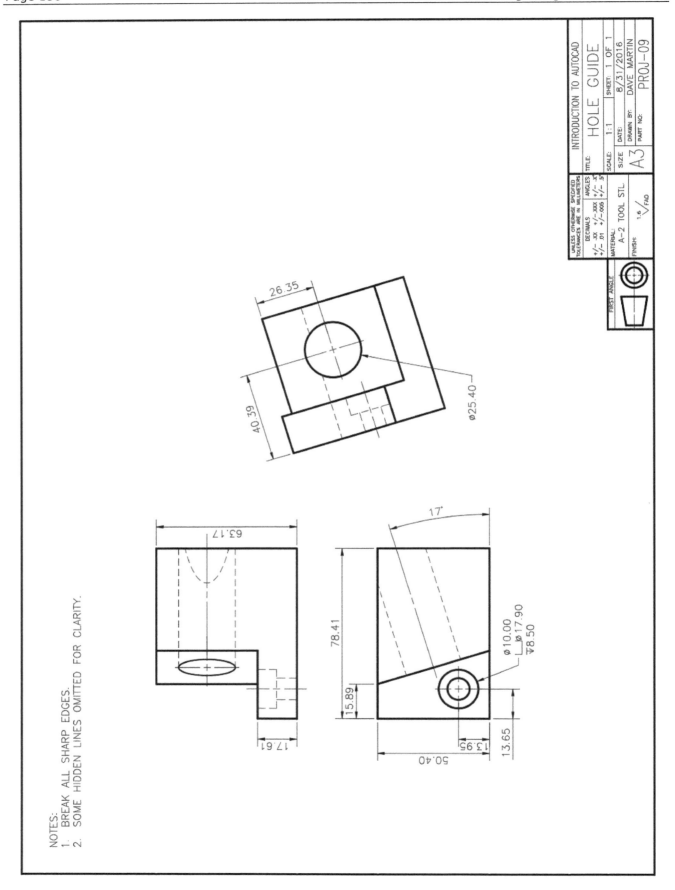

NOTES:
1. BREAK ALL SHARP EDGES.
2. SOME HIDDEN LINES OMITTED FOR CLARITY.

26.35

40.39

Ø25.40

63.17

17.61

17°

78.41

15.89

50.40

13.95

13.65

Ø10.00
⌴Ø17.90
▽8.50

| UNLESS OTHERWISE SPECIFIED TOLERANCES ARE IN MILLIMETERS | |
|---|---|
| DECIMALS | ANGLES |
| +/- .XX  +/-.XXX | +/- .x° |
| +/- .01  +/-.005 | +/- .5° |

| INTRODUCTION TO AUTOCAD | |
|---|---|
| TITLE: HOLE GUIDE | |
| SCALE: 1:1 | DATE: 8/31/2016 | SHEET: 1 OF 1 |
| SIZE A3 | DRAWN BY: DAVE MARTIN |
| PART NO: PROJ-09 | |

MATERIAL: A-2 TOOL STL.
FINISH: ¹·⁶√FAO

FIRST ANGLE

# Project #10 – Cover Plate

**Filename:** PROJ-10.dwg
Note: All screenshots are from the Autodesk® AutoCAD® software.

**Description:** This will introduce you to creating a rectangular array and ordinate (arrowless) dimensioning. You will also use the Table tool to create a table to document the sizes of features.

The UCS (Universal Coordinate System) tool will be introduced in the tutorial. Since this drawing will be printed at 1:2 scale, you will need to create new dimension styles.

## Beginning the Project

1.  Open PROJ-08.dwg and save the drawing as PROJ-10.dwg.

    The reason you will not be using PROJ-09 is that PROJ-10 is in imperial units.

    You will be changing the scale of the border and title block to twice the original size. This is because the drawing will be printed at 1:2 scale.

2.  Delete the views and dimensions from the previous drawing.

3.  Select the border, title block, and general notes.

    Click the Scale tool.

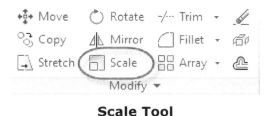

**Scale Tool**

4.  Key-in the base point at the 0,0 location. Use the # symbol for absolute coordinates.

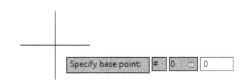

**Use 0,0 for Base Point**

5.  Type 2 for the scale factor.

    Press Enter to scale the elements.

    **Note:** Since you will not be using any other linetypes beside Continuous, there is no need to set the Linetype Scale to 2.000.

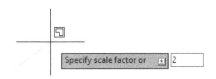

**Scale Factor set to 2**

6.  Set the Grid dot spacing to .5000 (2 x .2500).

7.  Fill out the title block and general notes.

Drawing the Object

1.  Begin by laying out the outside shape of the front view of the project.

2.  Once you have added the view, you will move the UCS to the lower left corner of the shape.

    This will be the new origin for the holes and rectangle.

    Type UCS to access the options to modify the UCS.

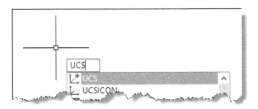

**UCS Key-in Command**

3.  Snap to the lower left corner of the shape for the origin.

    Your number values will be different than the example.

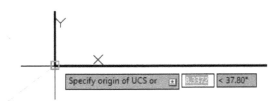

**New Origin for the UCS**

4.  Drag to the right to accept the X-Axis direction. Polar tracking should be on to insure that the direction is horizontal.

    Press Enter to accept the XY plane.

    The UCS is now located at the corner of the view.

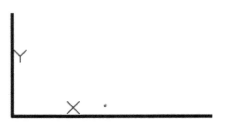

**UCS Relocated to Corner**

5.  To move the UCS again, type in the key-in command.

    To return the UCS to 0,0, use the World option.

6.  Begin by placing the holes at the locations given in the table.

    Since you have moved the UCS, do not use the # symbol for absolute coordinates.

| HOLE CHART | | |
|---|---|---|
| HOLE | DIA. | QTY. |
| A | 1.91 | 1 |
| B | 2.36 | 1 |
| C | .88 | 2 |
| D | 1.33 | 1 |

**Use Hole Chart for Hole Locations**

7.  Using the Circle tool to add the holes, type in the X and Y coordinates for their locations.

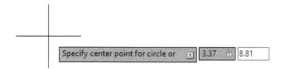

**Hole Location for First Hole**

8.  Repeat the process for the other four holes.

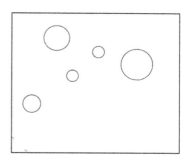

**Five Holes Added**

9.  Next you will place the first hole for the rectangular array.

    Place this hole at 6.69, .97. The diameter will be .65 inches.

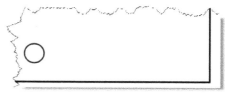

**First Hole of Array Placed**

10. Click on the down arrow next to the Array tool in the Modify panel. This is the same tool that was used for the polar array in PROJ-07.

    Choose the Rectangular Array option.

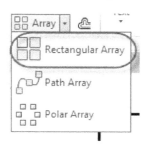

**Rectangular Array Option**

11. Select the circle and press Enter, a preliminary array will appear.

    Change the column spacing to 1.42 and the row spacing to 1.17.

    Verify the number of columns is set to 4 and the number of rows is set to 4.

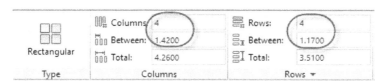

**Rectangular Array Settings**

12. Press Enter to exit the tool and place the array.

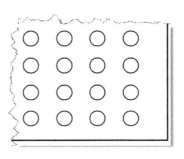

**Array Placed**

13. That last element you will place will be the rectangle.

Click on the Rectangle tool.

Enter 2.92,.73 for the first corner point and 5.49,2.62 for the second corner point.

Use the # symbol for the second point.

All the object lines are now placed.

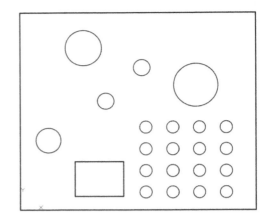

**All Object Lines Placed**

Dimensioning the Views (Adding the Center Marks)

1. Before dimensioning you will create and edit a new dimension style.

   Open the Dimension Style Manager dialog box.

   Start with the Mech 1-1 dimension style and create a new style called: Mech 1-2.

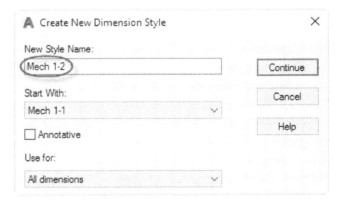

**Mech 1-2 Style Created**

2. Click on the Fit tab and set the "Use overall scale of" setting to 2.0000.

   This will be the only change made to the new style.

**Overall Scale set to 2.000**

3. Modify the Center Mark style.

   Set the center cross size to .25 and the center cross gap to .125.

4. Add the center marks for the holes.

   When adding the center mark for the first arrayed hole, stretch the two outside horizontal lines .385 inches from the edge of the circle.

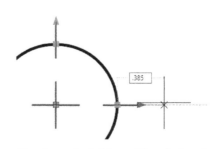

**Horizontal Line Stretched**

5.  Stretch the vertical outside lines .26 inches.

    This is done so that the center marks will overlap
    after arraying them in the next step.

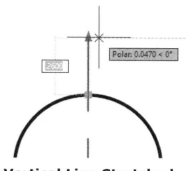

**Vertical Line Stretched**

6.  Use the Rectangular Array tool to create the
    remaining center marks.

    Set the number of columns to 4 and the rows to 4.

    Set the spacing or try using the triangular grips to
    space the copies to line up with the hole centers.

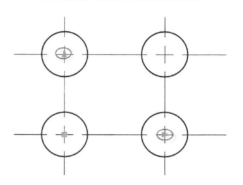

**Triangular Grips**

7.  The center marks are placed.

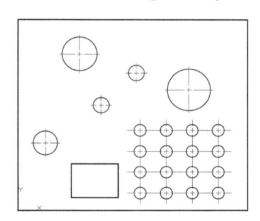

**Center Marks Placed**

Dimensioning the Views
(Placing the Ordinate Dimensions, Linear Dimensions, and Labels)

1. Click on the Ordinate dimension tool in the Home tab, Annotation panel.

   You may also click on the Dimension tool, then right-click and select the Ordinate option.

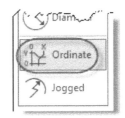

**Ordinate Dimension Tool**

2. Snap on the lower left corner of the view. The value will be .00. This value is based on the location of the UCS when you begin dimensioning.

   Drag the end of the extension line 1 1/2 grid dots (3/4") from the edge of the view.

   **Note:** The dimensions will not change if the UCS is moved later.

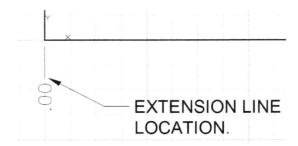

**Location of Extension Line**

3. Add the next dimension.

   Without clicking, snap on the endpoint of the first extension line and drag to the right.

   Use Object Snap Tracking to line up the extension line endpoints.

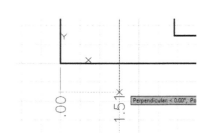

**Use Object Snap Tracking**

4. Repeat the process for the remaining ordinate dimensions.

   Some dimensions will be placed inside the view to avoid long extension lines.

   The ordinate dimensions are now placed.

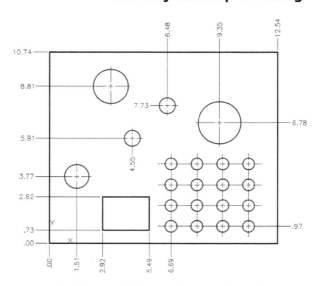

**Ordinate Dimensions Placed**

5.  Add the two linear dimensions for the row
    and column spacing of the holes.

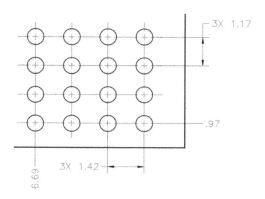

**Linear Dimensions Placed**

6.  Add the text below each of the holes. This will be used to identify the holes in the
    hole chart.

    Use .25 high text for the labels.

    You do not need to label all of the holes marked "E".

Creating the Hole Chart

A hole chart is used to consolidate multiple dimensions on a drawing. In this case you will use the hole chart to indicate the diameters and quantities of each of the holes.

AutoCAD has a special tool that is used for tables and is similar to the tools used in spreadsheet programs. You can also use this tool to upload and download data from/to an external source such as an Excel spreadsheet file.

1. Click on the Table tool in the Annotate tab, Tables panel.

   This tool may also be accessed from the Home tab.

**Table Tool**

2. The Insert Table dialog box opens.

   Set the Column & Row settings as shown.

**Insert Table Dialog Box**

3. Press the OK button.

   The dialog box will close and the table will be attached to the cursor.

   Place the table in the open area to the right of the view.

**Table Placed**

4.  Begin filling out the table starting with the title.

    Use .375 high text for the title.

    Click outside the table when finished with the title. The height of the row will become larger to accommodate the text.

    **Note:** Your font may be different. Later you will change the text style to MECHANICAL.

**Title Filled Out**

5.  Click inside the first cell beneath the title.

    Type in the word "HOLE" for the first header. The height of the text will be .25.

    Continue with the remaining text for the table.

    **Note:** You can use the properties window to modify the size and justification of the text after placing. You can also use the fence tool to select multiple cells to change properties.

**Remaining Cells Filled Out**

6.  Next you will set up the number format and justification for the cells.

    Click on the cell beneath the DIA. column.

**Cell Selected**

7.  In the Table Cell tab, select the Data Format tool and pick Custom Table Cell Format… in the drop-down menu.

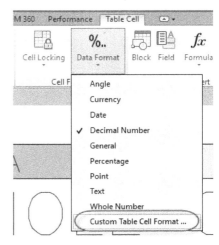

**Custom Table Cell Format…**

8. The Table Cell Format dialog box opens.

   Select "Decimal in the Format:" area.

   Then click the Additional Format... button.

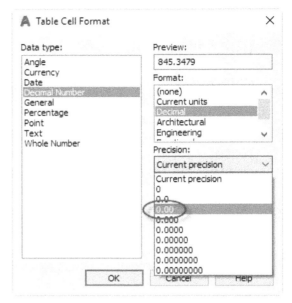

**Setting the Precision to 0.00**

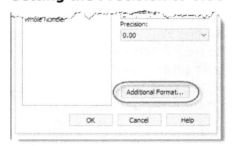

**Additional Format... Button**

9. The Additional Format dialog box opens.

   Check the Leading Zero Suppression check box to remove the leading zero.

**Additional Format Dialog Box**

10. Select the remaining cells using a crossing fence and update the properties to match the first cell.

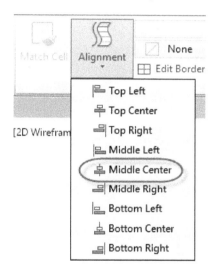

**Cells Updated**

11. Select all of the cells under the title.

    Change the Alignment to Middle Center in the Cell Styles panel.

**Alignment Set to Middle Center**

12. In the Properties window in the Content section, set the Text height to .25.

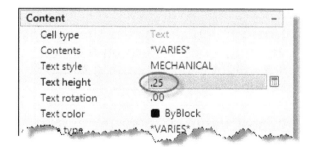

**Text Height Set to .25**

13. Next, you will set the lineweight to .50 for the title and header rows and the outside of the table.

    Select the title and header rows and click the Edit Borders tool in the Cell Styles panel.

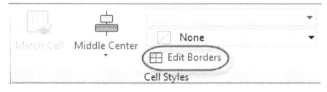

**Edit Borders Tool**

14. The Cell Border Properties dialog box opens.

Set the Lineweight to 0.50 mm in the drop-down window.

Click the Outside Borders and Inside Horizontal Border buttons.

Click OK to make the changes and close the dialog box.

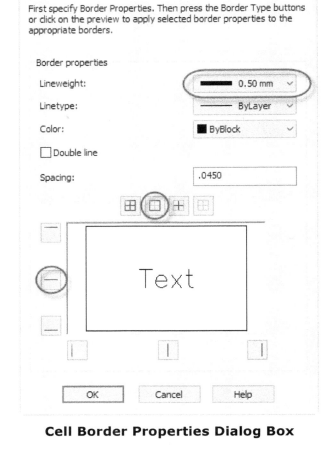

**Cell Border Properties Dialog Box**

15. The outside and inside horizontal lines are now thicker.

**Note:** If you cannot see the changes you may need to turn on the lineweight toggle by using the LWT key-in.

16. Repeat the process for the outside border of the remaining cells.

| HOLE CHART | | |
|------|------|------|
| HOLE | DIA. | QTY. |
| A | 1.91 | 1 |
| B | 2.36 | 1 |

**Lines Thicker**

| HOLE CHART | | |
|------|------|------|
| HOLE | DIA. | QTY. |
| A | 1.91 | 1 |
| B | 2.36 | 1 |
| C | .88 | 2 |
| D | 1.33 | 1 |
| E | .65 | 16 |

**Remaining Lines Thickened**

17. The last step is to set the height of the rows.

Select the title cell and change the height of the cell to .75 inches in the Cell portion of the Properties window.

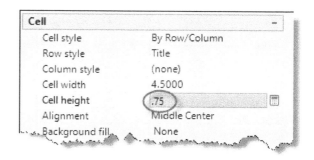

**Changing the Cell Height**

18. Repeat the process for the remaining cells

Change their height to .50 inches.

The table is now complete.

| HOLE CHART | | |
|---|---|---|
| HOLE | DIA. | QTY. |
| A | 1.91 | 1 |
| B | 2.36 | 1 |
| C | .88 | 2 |
| D | 1.33 | 1 |
| E | .65 | 16 |

**Table Complete**

19. You may use this table format for future projects.

If you wish to save the style of the table, begin by selecting the entire table.

Click the Table tool and then click the Launch the Table Style Dialog button.

**Launch the Table Style Dialog Button**

20. Create a new table style in the Table Style dialog box.

Name the style: Hole Chart

Click Continue to modify the settings.

**Create New Table Style Dialog Box**

21. In the New Table Style dialog box, click the button next to the "Select table to start from:" area.

    The dialog box will close temporarily, select the table you just created.

    Click the OK button to save the table style and close the dialog box.

    A new table with the updated style is attached to your cursor. Press the ESC button to end the command.

    **Note:** When inserting the new table, the Title and Header cells will already be filled out.

22. Save the project. This concludes the tutorial.

    Create a PDF of the project and print if desired.

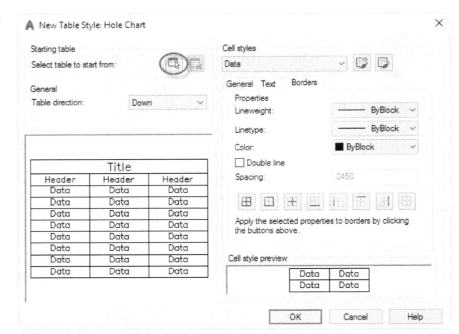

**New Style Table Dialog Box**

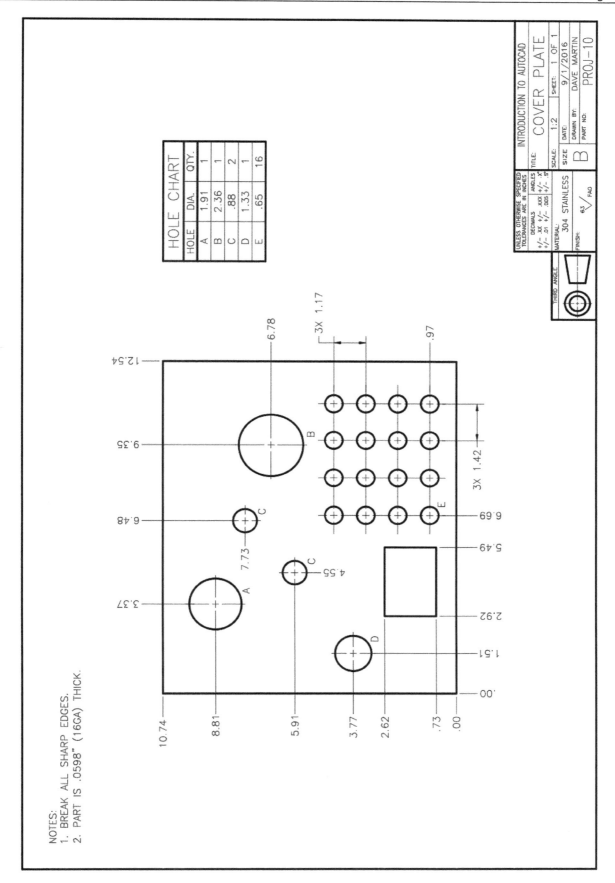

HOLE CHART

| HOLE | DIA. | QTY. |
|------|------|------|
| A | 1.91 | 1 |
| B | 2.36 | 1 |
| C | .88 | 2 |
| D | 1.33 | 1 |
| E | .65 | 16 |

NOTES:
1. BREAK ALL SHARP EDGES.
2. PART IS .0598" (16GA) THICK.

INTRODUCTION TO AUTOCAD

TITLE: COVER PLATE

SHEET: 1 OF 1
SCALE: 1:2
DATE: 9/1/2016
DRAWN BY: DAVE MARTIN
PART NO: PROJ-10
SIZE: B

UNLESS OTHERWISE SPECIFIED
TOLERANCES ARE IN INCHES
DECIMALS        ANGLES
+/- .XX    +/- .XXX    +/- .X°
+/- .01    +/- .005    +/- .5°

MATERIAL: 304 STAINLESS
FINISH: 63 √ FAO

THIRD ANGLE

# Project #11a – Weld Symbols

**Filename:** PROJ-11a.dwg
Note: All screenshots are from the Autodesk® AutoCAD® software.

**Description:** The project will introduce you to the process of creating the weld symbols. Symbols are known as Blocks in the AutoCAD software. For this project a folder will be created containing the different weld symbols. These blocks will be used for the next project that shows parts welded together into an assembly called a weldment.

## Beginning the Project

1.  Open PROJ-08.dwg and save the drawing as PROJ-11a.dwg.

2.  Delete the objects and general notes left over from PROJ-08.

3.  Fill out the title block.

## Drawing the Weld Symbols

Before you can create the blocks, you will need to create the elements for the weld symbols. Begin with the Fillet Weld symbol.

1.  The weld symbols don't have exact sizes but they should be consistent in size with each other.

    Use the PDF drawing from the website to draw the elements for the Fillet Weld and other symbols.

    The text will serve as placeholders. They may be changed depending on the size of the weld.

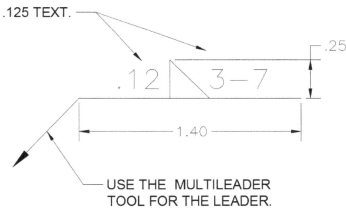

**Fillet Weld Symbol Dimensions**

2.  When adding the leader line, you will need to create a new multileader style.

    Start with the Mech 1-1 and create a new style called: Weld Leader

**New Multileader Style Created**

3. In the dialog box, click on the Leader Structure tab and uncheck the "Set landing distance" checkbox

**Set Landing Distance Unchecked**

4. Click on the Content tab and set the Multileader type to None.

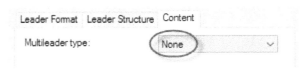

**Multileader Type set to None**

5. Click Ok to close the dialog box and save the new style.

   Add the reference line to the left end of the reference line.

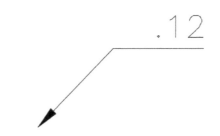

**Leader Line Added to Reference Line**

6. Draw the field weld flag and the all-around symbol.

   When drawing the filled in shape, draw the lines then use the Hatch tool with the fill set to Solid to fill-in the triangle.

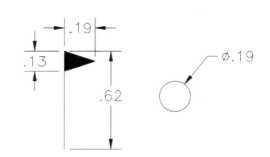

**Field Weld Flag and All-Around Symbols**

7. Draw the Notes symbol.

   This will go on the end of the weld symbol.

   Use Middle Left justification for this text.

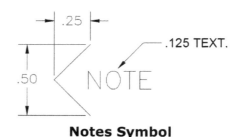

**Notes Symbol**

8. Draw the remaining symbols.

   To make the process efficient, copy the previous symbol and modify the elements.

   There are no specific dimensions for each symbol, approximate the sizes based on the example drawing.

9.  When locating the symbols for
    the chart, space the symbols .62
    inches from one another.

    Add the name of the symbol to
    the right.

    Use .125 for the text height.

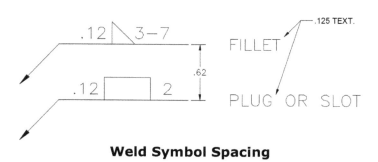

**Weld Symbol Spacing**

10. Draw the text and the lines for the chart.

    The height of the chart is 7.75 inches.

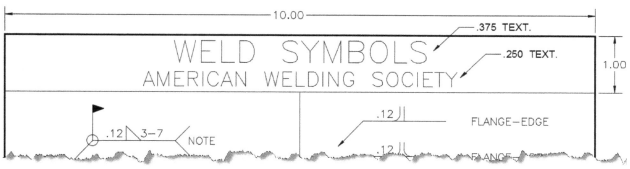

**Chart Text and Border Dimensions**

## Creating the Blocks

Now that you have completed the drawings of the weld symbols, you will create groups
of elements known as blocks. You will also save the blocks as individual files.

1.  The process to create blocks is to select the elements for the block, define the
    origin and create a name for the block.

    You will begin by creating blocks for the following:

| Name | Block Name | Description |
|------|------------|-------------|
| Field Weld Flag | 1 – Field Weld | Field Weld Flag |
| Tail with Note | 2 – Note | Tail Symbol with Note |
| All Around Symbol | 3 – All Around | All Around Symbol |

2.  Click on the Create tool in the Home tab, Block panel.

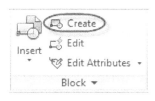

**Create Tool**

3.  The Block Definition
    dialog box opens.

    The Name area is used to
    name the block.

    The Base Point area is
    used to set the handle
    point for the block.

    The Objects area is used
    to select the objects that
    will be part of the block.

    These are the only
    options you will use at
    this point.

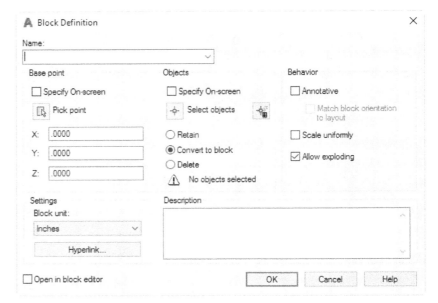

**Block Definition Dialog Box**

4.  Type in "1 – Field Weld" in the name area.

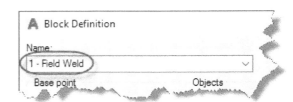

**Entering the Name of the Block**

5.  Click the Select Objects tool.

    The dialog box will close temporarily.

    Select the filled triangle and the vertical line for the field
    weld symbol and then press the Enter key to reopen the
    dialog box.

**Select Objects Tool**

6.  Click the Pick Point tool.

    Again, the dialog box will close temporarily.

    Snap on the bottom endpoint of the vertical line and
    press the Enter key to reopen the dialog box.

**Pick Point Tool**

7. Type in the description of the block in the Description window.

   **Note:** Adding the description is not required when creating the block.

**Description Window**

8. Repeat the process for the other two blocks.

   The origin for the Notes block will be at the left end of the angled lines.

   The origin for the All-Around block will be at the center of the circle.

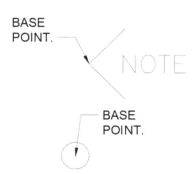

9. Create the remaining blocks.

   Pick the weld symbol, text and the leader line for the blocks.

   The base point will be at the left endpoint of the reference line.

**Base Point for Fillet Weld Symbol**

10. When you are finished, you will have a list of blocks available for use on your drawing.

    **Note:** The Title Block Text (B-Size) block was loaded with the title block file.

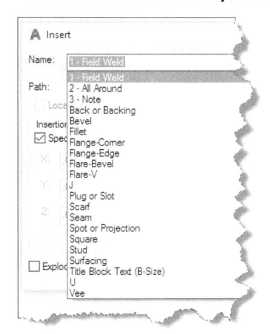

**List of Blocks Available**

## Using the Blocks

Now that the blocks are created, practice using them on the drawing.

1.  Pick an open area of the drawing.

    Click on the Insert tool in the Insert tab.

    Then click on the More Options... text at the bottom of the drop-down area.

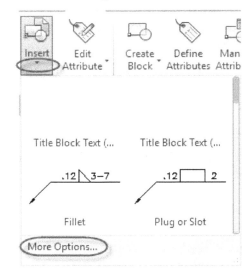

**Insert Tool and More Options...**

2.  The Insert dialog box opens.

    You can use this dialog box to select the block to add to the drawing, the insertion point, the scale, and the rotation.

    Select the Fillet block in the Name drop-down menu.

    Check the Explode checkbox at the bottom left of the dialog box.

    This will automatically break the block into individual elements after placement.

**Insert Dialog Box**

3.  Press the OK button.

    Click a point for the block.

    The Fillet weld symbol will appear.

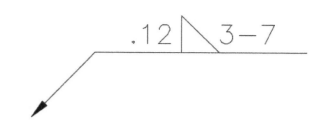

**Fillet Weld Symbol**

4.  Double-click on the text to edit.

    You can also click on the leader line to stretch and move the location of the arrowhead and add a vertex (additional line) to the leader.

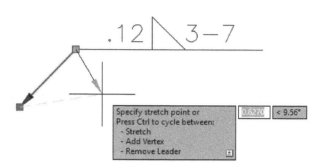

5.  Add the Field Weld and All-Around blocks to your weld symbol. These blocks do not need to be exploded.

    Add the Note block to your symbol. This will need to be exploded in order to edit the text.

    **Note:** The Explode tool is located in the Home tab, Modify panel.

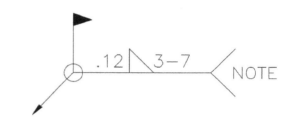

**Field Weld, All-Around, and Note Blocks Added to Weld Symbol**

**Explode Tool**

6.  Save the project. This concludes the tutorial.

    Create a PDF of the project and print if desired.

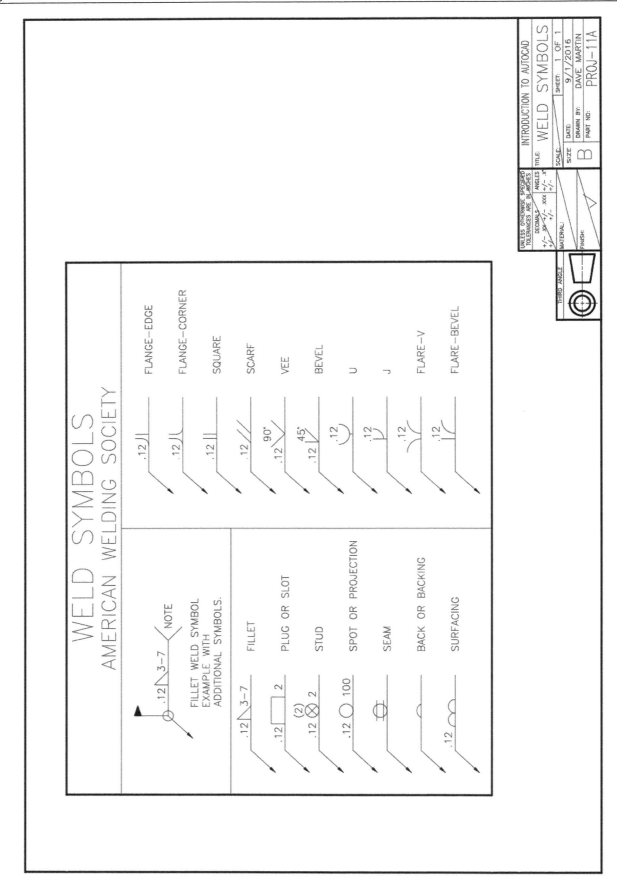

# Project #11b – Weldment

**Filename:** PROJ-11b.dwg

Note: All screenshots are from the Autodesk® AutoCAD® software.

**Description:** Now that the weld symbols have been created, you will now apply them to a drawing. This project is a collection of parts called a weldment. The drawing will not only show the sizes of the parts but will also show the types of welds that are used to join them together.

Beginning the Project

1.   Open PROJ-10.dwg and save the drawing as PROJ-11a.dwg.

2.   Delete the view and the table left over from PROJ-10.

3.   Fill out the title block and the general notes.

Drawing the Object

This is the object you will draw. A three-dimensional drawing is shown to aid in visualizing the weldment. In Part Two of the book you will create your own 3D version.

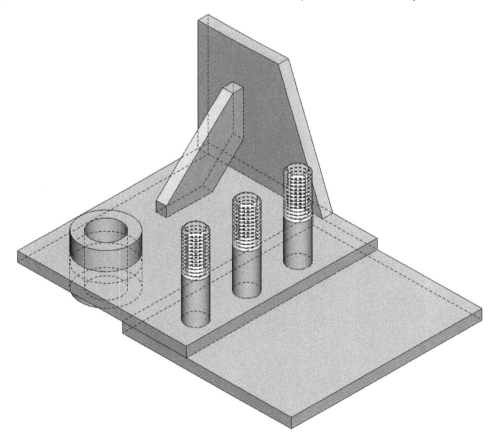

**Three Dimensional View of Weldment**

1.  Since you used PROJ-10 as your starting file, the settings for this project will be the same. If you had started from a full scale original drawing, you would have needed to made the following changes:

    a. Setting the grid dot spacing to .5000.
    b. Setting the linetype scale factor setting to 2.000.
    c. Selecting the title block and notes and scale to twice the original size.

2.  Change the UCS location back to the original origin.

    Type UCS to access the command.

    Type "W" to set the UCS location to World.

    The UCS is now back at the lower left corner of the border.

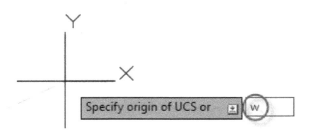

**World Option for UCS**

3.  Begin with the object lines for the top view.

    When adding the phantom lines for the existing part. Extend the lines 2.56 from the right edge of the part.

    You will need to use the PHANTOM-X-Short linetype to make the dashes visible.

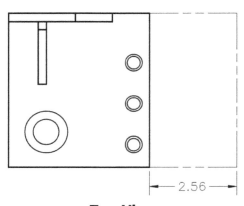

**Top View**

4.  Add the object lines for the front view.

    The chamfer for the top of the .500 stud is
    .0625, The length of the threaded portion
    is .50.

    You may use the Chamfer tool to create
    the chamfer for the end of the stud.

    This tool is located in the Modify panel with
    the Fillet tool.

    Set the distances of the chamfer to .063
    inches.

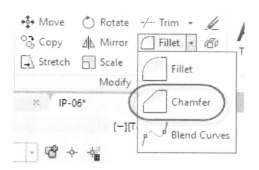

**Chamfer Tool**

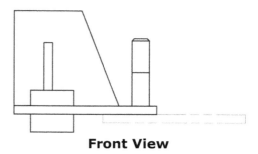

**Front View**

5.  Add the objects lines for the right side
    view.

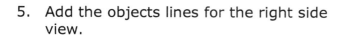

**Right Side View**

6.  Draw the detail view of Part A and place
    above the right side view.

    This view will be drawn at the same scale
    as the main drawing.

**Detail View of Part A**

7.  Add in the hidden lines.

    The hidden lines for the threaded portion of the studs are drawn at the depth of the chamfer (.063 inches).

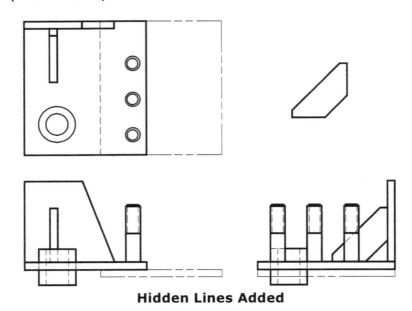

**Hidden Lines Added**

8.  Add the lines for the existing part.

    To create the break lines, use the Break-line Symbol tool located in the Express Tools tab, Draw panel.

    Set the size of the break-line symbol to .1250. Press "S" to set the size after clicking the tool.

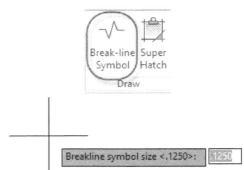

**Break-line Tool and Size**

9.  The lines for the Existing Part are added.

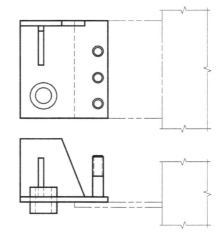

**Existing Part Lines Added**

10. Add the centerlines and center marks.

    Use the dimension style for the double-sized center marks created in PROJ-10.

    Use the Continuous linetype for the center marks for the studs.

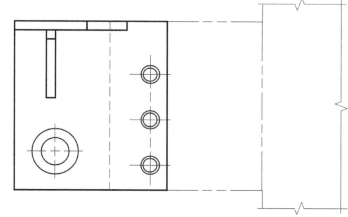

**Center Marks for Top View**

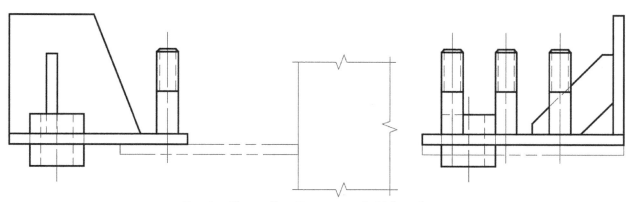

**Centerlines for Front and Side Views**

11. When dimensioning the views add the linear dimensions first, then the radial dimensions, and then the text notes.

Using the Autodesk Design Center to add the Weld Symbols

In this section you will use the Autodesk Design Center to add the blocks to the drawing. This will allow you to inserts the symbols without having to return to PROJ-11a to copy/paste the blocks into this drawing.

1.   Type ADC to open the Design Center dialog box.

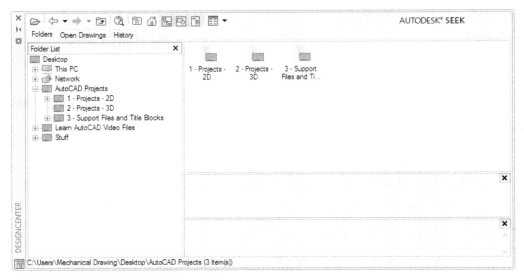

**Autodesk DesignCenter**

2.   On the left is the Folder List.

     Navigate to the PROJ-11a.dwg file and click the "+" next to the file name.

     Click the icon for Blocks under the file name.

     On the right you will see icons for the blocks that were created in the previous tutorial.

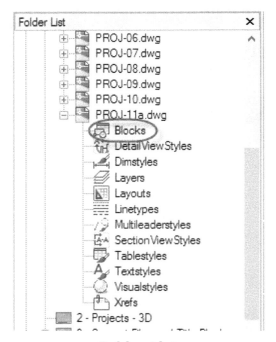

**Folder List**

3.  Click, hold, and drag the icons for the Field Weld, All Around, Fillet, and Stud blocks into the drawing area.

    You will need to drag the symbols one at a time.

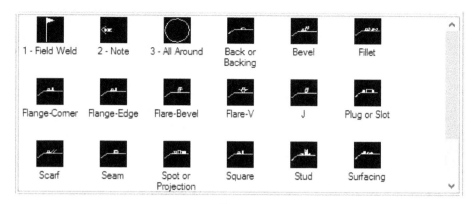

**Icons**

4.  After the blocks have been added to the drawing area you may delete them.

    Use will use the Insert block tool to add the blocks to the drawing.

    Close the Design Center dialog box.

5.  Open the Insert dialog box. Insert the blocks into your drawing. Set the Scale to 2 to account for the 1:2 scale of the drawing.

    Hook the leader lines so that they are pointing at the weld.

    If you have welding experience, it may help to think of the arrow as the electrode of the welder.

6.  The stud weld symbol indicates the size of the weld (.06 inches) and the number of studs to be welded (3).

    The fillet weld symbol indicates the size of the weld (.12). If the symbol is below the reference line, then the weld is on the same side as the arrow. If is above the reference line then the weld is on the opposite side.

7.  In the notes the American Welding Society (AWS) standard for welding symbols is referenced.

8.  Save the project. This concludes the tutorial.

    Create a PDF of the project and print if desired.

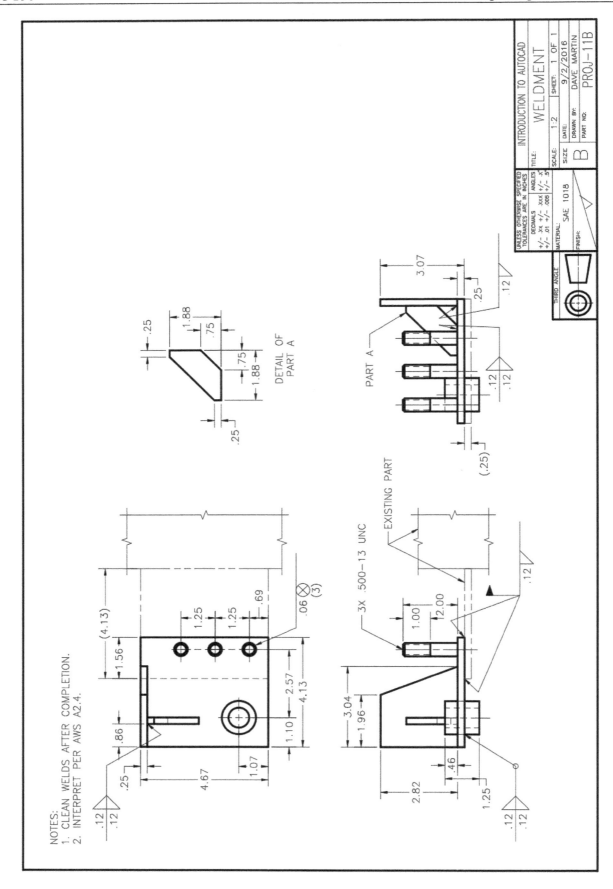

# Part Two

## Projects
## 3D Versions

# Projects – 3D Versions

**Congratulations on completing the first part of the book!**

<u>Introduction</u>

Now that you have completed the 2D version of the projects, you will now be instructed in the process of completing three-dimensional (3D) versions of the same projects. Once you are experienced with the software you would typically complete the 3D model of the project first and then use the software to automatically create 2D views of the software. This procedure will be covered later in this part of the book. You will use the information created in the 2D files when creating some of the 3D features.

When creating a 3D solid of an object there are two basic methods; the Extrusion Method and the Primitive Method. The Extrusion Method is typically used where the part is a shape with a uniform thickness. The Primitive Method is used when the object is comprised of primitive solids. The AutoCAD program has tools to create these primitives. They are the: box, cylinder, cone, sphere, pyramid, wedge, and torus. Both of these methods will be covered as part of the tutorials to create the 3D versions of the projects.

You will also create a 3D assembly of the Geneva Cam. This will introduce you to the use of reference files when adding the individual part files to the assembly file.

# Project #1 – 3D – Absolute Coordinate Exercise

**File Name:** PROJ-01-3D.dwg
Note: All screenshots are from the Autodesk® AutoCAD® software.

**Description:** This is the first 3D project. You will use the elements created as part of the 2D version. After completing the project, you will check the volume of the project to verify that you created the solid accurately. Refer to the Project Volumes on the 3D Projects page at the beginning of the book for these volume measurements.

> **Note:** If you have decided to start Part Two after completing PROJ-03.dwg in Part One of the book, keep in mind that some of these projects will require elements that have been drawn in the 2D versions of the projects.

<u>Beginning the Project</u>

1.  Start a new drawing from scratch.

    For this first 3D drawing you will start from a blank file. Once you have completed the project, you will use this file to begin the next project.

2.  Save the file as: PROJ-01-3D.

    The 3D files will be contained in the Projects -3D folder that you created at the beginning of the book.

3.  For the 3D projects you will need to change the workspace from the Drafting and Annotation workspace to the 3D Modeling workspace.

    The Workspace Switching tool is located at the bottom right corner of the screen in the Status Bar.

    As with the 2D projects, we will discuss the 3D tabs and panels as we need them for the tutorials.

    **Note:** To save changes made to the Workspace after closing it, select the Workspace Settings… option and check the "Automatically save workspace changes" button.

**Workspace Switched to 3D Modeling**

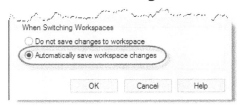

**"Automatically save workspace changes" Button**

Preparing the Views

1. Begin by setting up multiple viewports for the drawing.

   The basic method is to use the Multiple viewports tool in the Home tab, View panel.

   You may also create other viewport layouts by using the Viewport Configuration tool in the Visualize tab, Model Viewports panel.

   For the 3D tutorials, the Four Equal viewport set-up will be used.

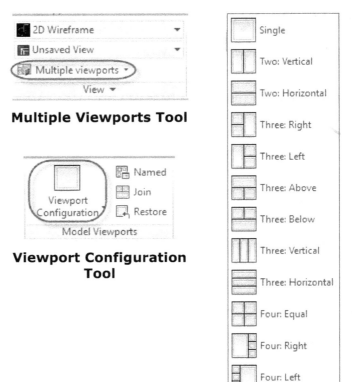

**Multiple Viewports Tool**

**Viewport Configuration Tool**

**Viewport Configuration Choices**

2. Your screen should look like this…

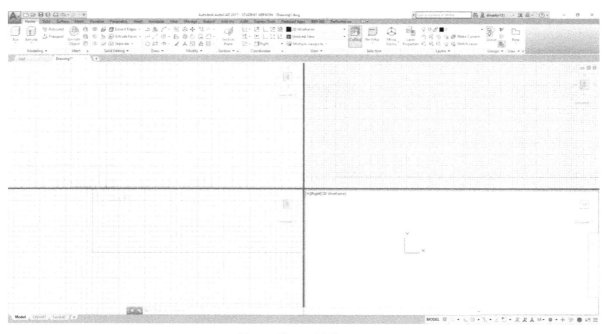

**Four Equal Views**

3.  As you click on each of the
    four views, you will see that
    the edges of the view
    window turn blue.

    This shows that the view is
    active.

    Also, the name of the view
    will appear at the top left of
    the window along with its
    display style.

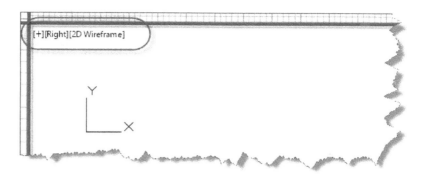

**Top Left of Active View**

4.  At the top right corner of the view you will see the
    ViewCube and a collection of view tools.

    Up to this point in the book, you may not have used
    these tools.

    You will use them now to rotate the view to a standard
    orientation.

**ViewCube and View Tools**

5.  Reorient the fours views.

    Set the top left viewport to Top. This is done by
    clicking on the triangles that surround the cube.

    Set the bottom left viewport to Front.

    Set the bottom right viewport to Right.

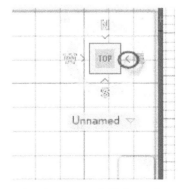

**Orthogonal Triangle**

6. Set the upper right viewport to Front, Right Isometric.

   This is done by click on the corner of the ViewCube where the Front, Right, and Top surfaces meet.

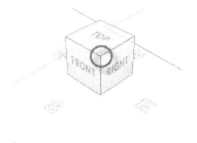

**Front Right Isometric Orientation**

7. You can also rotate the views by using the middle mouse button and the Shift key held down.

   This will orbit the view.

   Open the Navigation Wheel by clicking on the Full Navigation Wheel tool in the view tools.

   You can also use the Navigation Wheel to Zoom, Orbit, Pan, and Rewind to previous views.

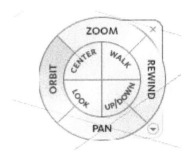

**Navigation Wheel**

**Full Navigation Wheel Tool**

8. Before beginning to draw, you will need to reorient the UCS so that the plane is in the Front view. By default, the UCS plane is oriented to the top view.

   Click in the Front view and type UCS to access the UCS options.

   Type "V" to reorient the UCS to the Front view. You will see the View Cube change to Top because the UCS rotation has been changed.

**UCS Options in the Command Line**

9. Save the UCS as "Front".

   Type UCS to access the options.

   Type "NA" for the named UCS.

   Type "S" to save the UCS.

   Type "Front" to name the saved UCS.

10. Beneath the View Cube is the UCS drop-down.

Click on the drop-down to see the saved UCS.

This way you will be able to switch between the World UCS (WCS) and the Front UCS.

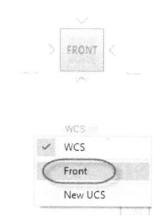

**Front UCS in Drop-Down**

11. Lastly, set up the grid spacing to .25 and the major line setting to 4.

12. Now you are ready to bring in objects from your 2D version of the project into this file.

## Creating the Model (Extruding the Outside Shape and Setting Up the Visual Style)

1. Open the 2D version of PROJ-01.

2. Turn off the Text layer in the Layer drop-down.

This will make it easier to select the object lines.

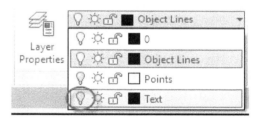

**Text Layer Off**

3. Select the objects lines.

Copy the lines to the Clipboard.

**Note:** There is no tool for Copy/Paste in the Ribbon. You may either right-click after selecting the elements and choose Clipboard, or open the Menu bar at the top of the screen to access the Edit menu.

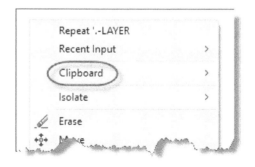

**Clipboard Option in Menu**

**Down Arrow to Access Menu Bar**

**Show Menu Bar**

4.  Switch to the 3D version of the file.

    Confirm that the view is set to the Front UCS.

    Paste the elements in the lower left viewport.

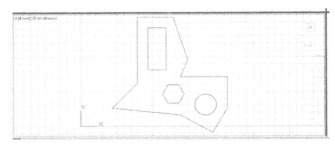

**View Placed in Front View**

    The other views are still oriented to the WCS. You will see the shape as a line (edge view) in the top and right views.

    **Note:** Even though this is the Front view, the ViewCube will be oriented to the Top view. This will change as the UCS is changed back to WCS.

5.  Now that you have the elements in the 3D file, you will change the individual lines to regions.

    Click on the Region tool in the Home tab, Draw panel.

    This will convert the lines forming the perimeter of the shape into a single element.

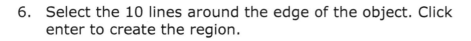

**Region Tool**

6.  Select the 10 lines around the edge of the object. Click enter to create the region.

    To verify that you have a region, click on one of the lines around the edge. All of the lines will highlight.

    Repeat the process for the rectangular shape.

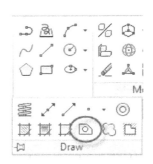

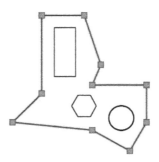

**Region Highlighted**

7.  You will not need to repeat the process for the hexagon or circle.

    Since these are shapes, they are also regions.

    Click the Extrude tool in the Home tab, Modeling panel.

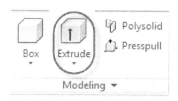

**Extrude Tool**

8.  Click on the edge of the shape in the Top view.

    Press Enter.

    Drag the mouse up in the Top view. You will see the shape becoming a solid.

    Type 1.25 of the height of the extrusion.

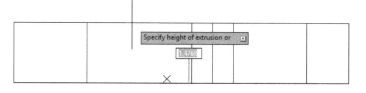

**Extruding the Shape**

9.  The shape is now extruded.

    You will be able to see this clearly in the Isometric view.

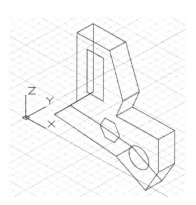

**Extruded Shape in the Isometric View**

10. To see the shape in a more realistic style, you will change the display style.

    Activate the Isometric view by clicking inside the view.

    In the View panel, click on 2D Wireframe in the drop-down menu.

    Select the Visual Styles Manager... text at the bottom.

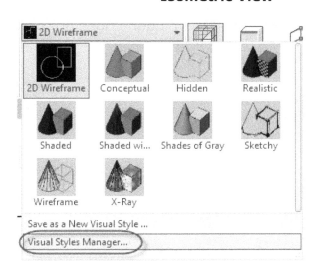

**Visual Styles Manager...**

11. The Visual Styles Manager dialog box opens.

    Double-click on the Hidden visual style.

    This will update the Isometric view style.

    You will make two changes to the style.

    Click on the word "No" in the Occluded Edges section and change it to "Yes".

    Change the Linetype to Dotted.

    The style will update as you make these changes.

    **Note:** You may have difficulties getting the occluded edges to display. Make sure you have installed AutoCAD 2017 Service Pack 1 to solve this issue.

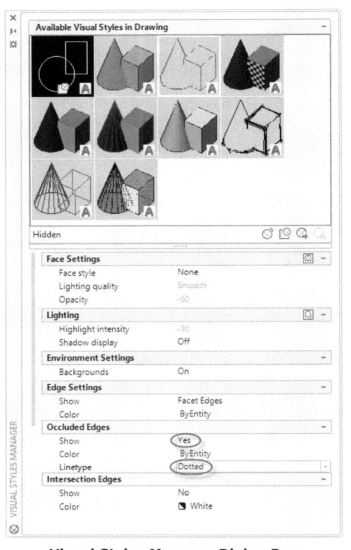

**Visual Styles Manager Dialog Box**

12. You will now be able to see the shape as shaded and the hidden edges are dotted.

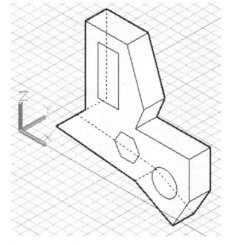

**View Shaded and Hidden Edges Dotted**

## Creating the Model (Extruding the Interior Shapes and Creating the Voids)

1. Next you will create the voids for the rectangle, hexagon, and circle.

   Click on the Extrude tool.

   Select the three inside shapes and press Enter.

   Drag the other end of the extrusions through the solid. The distance will not matter as long as the extrusions extend through the larger solid.

   Click to accept the extrusions.

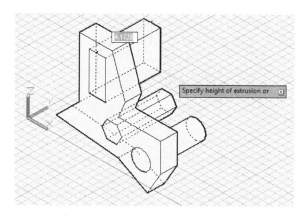

**Dragging the Extrusion End Through the Solid**

2. Click on the Solid, Subtract tool in the Solid Editing panel.

   This tool is used to remove material where two solids intersect.

**Solid, Subtract Tool**

3. Select the larger solid first and press Enter.

   Select the three smaller solids to subtract and press Enter.

   The extruded solids disappear and the voids are created.

   Orbit the view to make sure that the voids are through to the other side.

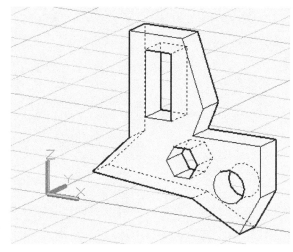

**Voids Created**

4. The solid is finished.

   Check the volume with the VOLUME key-in.

   This is part of the MASSPROP command.

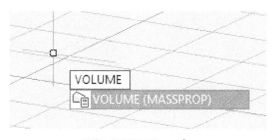

**VOLUME Key-in**

5.  Select the solid.

    A text window will appear with geometrical information about the solid.

    The volume should be 32.8393. The other values will be different since they depend on the location of the solid in 3D space.

    Since the project is in inches, the volume is in cubic inches.

    If you would like to write the analysis to a text file, press Enter to continue otherwise, press ESC twice to end the command.

    **Note:** The volume will be given at the end of each 3D project. If your volume is different from the volume given, it may be due to using a different method to complete the solid than the method shown.

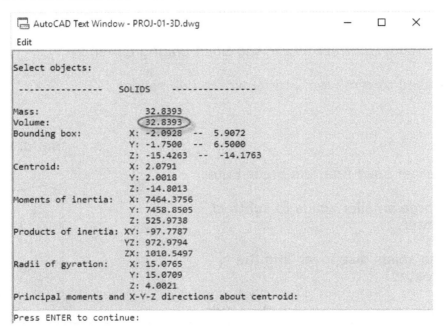

**Text Window Showing Volume**

6.  Save the project. This concludes the tutorial.

    Later, you will create a PDF of the solid.

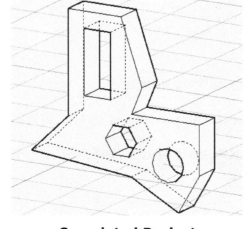

**Completed Project**

# Project #2 – 3D – Relative Coordinate Exercise

**File Name:** PROJ-02-3D.dwg
Note: All screenshots are from the Autodesk® AutoCAD® software.

**Description:** The procedure for this project is very similar to PROJ-01-3D. The same extrusion method will be used to create the solid.

## Beginning the Project

1. Open PROJ-01-3D.dwg and save the drawing as PROJ-02-3D.dwg.

    If you just completed PROJ-01-3D.dwg, save the file before saving it under a new file name.

2. Delete all the objects in the file.

    You will not need any elements from the previous project.

## Creating the Model

1. Open the 2D version of PROJ-02.

2. Select the object lines for the shape and copy the elements to the clipboard.

3. Switch to the PROJ-02-3D file and paste the elements into the front view.

    Make sure that the Front view is set to the Front UCS created in the last project.

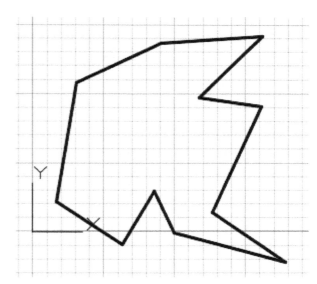

**Lines Pasted to Front View**

4. Set the current layer to Object Lines.

5. Create a region from the lines.

    The new region with be placed on the Object Lines layer.

6.  Click on the Extrude tool and extrude the shape .25 inches.

7.  Use the VOLUME command to check the volume.

    The volume should be 9.4599 cubic inches.

**Volume of Solid**

8.  The project is completed.

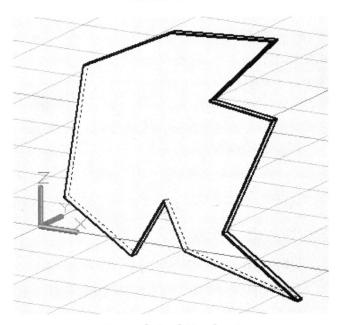

**Completed Project**

9.  Save the project. This concludes the tutorial.

# Project #3 – 3D – Bracket

**File Name:** PROJ-03-3D.dwg
Note: All screenshots are from the Autodesk® AutoCAD® software.

**Description:** For this project you will use the extrusion method for the individual parts of the solid. Then you will join them together into one. After that, you will use a primitive solid to add the holes to the solid.

Beginning the Project

1.  Open PROJ-02-3D.dwg and save the drawing as PROJ-03-3D.dwg.

    If you just completed PROJ-02-3D.dwg, save the file before saving it under a new file name.

2.  Delete all the objects in the file. You will not need any elements from the previous project.

Creating the Model (Extruding the Front View and Rotating the Elements)

1.  Open the 2D version of PROJ-03.

2.  To quickly select only the object lines from the 2D you will use the Isolate tool to isolate the Object Lines layer.

    Click on the Isolate tool in the Layers panel.

**Isolate Tool**

3.  Click one of the object lines in the drawing.

    The rest of the elements will turn gray and will not be able to be selected.

    Select all three views. You will see only the object lines with handles indicating that they are selected.

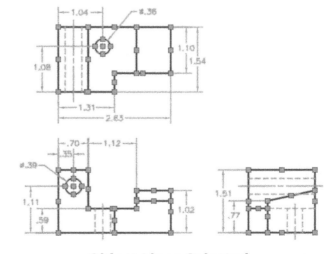

**Object Lines Selected**

4.  Copy the elements to the clipboard.

5.  Click on the Unisolate tool to unisolate
    the Object Lines layer.

    The other layers are no longer gray.

    **Unisolate Tool**

6.  Switch to the PROJ-03-3D file and
    paste the elements into the front
    view.

    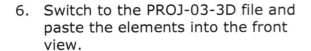
    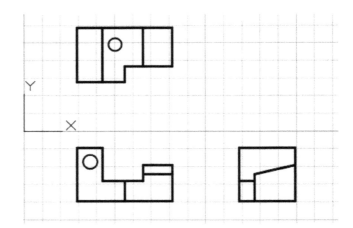

    **Lines Pasted to Front View**

7.  You will be using some of the
    elements from each view for the
    extrusions.

    Create a region from the exterior lines
    of the front view and extrude the
    depth of the model (1.54 inches).

    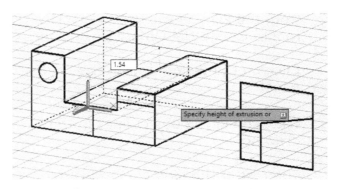

    **Shape Extruded 1.54 Inches**

8.  Click inside the right view and create a new UCS based on the view.

    Use the View option in the UCS command.

    Name the UCS "Right".

9.  In the right view, select the elements from the pasted top view and rotate them 90 degrees clockwise.

    Snap to the bottom edge for the base point of the rotation.

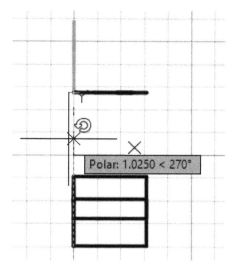

**Rotating Elements from Top View**

10. Switch to the top view and rotate the elements from the pasted right view 90 degrees counter-clockwise.

    Snap to the left edge for the base point.

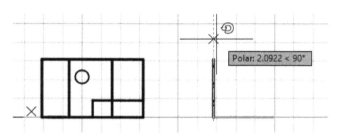

**Rotating Elements from Right View**

11. The pasted elements are rotated and aligned to the solid.

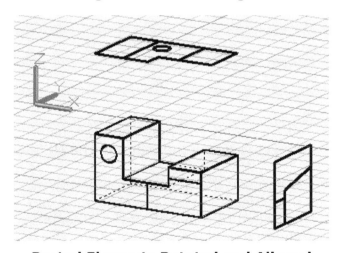

**Pasted Elements Rotated and Aligned**

Creating the Model (Creating the Regions and Subtracting the Solids)

1.  In the top view, you will create a region from a portion of the top view lines.

    Click on the Line tool in the Draw panel.

    Draw two lines below and to the right of the top view. Use Object Snap Tracking to make sure that the new lines are on the same level as the other lines.

    **Note:** If you have difficulty snapping to the top view line, snap to the line in the Isometric view first.

2.  Draw the second line from the first line endpoint.

    Check the other views to make sure that the lines are at the same level.

3.  At this point you may see that the object is below the plane of the UCS.

    If you see the grid squares on top of the objects in the Isometric view you will need to move all of the objects above this plane.

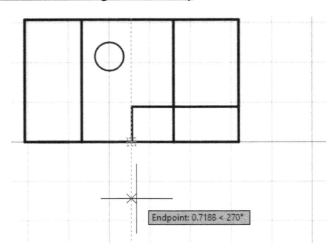

**Using Object Snap Tracking to Draw the Line**

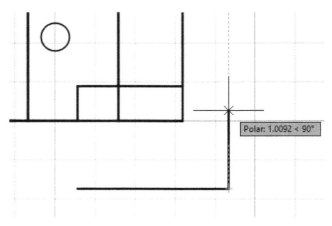

**Second Line Drawn**

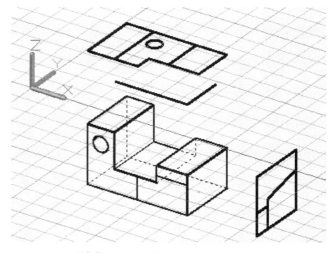

**Objects Below Grid Plane**

4.  Switch to the Right UCS in the view using the drop-down below the ViewCube.

    You can tell that the UCS is changed because the grid squares are visible.

    Click in the right view and select all of the objects.

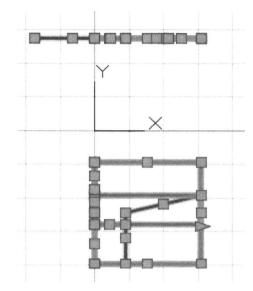

**All Objects Selected**

5.  Click on the Move tool and move the objects so they are above the UCS icon in the right view.

    If you cannot see the UCS icon, move the objects above the red line.

    As you move the elements, watch the Isometric view to see the objects move above the grid plane.

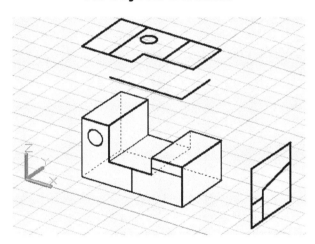

**Solid and Other Lines Above Grid Plane**

6.  In the top view elements, use the Fillet tool set to a zero radius to form the shape.

    Delete the other lines from the view but keep the circle.

    You will need the circle to create the cylinder solid to make the hole.

    Create a region from the rectangular shape.

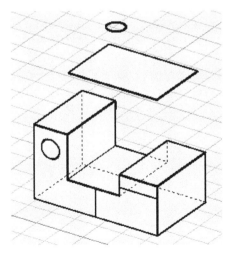

**Region Created and Lines Deleted**

7.  Extrude the region through the solid.

    The distance will not matter, make
    sure that the extrusion extends below
    the other solid.

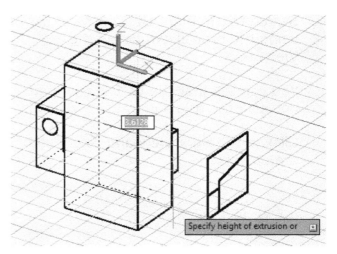

**Region Extruded Through Solid**

8.  Click on the Solid, Subtract tool to
    create the cut in the main solid.

    Delete the extra line from the front
    view.

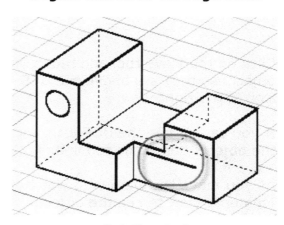

**Cut Created**

9.  You will use the same method to
    create the angled surface from
    elements in the right view.

    Draw four lines to create a shape from
    the angled line in the right view.

    As before, use Object Snap Tracking
    to make sure that the lines are planar
    with the angled line.

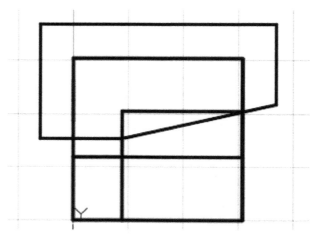

**Additional Lines for Shape Drawn**

10. Delete the extra lines from the right side elements and create a region from the shape.

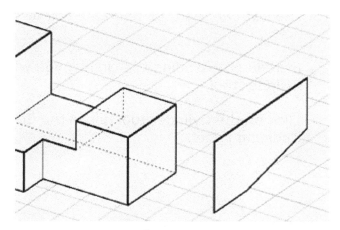

**Region Created**

11. Extrude the region into the main solid.

    This time, do not extrude all the way through.

    Stop around the middle of the solid.

    You can check the distance in the front view.

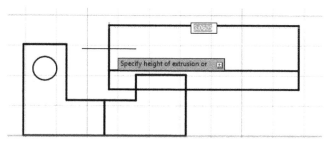

**Edge of Extrusion in Front View**

12. Use the Solid, Subtract tool to create the angled surface.

    **Note:** If you complete the extrusion in the front view, the UCS will change in the Isometric view. If this happens, reset the UCS in the Isometric view to the WCS in the drop down menu.

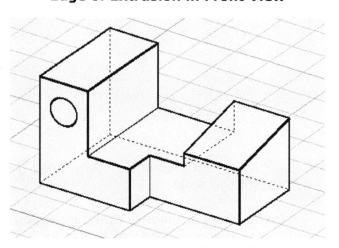

**Angled Surface Created**

13. The last two features to create will be the two holes.

    Instead of extruding the circles, you will use the Cylinder tool.

    Click on the Cylinder tool under the Box tool in the Modeling panel.

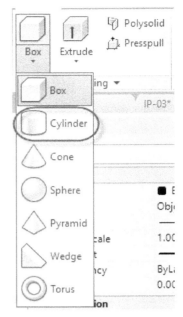

**Cylinder Tool**

14. In the front view, snap to the center of the circle at the upper left corner of the view.

    Snap to the edge of the circle for the radius.

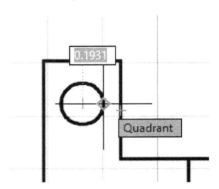

**Center and Radius of Cylinder Located**

15. Click in the Isometric view and drag the cylinder through the solid.

    As with the extrusions, make sure you drag through the other side of the solid.

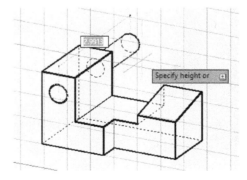

**Cylinder Dragged Through the Solid**

16. Complete the cylinder.

    Use the Solid, Subtract to create the hole.

    Reset the UCS to WCS in the Isometric view.

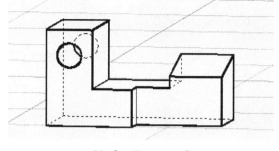

**Hole Created**

17. Repeat the process for the top hole.

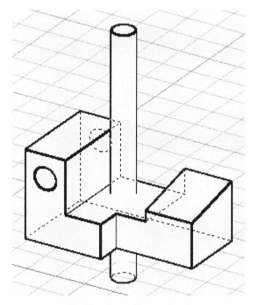

**Cylinder Created**

18. Create the hole using Solid, Subtract.

    Delete the two circles from the pasted elements and any other extra lines.

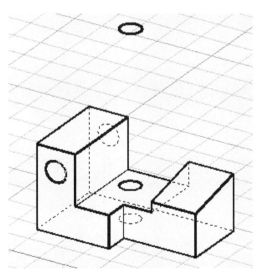

**Second Hole Created**

19. Use the VOLUME command to check the volume.

    The volume should be 3.0664 cubic inches.

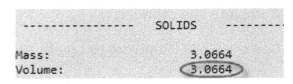

**Volume of Solid**

20. Save the project.

    This concludes the tutorial.

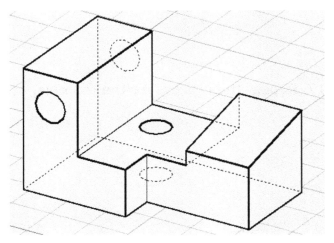

**Completed Project**

# Using a 3D Solid to Create Orthographic Views

**Description:** Now that you have finished the first three 3D versions of the Projects, you will now convert the 3D solid to a set of 2D orthographic views. The procedure will use Project #3 as the example.

This tutorial will also introduce you to the concept and use of Paperspace. This is used as an alternate method to create sheet views of orthographic drawings.

## Beginning the Project

1.  Open PROJ-03-3D.dwg. This will be a continuation of the project and will not need to be saved under a different file name.

2.  Since the 3D projects were started from a blank file, you will need to import the layers and linetypes from the 2D drawing file.

    You will use the Design Center application in AutoCAD to transfer the layers and linetype from the 2D file to the 3D file.

    Type "ADC" to open the Design Center application.

    **Note:** You last used the Design Center in Project #11b to add the weld symbol blocks to the drawing file.

3.  On the left of the dialog box is the folder list.

    Navigate to your PROJ-03.dwg file (2D version).

    Click the "+" sign next to the file to expand the elements contained within the file.

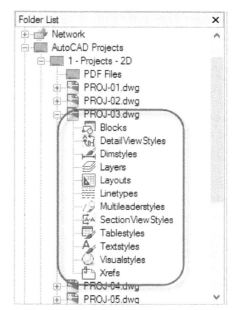

**Elements in the PROJ-03.dwg File**

4. Click on the Layers category under the file.

   You will see the layers in the drawing inside to Content Area to the right.

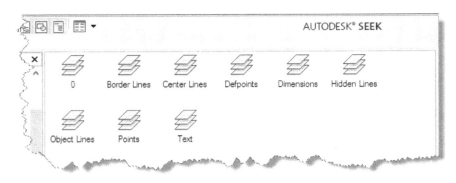

**Content Area Showing the Layers**

5. To add the layers to the 3D file, select the layers within the content area and drag-and-drop them into the drawing area of the file.

   Check the Layer drop-down to see if the layers have been added.

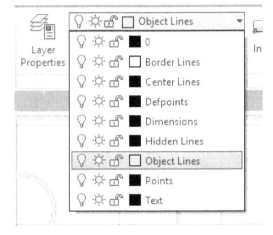

**Layers Added to PROJ-03-3D.dwg**

6. Repeat the process for the Linetypes.

   Open the Linetype Manager with the LTYPE key-in to see if the linetypes have been added.

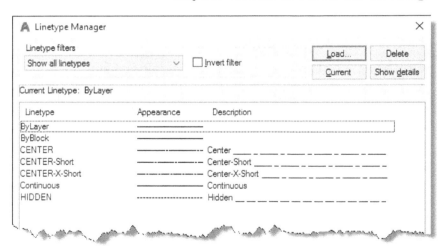

**Linetypes Added to PROJ-03-3D.dwg**

7. You may also load Dimension Styles, Multileader Styles, Text Styles, and any other elements/styles created within the 2D file.

## Setting Up the Orthographic Views

For this portion of the tutorial you will use the Solid View tool to create the views of the solid. This tool will take "snapshots" of the solid in various orientations.

1. Click on the Layout1 tab at the bottom left corner of the screen.

   You will see that the UCS icon has changed to the Paperspace Icon.

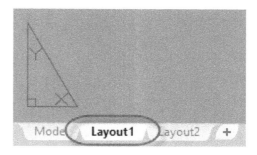

**Layout1 Tab**

2. You will see one of the views from model space with a box surrounding it.

   This is called the Viewport.

   Think of it as a window into Model Space where the 3D solid is located.

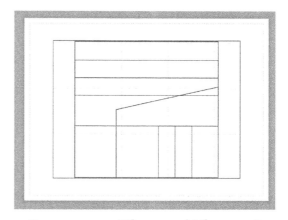

**Paperspace View and Viewport**

3. Click on the edge of the viewport surrounding the view and delete it.

   You will be making new viewports for each of the standard views and the isometric view.

   The dashed line is the edge of the printable area for the page size and the edge of the white rectangle is the edge of the paper.

   This page size is setup for "A" size (8.50" x 11").

**Viewport Deleted**

4. Click on the Solid View tool in the Model panel.

   You can also access this tool with the SOLVIEW key-in command.

**Solid View Tool**

5.  An option menu will appear attached to the cursor.

    Choose the Ucs option with the cursor.

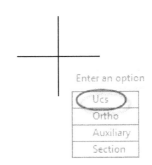

**Ucs Option**

6.  Choose the Named option.

    Type in the saved UCS, Front that was created in the last tutorial.

    This will be your base view.

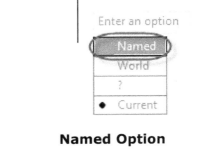

**Named Option**

7.  Press Enter to accept the view scale at 1.000.

**View Scale set to 1.0000**

8.  Specify the view center at a point in the lower left corner of the page.

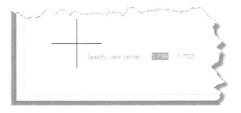

**View Center Location**

9.  The front view of the solid will appear on the sheet.

    The viewport will cover the entire sheet.

    You may click a new location if the first one was not in the correct place.

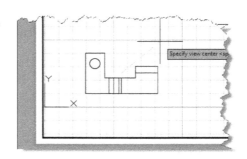

**View Placed on Sheet**

10. Press Enter to accept the location.

    At the next step you will click the upper left corner of the viewport.

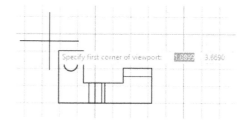

**Upper Left Corner of Viewport**

11. Drag down and to the right for the lower right corner of the viewport.

    Leave a small space around the edge of the view.

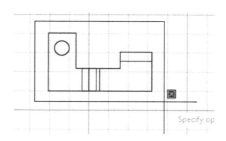

**Lower Right Corner of Viewport**

12. The next prompt is to name the view.

    Type "Front" for the view name.

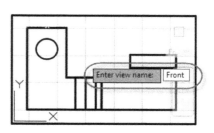

**Name the View: Front**

13. The Viewport is resized and placed around the view.

    Once the Viewport is placed and named, you may lock it. You will need to be in Model space to lock the view.

    This will keep from accidentally changing the scale or panning the view.

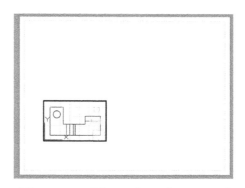

**Viewport Placed and Named**

    The Viewport Lock tool is located in the Status Bar at the bottom right corner of the screen.

**Viewport Lock Tool**

14. Now you have placed the Front View.

    Now you will use the Ortho option in the Solid View tool to create the Top and Side views.

    Click on the Solid View tool, then right-click and select the Ortho option.

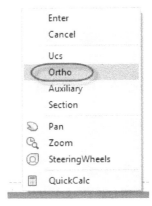

**Ortho Option**

15. The drawing will automatically switch to Paperspace.

    Click or snap on the top edge of the viewport for the front view.

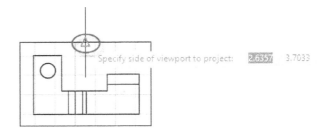

**Specify Side of Viewport for New View**

16. Drag up to locate the view center for the Top view.

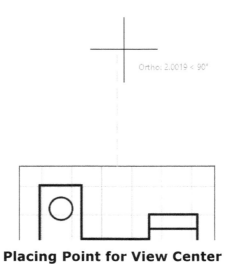

**Placing Point for View Center**

17. Click the point and press Enter.

    Draw the corners of the viewport as before.

    The Top view is placed.

    Name the view: Top

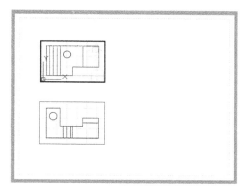

**Top View Placed**

18. Repeat the process for the Right Side view.

    When using the Ortho option, click on the right side of the front viewport.

    Name the view: Right

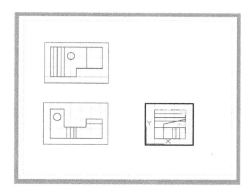

**Right View Placed**

19. The last view that you will place in the Isometric view. This view will require creating a new saved UCS.

    Click the Model tab at the bottom of the screen to return to Modelspace.

20. Click in the Isometric view to make the view current.

    Type UCS to begin the UCS tool.

    Right-click and select the View Option.

    This will align the UCS to the view rotation.

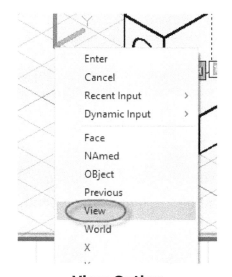

**View Option**

21. The UCS is now oriented to the view.

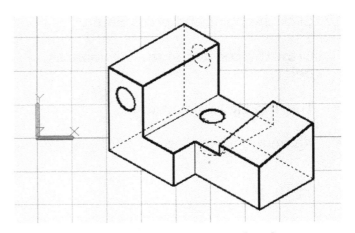

**UCS Oriented to Isometric View**

22. Save the UCS as: Iso.

23. Click the Layout1 tab to return to the sheet view.

    **Note:** If you accidentally change the view scale in one of the views, you can use the UNDO command to go back to the original view. You can also use the key-in command, MVSETUP to re-align the views.

24. Click the Solid View tool.

    Use the Ucs option for the new isometric view.

    Right-click for the Named option.

    Type Iso as the UCS to restore.

    Use 1.000 for the view scale.

    Specify the view center at the upper right corner and place the viewport corners.

    Name the view: Iso

    The Isometric view is placed

**Isometric View Placed**

25. Now all of the views are placed.

    In the next section you will create hidden line views.

### Creating Hidden Line Views of the Viewports

1.  Now you will use the Solid Drawing tool to create the hidden line views.

    Click on the Solid Drawing (SOLDRAW) tool in the Modeling panel.

    The Layout1 view will automatically open if you were in the Model view.

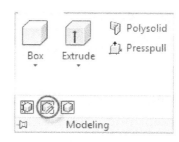

**Solid Drawing Tool**

2.  The prompt will ask you to select objects.

    Select the edges of the four viewports for each of the views.

    Press Enter when finished selecting.

    **Note:** In the previous section, if you did not name the views as they were created this step will not work. You will need to re-create the views with names.

3.  You will see that the object lines and hidden lines for each of the views have been created.

    The solid model has been automatically hidden in each view.

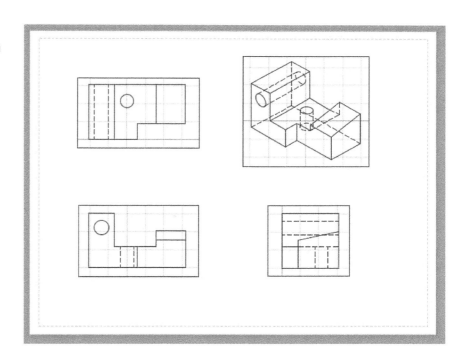

**Hidden Line Views Created**

4. Open the Layer Properties dialog box.

   At this point you will need to set up the layer attributes for each layer.

   Refer to the screenshot of the Layer Properties Manager dialog box for the attributes of each layer.

   The primary change you will make is to change the Visible layers to the correct color and lineweight. The Hidden and Dimension layers will need to have their lineweights changed.

   Each view has its own set of layers. Example: Front view has Front-DIM, Front-HID, and Front-VIS. The DIM layer is for Dimensions, the HID layer is for hidden lines, and the VIS layer is for visible (object) lines.

   **Note:** You can use the Ctrl key to select multiple layers at once.

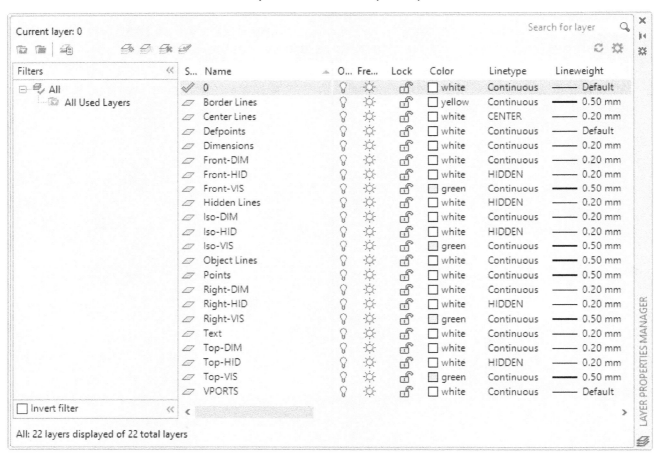

**Layer Attribute for New Layers (Not all Columns are Shown.)**

5. The views are now set up with the correct attributes.

## Pasting the Border/Title Block into Layout1

This portion of the procedure covers the method to add the A-Size Border file to Layout1.

1. Open the A-Size Border.dwg file.

   Select all of the elements and copy them to the clipboard.

2. Switch to the PROJ-03-3D file.

   Open the Layout1 tab and switch to Paper space. Use the Paper/Model Space toggle on the status bar.

**Paper Space Toggle**

3. Paste the elements into the view by using the Paste to Original Coordinates option.

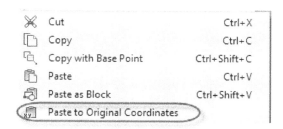

**Paste to Original Coordinates**

4. The elements will be located at the edge of the paper boundary.

   If you cannot see the points at the corners, use the PTYPE key-in command to change the point style and size.

   The border is placed.

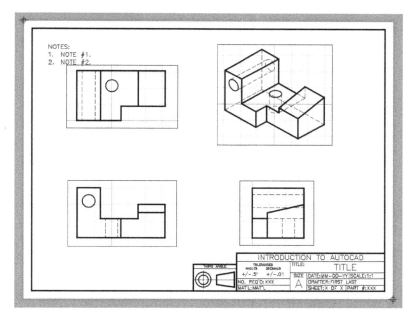

**Border Placed**

Dimensioning the Views

1.  Now that you are finished with the 3D elements,
    change your Workspace back to Drafting &
    Annotation.

    You may be switched to the Model tab. If so,
    switch back to Layout1.

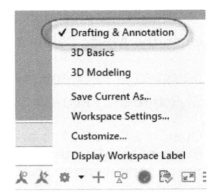

**Workspace Switched to
Drafting & Annotation**

The process to dimension the views will be the same as with the 2D version.

The main difference is that you will place the dimensions into Paperspace while the
views will be in Modelspace.

2.  Before dimensioning you may need to
    move the views within the border.

    Turn on the Polar Tracking toggle.

    While in paperspace, move the
    viewports to their appropriate
    location.

    Make sure to keep the views aligned
    with each other.

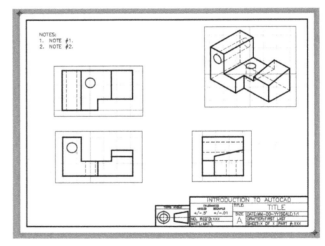

**Views Moved**

3.  Click on the Paper toggle at the bottom of the screen.

    This will switch the drawing to model space.

4. Click in the front view viewport and turn off the Grid squares.

   Repeat the process for the other views.

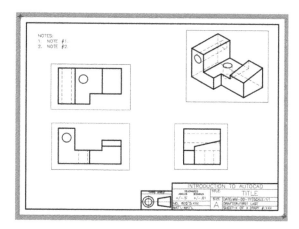

**Grids Off in Each View**

5. Switch back to paperspace.

   Open the Layer Properties Manager dialog box.

   Find the VPORTS layer at the bottom and scroll over to the VP Freeze column.

   Click the icon to freeze the VPORTS layer.

   **Note:** Freezing a layer is used to turn off a layer in only one layout tab.

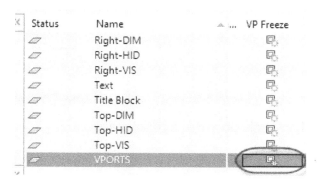

**VPORTS Layer VP Freeze Icon**

6. Now the drawing will look the same as it does in the 2D version.

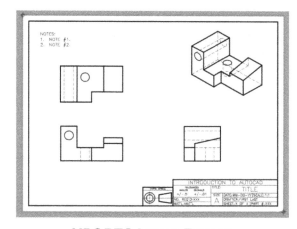

**VPORTS Layer Frozen**

7. To plot the drawing you will use the same settings as with the 2D version of the project.

8. Add the dimensions and fill out the title block if you wish.

   From here on you have the option of using the 3D solid to create 2D dimensioned views of the projects.

Creating a 3D Layout View

This last section is a workaround to view the 3D solid correctly. In the model tab you will see both the solid and the individual views. You have the choice of either turning off the views and viewing the solid or you may decide to create a 3D layout view. This section will cover the steps to do this.

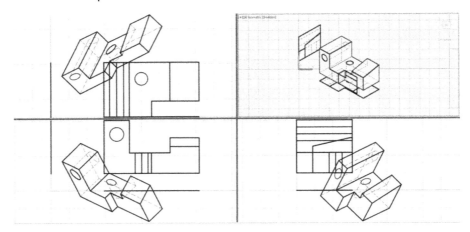

**Solid and Individual Hidden Line Views**

1.  Click on the Layout2 tab.

**Layout2 Tab**

2.  The Layout2 tab opens.

    Right-click on the tab and select Rename.

    The text for the layout tab will highlight.

    Rename the tab, 3D Views.

    Also rename the Layout1 tab, 2D Sheet.

    This will make it easier to identify the function of the tabs.

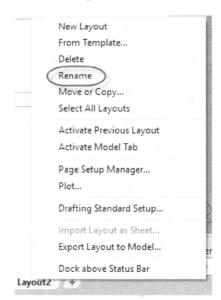

**Renaming the Layout Tab**

**Tabs Renamed**

3. Delete the viewport in the layout so that you have a blank view.

4. Zoom into the view so that the entire area is filed by the paper boundary.

5. Use the VPORTS key-in command to open the Viewports dialog box.

   Change the Setup: field to 3D.

   Set the Standard viewports setting to Four:Equal.

   Click in the SE Isometric view and change the Visual style to Hidden.

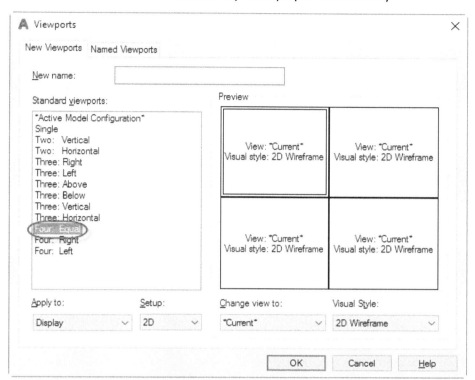

**Viewports Dialog Box Settings**

6. Press the OK button to close the dialog box and place the corners.

   Depending on the size and set-up of your screen the points will vary.

   Click at the upper left edge of your display area and then at the lower right so that the views fill the entire space.

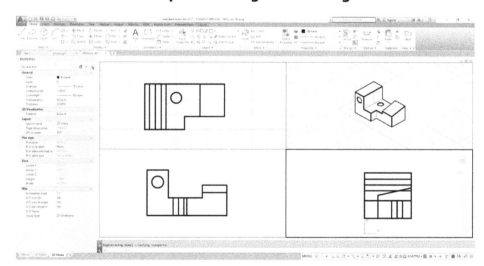

**Four Viewports Placed**

7. Toggle to modelspace.

   Now you may click in each view to modify the solid.

8. Save the project. This concludes the tutorial.

# Project #4 – 3D – Plate

**File Name:** PROJ-04-3D.dwg
Note: All screenshots are from the Autodesk® AutoCAD® software.

**Description:** For this project you will use the extrusion method. Instead of projecting each shape individually, you will extrude all shapes together. Then the voids will be created from the intersecting solids.

Beginning the Project

1.  Open PROJ-03-3D.dwg and save the drawing as PROJ-04-3D.dwg.

    If you just completed PROJ-03-3D.dwg, save the file before saving it under a new file name.

2.  Delete all the objects in the file. You will not need any elements from the previous project.

    Use Ctrl+A to select any elements that may be hidden or frozen.

Creating the Model

1.  Open the 2D version of PROJ-04.

2.  Select only the object lines from the 2D view.

    Use the Isolate tool to isolate the Object Lines layer.

3.  Switch to PROJ-04-3D.

    Paste the elements in the Front View.

    Make sure you are in the Front UCS that was created in the previous project.

    Set up the location so that the lower left circle is at the origin (0,0).

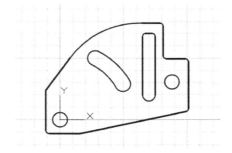

**Objects Placed in Front View**

4.  Fit the objects in the other views.

    Set the UCS to WCS in the other three views.

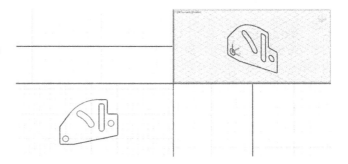

**Object Fit in Other Views**

5.  Set the current layer to Object Lines.

    Use the Region tool to create regions of the exterior shape and the two slots.

    The circles are already regions.

    In the Isometric view, you will see that the grid squares are hidden behind the regions.

    **Note:** You may pick the entire view to create the regions all at once.

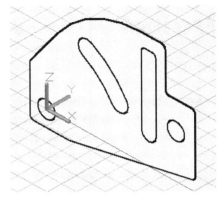

**Regions Created**

6.  Click the Extrude tool.

    Pick all of the regions at once and extrude .375 inches.

    The direction of the extrusions will be upward in the top view.

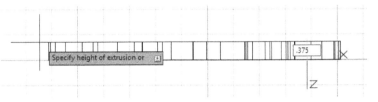

**Direction and Height of Extrusions**

7.  All of the extrusions are created as separate solids that overlap one another.

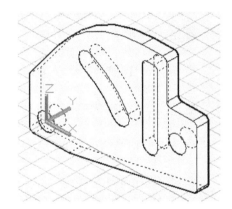

**Extrusions Created**

8.  Use the Solid, Subtract tool to create the voids.

    Click the tool and then select the outside larger solid.

    Press Enter and then select the smaller solids that overlap with the larger solid.

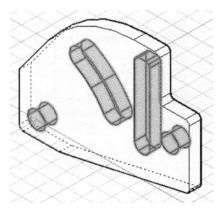

**Smaller Solids Selected**

9. Press Enter to accept the selection and end the command.

   The voids are created.

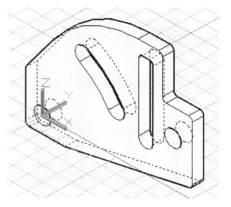

**Voids Created**

10. Use the VOLUME command to check the volume.

    The volume should be 5.7910 cubic inches.

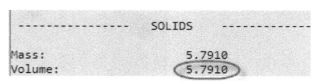

**Volume of Solid**

11. Save the project. This concludes the tutorial.

If Creating a Dimensioned View:

If you have not created the 2D views for the project yet, you should do so now. The 2D sheet view is set up from the previous project, but the views will need to be deleted and re-created for the new project. Refer to the 2D tutorial for dimension set-up and placement.

Before creating the 2D views using the Solid View tool, you will need to merge the four VIS layers into the Object Lines layer. This is done in the Layer Properties Manager by right-clicking on the layer and selecting "Merge selected layers(s) to…" in the drop-down menu. This will also delete the original layer(s). Repeat the process for the HID and DIM layers.

**Merge Selected Layer(s) to… Command**

# Project #5 – 3D – Saw Handle

**File Name:** PROJ-05-3D.dwg
Note: All screenshots are from the Autodesk® AutoCAD® software.

**Description:** For this project you will use the extrusion method. You will also use the Fillet tool to create rounded corners on the solid.

### Beginning the Project

1.  Open PROJ-04-3D.dwg and save the drawing as PROJ-05-3D.dwg.

    If you just completed PROJ-04-3D.dwg, save the file before saving it under a new file name.

2.  Delete all the objects in the file. You will not need any elements from the previous project.

    Use Ctrl+A to select any elements that may be hidden or frozen.

3.  Merge the layers generated by the Solid View tool into the Object Line, Hidden Line, and Dimension layers.

### Creating the Model (Extruding the Shapes and Creating the Voids)

1.  Open the 2D version of PROJ-05.
2.  Select the object lines and the single hidden line from the 2D view. Only select the elements in the front view.

    Use the Isolate tool to isolate the Object Lines layer.

3.  Copy the elements to the clipboard.
4.  Switch to the 3D file and paste the elements to the front view.

    Locate the objects above and to the right of the UCS origin in the front view.

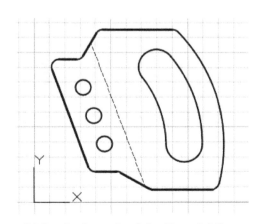

**Objects Located in Front View**

5.  Use the Region and Extrude tools to extrude the elements .75 inches.

    When extruding, do not select the hidden line.

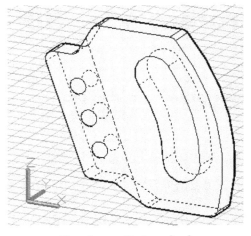

**Regions Extruded**

6.  Use the Solid, Subtract tool to create the voids.

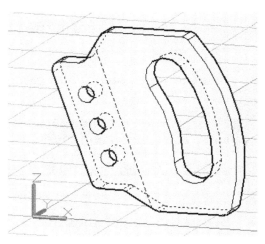

**Voids Created**

Creating the Model (Rounding the Corners)

1.  Click inside the Isometric view to make it current.
2.  Click on the Single Viewport tool in the View panel to make the Isometric view the only view.
3.  You may notice that the arcs have facets.

    If this is an issue with your drawing, use the VIEWRES command to make the arcs appear smoother. Type VIEWRES to change the view resolution.

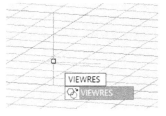

**VIEWRES Command**

4.  Press Enter to accept yes for Fast Zooms.

    Type 10000 for the zoom circle percent.

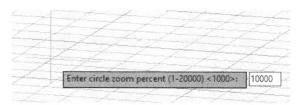

**Zoom Circle Percent set to 10000**

5.  Zoom in and out to see the changes.

    The arcs should appear smoother.

6.  Click on the Fillet tool in the Modify panel.

    Select the upper corner of the solid.

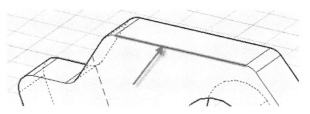

**Edge Selected**

7.  Type .25 for the radius and press Enter.

8.  Right-click and select the Chain option in the menu.

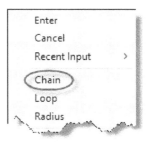

**Chain Option**

9.  Click the small arc next to the line.

    The entire edge around the front of the solid will highlight.

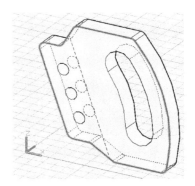

**Edge Highlighted**

10. Press Enter to accept the selection and end the tool.

    The corners are now rounded.

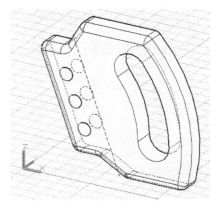

**Corners Rounded**

11. Repeat the process for the other side of the solid and for the two inside corners of the finger slot.

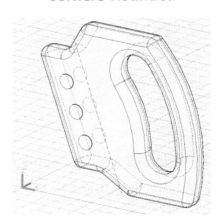

**Remaining Corners Rounded**

<u>Creating the Model (Creating the Kerf)</u>

1.  The last feature you will add to the solid will be the kerf (narrow slit) to hold the saw blade.

    You will use the hidden line for the edge of the shape.

    Change the hidden line to the object line layer.

2.  Draw a shape starting at the angled line.

    Use Object Snap tracking to make sure that the lines are on the same plane.

    The length of the lines do not matter as long as the left edge of the shape extends past the edge of the solid.

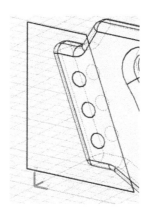

**Shape Drawn**

3.  Make the shape into a region.

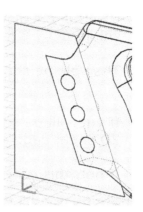

**Region Created**

4.  Move the shape into the part .34 inches so that the shape and solid intersect.

    Use Object Tracking to move the shape along the Y axis.

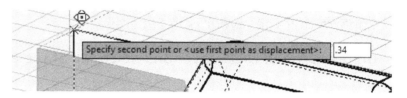

**Move the Shape Along the Y Axis**

5.  Extrude the region .06 inches along the Y axis towards the back side of the solid.

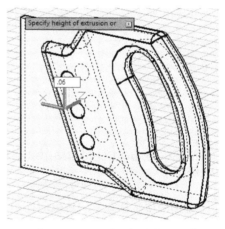

**Region Extruded .06 Inches**

6.  Use the Solid, Subtract tool to create the kerf.

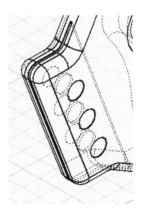

**Kerf Created**

7.  Use the VOLUME command to check the
    volume.

    The volume should be 12.4649 cubic inches.

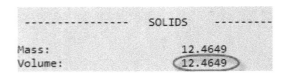

**Volume of Solid**

8.  If you will be creating the 2D views and dimensions, you will need to modify the
    2D sheet page set-up. This is covered in the next section.

    If not, this concludes the tutorial.

Setting up the 2D Sheet Layout Tab (Optional)

1.  Click on the 2D Sheet tab to open the layout tab.

2.  Confirm that the layout is in Paperspace.

    Unfreeze the VPORTS layer and delete all of the elements.

3.  Right-click on the 2D Sheet tab and
    select the Page Setup Manager...
    choice.

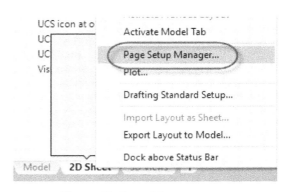

**Page Setup Manager...**

4.  The Page Setup Manager dialog box
    opens.

    This dialog box is used to change the
    settings for the layout page setup.

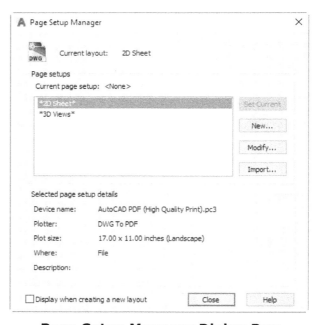

**Page Setup Manager Dialog Box**

5.  Click the Modify... button.

    The Page Setup – 2D Sheet dialog box opens. This is similar to the Plot dialog box.

    Match the changes to the example below.

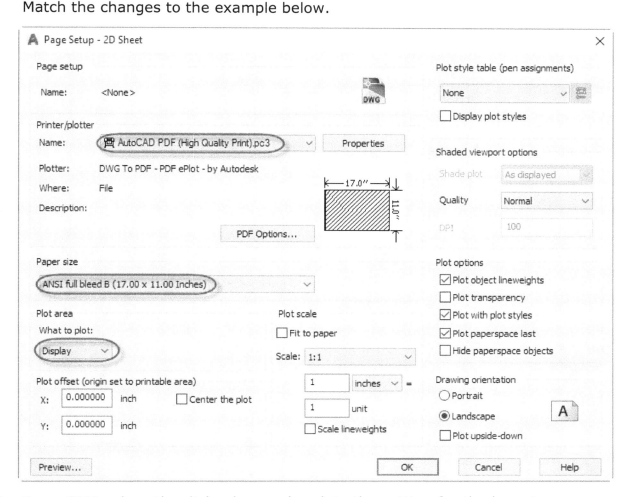

6.  Press OK to close the dialog box and update the setting for the layout.

    You will see that the page boundary has increased to 17" x 11".

7.  Open the B-Size Border file.

    Select the elements and copy paste into the 2D Sheet layout in PROJ-05-3D.

8.  The pasted elements will most likely not be centered on the edges of the paper boundary.

    Re-open the Page Setup manager and change the Plot area setting to Window.

    Use the points at the corners for the boundary of the window.

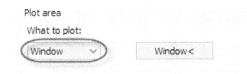

**Plot Area set to Window**

Setting up the 2D and Isometric Views

This is a continuation from the previous section. A new method of generating the hidden line view will be covered. The reason for this is that the Solid View and Solid Drawing tools are not able to create hidden line views with tangential edges. Since the edges of this project are rounded, the Solid Profile tool will be needed for the isometric view.

1. Using the Solid Drawing and Solid Views tools, set up the front and left side views using the same method covered in previous tutorials.

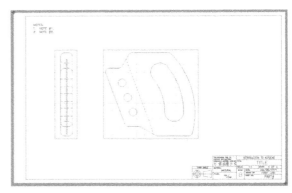

**Front and Left Views**

2. Before using the Solid Profile tool, you will need to create a viewport for the view.

   Use the VPORTS key-in command to open the Viewports dialog box to add a single viewport at the top right corner of the border.

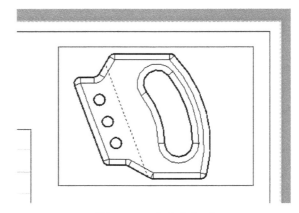

**Viewport Added**

3. Zoom in to the view.

   Switch to modelspace and click inside the view to make it current.

   Use the ViewCube to rotate the view to the Front Left Isometric orientation.

   Set the scale of the viewport to 1:2.

   This is done using the Viewport Scale tool in the status bar.

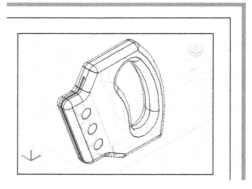

**View Rotated**

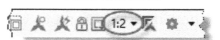

**Viewport Scale Tool**

4. Click on the Solid Profile tool in the Modeling panel.

   You will not need to create a new UCS for the tool. This tool will automatically project a profile of the object to a plane that is parallel to the view.

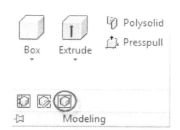

**Solid Profile Tool**

5. Click on the solid when asked to select objects. Press Enter to accept the selection.

   Press Enter to answer "Yes" when asked to display hidden profile lines on a separate layer.

   Press Enter to answer "Yes" when asked to project profile lines onto a plane.

   Press "N" to keep the tangential edges.

   The profile view is created.

   Freeze the Object Lines layer in the viewport to hide the solid and leave the profile view.

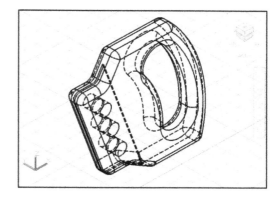

**Profile View Created**

6. Open the Layer Properties manager dialog.

   You will see two new layers. One layer has PH-XXXX for the name format and the other has PV-XXXX. PH means Profile Hidden and PV means Profile Visible.

   **Note:** The XXXX portion of the layer name represents the designation of the viewport handle. This designation will vary.

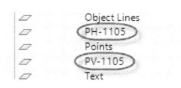

**PH and PV Layers**

7. Change the PV layer to Green and 0.50mm lineweight and the PH layer to White and 0.20mm lineweight.

   **Note:** If you do not see the lines change lineweight, you will need to explode the group of lines, isolate them, and change the lineweight setting to ByLayer in the Properties window. (You may need to re-open the Properties window.)

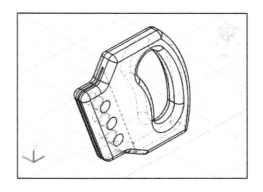

**Completed View**

8. This concludes this section and the tutorial. Dimension the drawing if needed.

# Project #6 – 3D – Guide

**File Name:** PROJ-06-3D.dwg

Note: All screenshots are from the Autodesk® AutoCAD® software.

**Description:** For this project you will only be using the base shape in the 2D file for the base of the solid. The Modeling tools will be used to create the cylinders, fillets, and rounds. You will also use the Chamfer tool to create a chamfered corner. Lastly, you will use the section view option to create the section view with the Solid View and Solid Draw commands.

## Beginning the Project

1. Open PROJ-05-3D.dwg and save the drawing as PROJ-06-3D.dwg.

    If you just completed PROJ-05-3D.dwg, save the file before saving it under a new file name.

2. Delete all the objects in the file. You will not need any elements from the previous project.

    Use Ctrl+A to select any elements that may be hidden or frozen.

3. Merge the layers generated by the Solid View tool into the Object Line, Hidden Line, and Dimension layers.

## Creating the Model

1. Open the 2D version of PROJ-06.

2. Select the outline of the top view. Include the outside circles

    Use the Isolate tool to isolate the Object Lines layer.

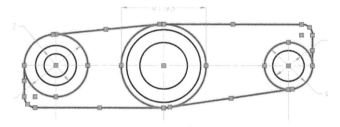

**Elements to be Copied**

3. Switch to PROJ-06-3D and paste the elements into the Top View.

    Locate the view with the center of the center circle at the origin of the view.

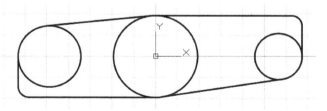

**Elements Pasted in Top View**

4.  Trim the lines to form a single profile.

    Create a region from the lines and
    extrude the up .54 inches.

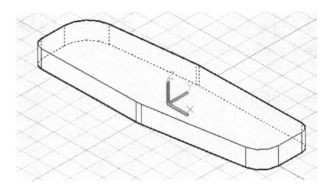

**Base Extruded**

5.  Use the cylinder tool to add the three
    cylinders at the bottom of the base
    solid.

    Locate the centers by snapping at the
    center of the arcs.

    The radius can be set by snapping to
    the edge of the arcs.

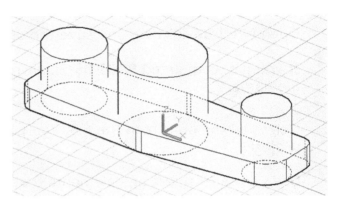

**Cylinders Added**

6.  Use the Solid, Union tool to union the
    base and the three cylinders together.

    After clicking the tool, select all four
    solids and press Enter.

**Solid, Union Tool**

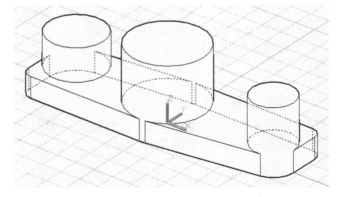

**Cylinders and Base Unioned**

7.  Use the Cylinder tool and the Solid,
    Subtract tool to create the holes
    through the cylinders.

    For the counterbored hole, start with
    the larger diameter.

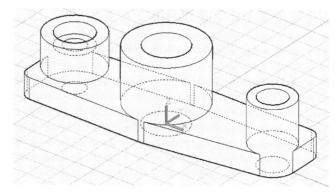

**Holes Created**

8.  Use the Chamfer tool for the countersink.

    Press "D" to use the Distance option and set
    both distances to .30 inches.

    Click on the top of the hole at the inside corner
    for the edge to be chamfered.

    The entire top surface will highlight.

    Press Enter for the next step.

    Press Enter twice to accept the distances.

    Click the edge again and press Enter to accept
    the chamfer and end the tool.

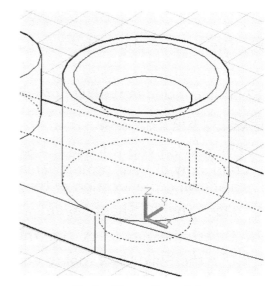

**Hole Chamfered to
Create Countersink**

9.  The last features to add will be the fillets and
    rounds.

    Use the Fillet tool to add these features.

    The radius is .25 inches for all rounds and
    fillets.

    When choosing the corners for the fillets and
    rounds pick at the intersection of the
    surfaces.

    You may pick all of the corners at once.

    **Note:** It is a good idea to make a copy of
    the solid before adding the fillets and
    rounds. This way if they do not come out
    correctly, you can try another method.

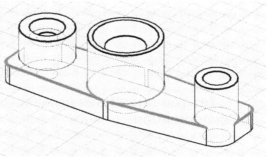

**Edges Chosen for Fillets and
Rounds**

10. Press Enter to accept the edges.

    The corners are now filleted and rounded.

    If they are correct, delete the copied solid.

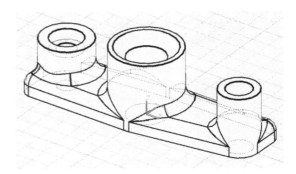

**Edges Filleted and Rounded**

11. Use the VOLUME command to check the volume.

    The volume should be 9.5502 cubic inches.

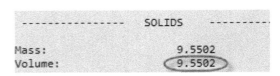

**Volume of Solid**

12. This concludes the 3D portion of the tutorial.

Creating the 2D Views

In this section you will use the Solid View and Solid Drawing tools to create a 2D section view of your project. This will create an additional layer that contains the hatch lines showing the location of the section.

1.  Open the 2D Sheet Layout view.

2.  Delete the viewports from the previous project.

3.  Use the Solid View tool to add the top view of the object.

    Use the UCS option and the World UCS.

    Name the view: Top

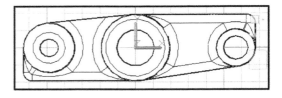

**Top Viewport Created**

4.  For the next viewport, use the Section option.

    **Note:** You must have at least one view placed to use the Section option.

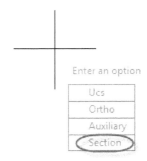

**Section Option**

5. The next step is to place the first point of the cutting plane.

   This will be located along the imaginary plane that shows the inside of the object.

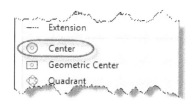

**Center Snap Mode
Selected**

   Snap at the center of the left hole in the top view. The Object Snap tool has been temporarily turned off. Use the snaps override to turn on the Center Snap Mode.

   This is done by holding the Ctrl or Shift key and right-clicking the mouse. Select the Center snap mode in the pop-up menu.

6. After snapping at the center of the circle, drag the mouse to the right and click the second point.

   Use Polar Tracking to make sure that the line is horizontal.

   The line does not need to go through the entire solid.

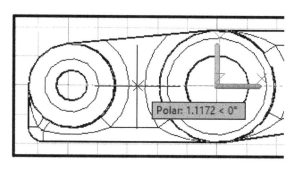

**Dragging Mouse for Second Point**

7. Click the next point below the solid to indicate which side to view the section from.

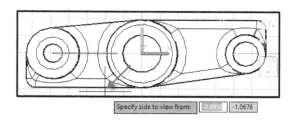

**Click Below View**

8. Press Enter to accept the view scale at 1.000.

9. Click below the view for the view center.

   Specify the corners of the viewport.

   The top view may temporarily disappear.

   Name the view: Section

   Press the Esc to end the command.

   **Note:** The view will not appear sectioned until the Solid Drawing tool is used.

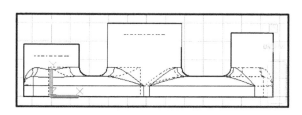

**Section View Placed**

10. Click the Solid Drawing tool.

    Select both viewports and press Enter.

    The hidden line and section views are created.

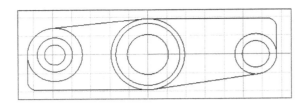

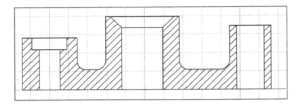

**Views Created**

11. Open the Layer Properties Manager dialog.

    You will see an additional layer created for the Section view called: Section-HAT. The letters HAT stand for Hatch.

    Use Red for the color, Continuous for the linetype, and 0.20 mm for the lineweight.

**Section-HAT Layer**

12. Create a new viewport at the upper right corner of the sheet using the VPORTS command.

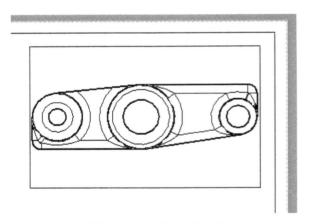

**Viewport Created**

13. Switch to Modelspace.

   Rotate the view to Right Front Isometric

   Set the viewport scale to 1:2 scale.

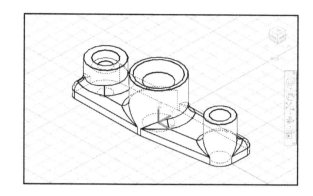

**View Scaled and Rotated**

14. Since the solid had rounded corners, use
   the Solid Profile tool to create a hidden
   profile view of the solid.

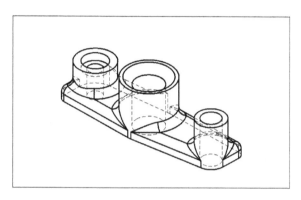

**Profile View of Solid**

15. This concludes the tutorial, dimension the drawing if needed.

# Project #7 – 3D – Gasket

**File Name:** PROJ-07-3D.dwg
Note: All screenshots are from the Autodesk® AutoCAD® software.

**Description:** This project will use the extrusion method. Only the outside shape will be extruded. The holes will be placed using the Cylinder tool and then subtracting the intersecting solids. Arraying the cylinders use the Array tool will also be covered.

Beginning the Project

1.  Open PROJ-06-3D.dwg and save the drawing as PROJ-07-3D.dwg.

    If you just completed PROJ-06-3D.dwg, save the file before saving it under a new file name.

2.  Delete all the objects in the file. You will not need any elements from the previous project.

    Use Ctrl+A to select any elements that may be hidden or frozen.

3.  Merge the layers generated by the Solid View tool into the Object Line, Hidden Line, Dimension layers, and Section Lines layers.

Creating the Model

1.  Open the 2D version of PROJ-07.

2.  Select the outline of the view.

    Do not include the eight circles around the larger hole.

    You may use the Isolate tool to isolate the Object Lines layer.

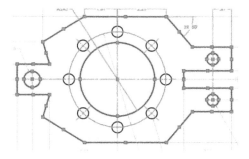

**Elements to be Copied**

3.  Switch to the PROJ-07-3D file.

    Paste the elements in the top view. Locate the objects with the origin at the center of the large circle.

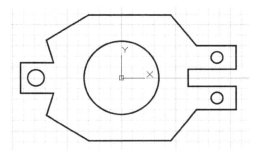

**Elements Pasted in Top View**

4. Create a region and extrude .06 inches upward.

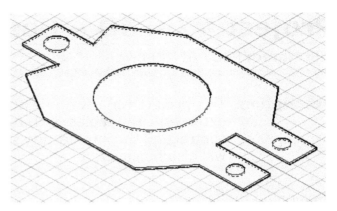

**Region and Circles Extruded**

5. Use the Solid, Subtract tool to create the holes.

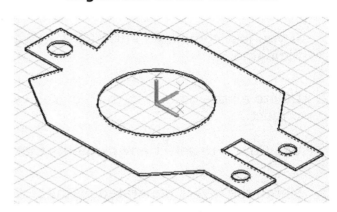

**Holes Created**

6. Add a .51 diameter cylinder up 2.23 from the center of the large hole.

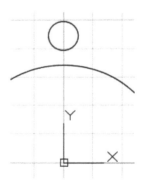

**.51 Cylinder Added**

7. Before subtracting to create the hole, array the cylinder to create eight cylinders total.

   Refer to the 2D procedure for PROJ-07 for the use of the Array tool.

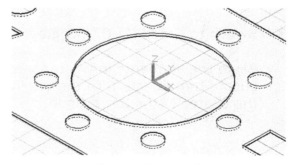

**Array Created**

8.  You will not be able to subtract the solids until the array is changed to individual cylinders.

    Click on the Explode tool in the Modify panel.

    Select one of the eight cylinders.

    Press Enter to explode the array into individual cylinders.

**Explode Tool**

9.  Use the Solid, Subtract tool to create the eight holes.

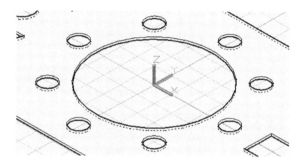

**Holes Created**

10. Use the VOLUME command to check the volume.

    The volume should be 1.7920 cubic inches.

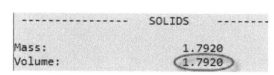

**Volume of Solid**

11. This concludes the tutorial, create a hidden line view and dimension the drawing if needed.

# Project #8 – 3D – Geneva Cam Assembly

**File Names:** See Chart
Note: All screenshots are from the Autodesk® AutoCAD® software.

**Description:** This project will be your first Assembly project. The assembly will consist of four parts. Each part will be created in a separate file and then inserted into the assembly drawing with the use of the Reference tool.

You will also create a 2D exploded isometric assembly drawing with a parts list.

Beginning the Project

1. Open PROJ-07-3D.dwg and save the drawing as PROJ-08-3D.dwg.

   If you just completed PROJ-07-3D.dwg, save the file before saving it under a new file name.

2. Delete all the objects in the file. You will not need any elements from the previous project.

   Use Ctrl+A to select any elements that may be hidden or frozen.

3. Merge the layers generated by the Solid View tool into the Object Line, Hidden Line, Dimension layers, and Section Lines layers.

4. Since this is an Assembly Project, you will need to create additional files for all of the parts. To keep things organized, use the following chart for the file names for the 3D and 2D files:

| **Part/Drawing Name** | **File Name** |
|---|---|
| Geneva Cam (3D) | PROJ-08-3D-1-Cam.dwg |
| Drive Wheel (3D) | PROJ-08-3D-2-Wheel.dwg |
| Base & Pin (3D) | PROJ-08-3D-3-Base.dwg |
| Shaft & Key (3D) | PROJ-08-3D-4-Shaft and Key.dwg |
| Assembly of Parts – Assembled (3D) | PROJ-08-3D-Assembled.dwg |
| Assembly of Parts – Exploded (2D and 3D) | PROJ-08-3D-Exploded.dwg |
| Cam & Drive Wheel (2D) | PROJ-08-02-Cam & Wheel |
| Base, Shaft & Key (2D) | PROJ-08-03-Base, Shaft & Key |

**Note:** The Base and the Shaft & Key do not have 2D files, dimensions for these parts will be given later in this tutorial. For now, create the 3D drawing files using the PROJ-08-3D-1-Cam.dwg as a starting point. You will also create a subfolder in the Projects – 3D folder called: Geneva Cam Assembly.

Creating the Model (Geneva Cam)

1.  Open the 2D version of PROJ-08.

2.  Select the outline of the Geneva Cam portion
    of the drawing.

    Use the Isolate tool to isolate the Object
    Lines layer.

    The outside shape of the cam may still be
    grouped as an array.

    Explode the array into individual elements
    before copying to the elements to the
    clipboard.

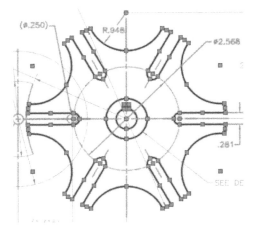

**Elements to be Copied**

3.  Paste the elements into the top view of the
    PROJ-08-01-Cam file.

    Locate the center of the part at the origin.

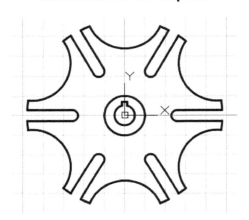

**Elements Pasted to Top View**

4.  Create a region for the outside edge of the cam and the inner hole and keyway.

    This can be done by selecting the entire group of elements.

    Three regions will be created.

5.  Extrude the outside shape .200 inches
    downward.

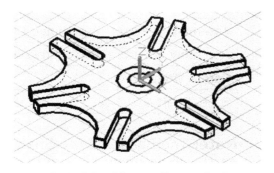

**Outside Shape Extruded**

6. So that the objects will be at the correct height in relation to the origin, you will move the elements upward in the isometric view.

   You will use the Gizmo tool to aid in doing this.

   In the isometric view, click the outside extruded shape.

   You will see the Gizmo appear near the center of the part.

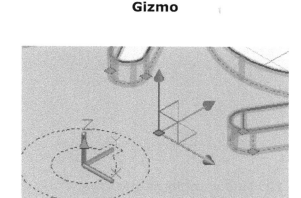

**Gizmo**

7. Click at the bottom of the Gizmo where the three axes intersect and move it out of the way.

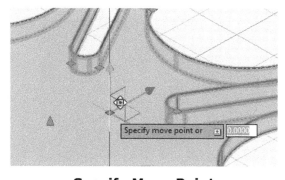

**Gizmo Moved**

8. Click on the vertical axis of the Gizmo.

   You will see a vertical line appear and a field appear asking to specify the move point.

   Type .263 for the distance.

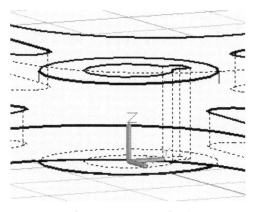

**Specify Move Point**

9. Next you will extrude the two inner shapes .525 upward.

   If you are working in the isometric view, you will need to rotate the view to see the shapes beneath the cam.

**Shapes Extruded**

10. Union the outside cylinder to the cam.

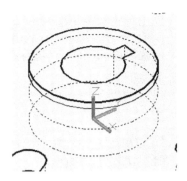

**Cylinder Unioned to Cam**

11. Subtract the inner shape from the solid.

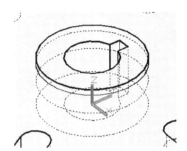

**Inner Shape Subtracted**

12. This completes the cam.

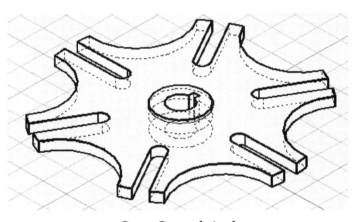

**Cam Completed**

13. Use the VOLUME command to check the volume.

    The volume should be 2.2996 cubic inches.

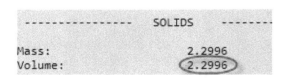

**Volume of Solid**

## Creating the Model (Drive Wheel)

1.  Starting with the 3D Cam file, create the next 3D file called PROJ-08-3D-2-Wheel.

    Switch to or open the 2D version of PROJ-08.

2.  Select the outline of the Drive Wheel portion of the drawing.

    Use the Isolate tool to isolate the Phantom Lines layer.

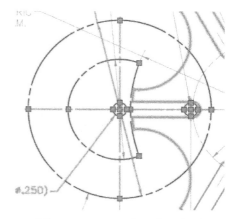

**Elements to be Copied**

3.  Paste the elements into the top view of the PROJ-08-02-Wheel file.

    Locate the center of the part at the origin.

    Change the elements to the Object Lines layer.

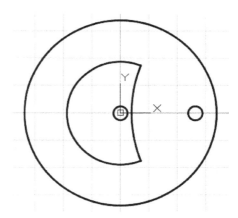

**Elements Pasted to Top View**

4.  Create regions of the four shapes.

    Extrude the two small circles and the inner shape .463 inches vertically.

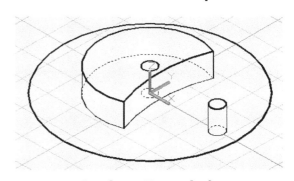

**Regions Extruded**

5. Extrude the outer circle .200 inches vertically.

   Union the outer solid, the inner shape, and the pin on the left together.

   Subtract the other small circle in the center to create the hole.

**Drive Wheel Completed**

6. Use the VOLUME command to check the volume.

   The volume should be 2.2619 cubic inches.

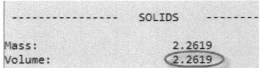

**Volume of Solid**

## Creating the Model (Base)

1. Starting from the previous file, create a new file named PROJ-08-3D-Base.

2. Use this drawing for the dimensions of the base.

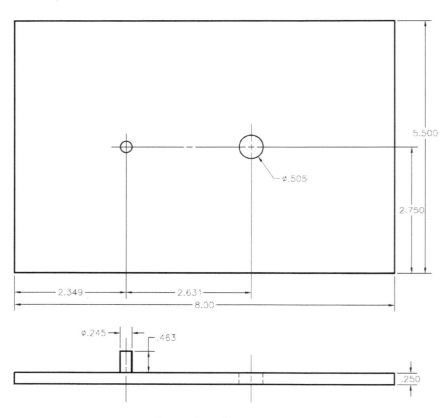

**Drawing for Base**

3. Draw the outline for the base and the two circles in the top view.

   Place the lower left corner of the rectangle at the origin.

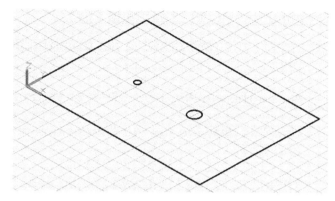

**Outline for Base**

4. Extrude the smaller circle on the left upward .713 (.250 + .463).

   Extrude the rectangle and other circle upward .250 inches.

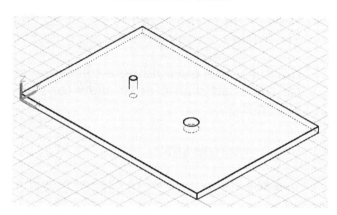

**Shapes Extruded**

5. Union the rectangular shape and the .713 high cylinder.

   Subtract the .505 cylinder on the right from the solid to create the hole.

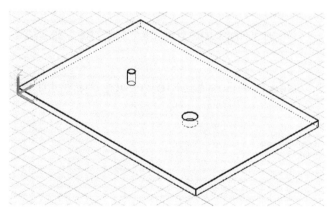

**Solids Unioned and Subtracted**

6. Use the VOLUME command to check the volume.

   The volume should be 10.9718 cubic inches.

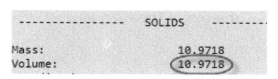

**Volume of Solid**

Creating the Model (Shaft and Key)

1.  Create the new drawing file from the previous
    file.

    Name the file PROJ-08-3D-4-Shaft and Key.

    Use this drawing for the dimensions of the Shaft
    and Key.

    These parts will be drawn as two separate solids
    within the same file.

    **Note:** The purpose of the key is to keep the
    Shaft from spinning inside the hole in the cam.

    Normally there would be a tolerance dimension
    for the shaft diameter to allow for the proper fit
    within the cam.

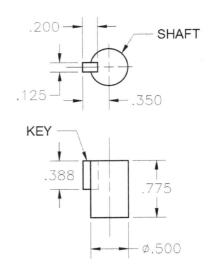

**Drawing for Shaft and Key**

2.  Begin with the shaft.

    Use the Cylinder tool to create a cylindrical
    solid.

    Use the dimensions from the drawing.

    Do not include the slot for the keyway.

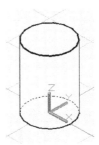

**Cylinder Created**

3.  Use the Box tool to create the solid for the key.

**Key Created**

4.  Place the key with the left side at the center of
    the top of the cylinder.

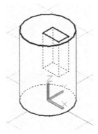

**Key Located at Top of Cylinder**

5. Use the Gizmo tool to move the key to the left along the X axis .350 inches.

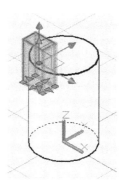

**Key Moved**

6. Before using the Solid, Subtract tool to create the keyway, make a copy of the key at locate it away from the shaft.

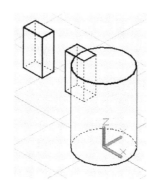

**Key Copied**

7. Use the Solid, Subtract tool to make the void for the keyway.

   Move the copied key into position inside the keyway.

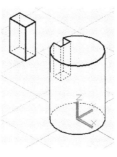

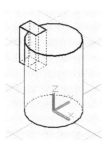

**Void Created**          **Key Moved into Position**

8. Use the VOLUME command to check the volumes for both parts.

   The volume should be 0.1474 cubic inches for the Shaft and 0.0097 for the Key.

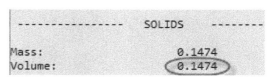

**Volume of Shaft**

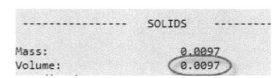

**Volume of Key**

<u>Creating the Assembly</u>

Now you will create an assembly drawing of the parts. There will be two versions, one with the parts touching each other and the other in an exploded version. You will then create a 2D drawing of the exploded version with a parts list and find numbers for the individual parts.

1. Open or Create the PROJ-08-Assembled file.

2. You will use the Attach tool in the Insert tab, Reference panel to reference the individual part files into the assembly file.

    This will create a link between the two files. This method is more efficient than using the copy/paste method.

    With the reference method, if the part dimensions are changed they will be updated in the assembly file as well.

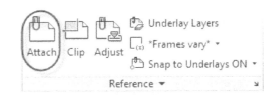

**Attach Tool**

3. The Select Reference File dialog box opens.

    You can attach the four reference files at the same time or one at a time.

    After attaching the files, you will move them into position.

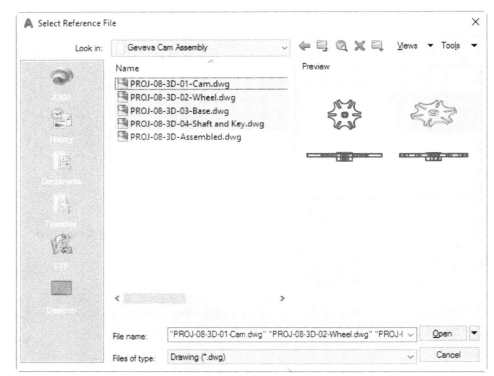

**Select Reference File Dialog Box**

4. The Attach External Reference dialog box opens.

   Click the Ok button to attach the files.

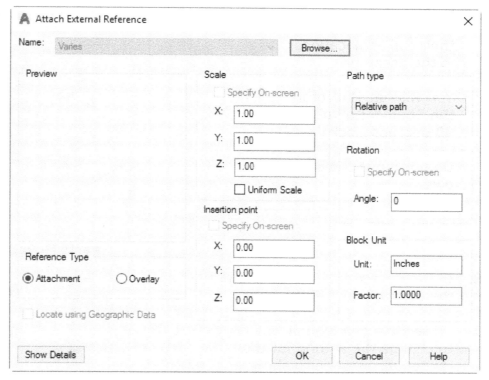

**Attach External Reference Dialog Box**

5. All of the parts are added to the drawing.

   You will notice that they appear in the same location relative to the origin as in the original drawings.

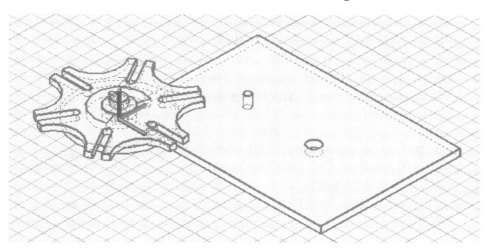

**Parts Added to Drawing**

6. The parts are gray in color because they have been referenced.

   This is due to the Xref Fading setting.

   Use the slider bar to change this setting to zero.

   The parts will now be black in color.

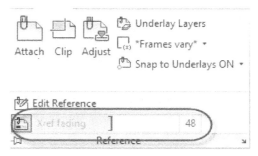

**Xref Fading**

7. Using the Move tool move the parts into their correct locations in the assembly.

   You will need to rotate the Shaft & Key part 90 degrees clockwise.

   Do not move the base part.

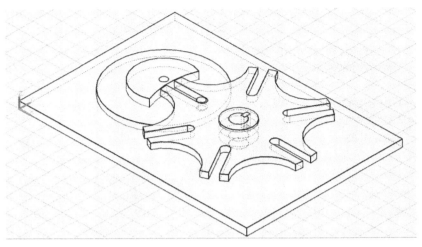

**Parts Moved**

8. In the next step, you will change the color of each of the parts.

   To see this change you will need to change the setting for the Hidden visual style to show colors.

   Open the Visual Styles Manager dialog box and change the Edge Setting Color to "By Entity".

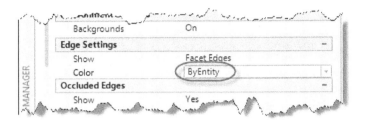

**Edge Settings Color Changed to By Entity**

9. Up to this point, the colors of the 3D versions of the projects have been green.

   To make the parts easier to see you will change the colors of each part. Since the parts are referenced, you will need to change.

   Double-click on the Cam part to edit it.

   The Reference Edit dialog box opens.

   **Note:** For this section of the tutorial, the screen shots will be in grayscale.

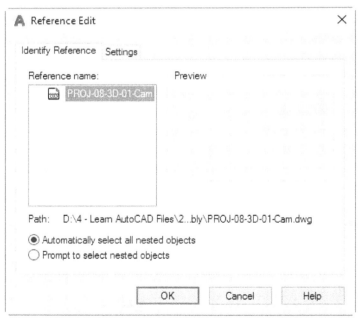

**Reference Edit Dialog Box**

10. Click the Ok button to edit the reference file.

    The other parts will turn gray.

    Click on the cam then right-click and select Properties to open the Properties window.

    Override the color in the General area to Red.

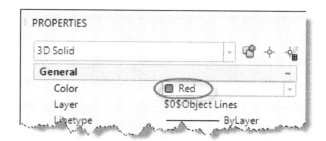

**Cam Part Changed to Red**

11. Click the Save Changes tool in the Edit Reference panel.

    Click OK in the Alert box to save the changes.

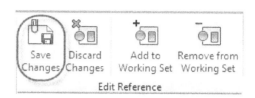

**Edit Reference Panel**

12. This not only changed the color of the part in the Assembly file but also in the original file.

    Open the PROJ-08-3D-01-Cam.dwg file.

    You will see that the solid has been changed to red.

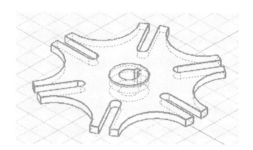

**Solid Changed to Red**

13. Close the Cam file.

14. Switch to the assembly file.

    You will see an alert box in the lower right corner of the screen stating that a referenced file has changed and will need to be reloaded.

    Click on the blue text to reload the file.

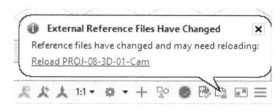

**Alert Box**

15. Repeat the process for the other parts.

    Change the parts to the following colors:

    Wheel – Green
    Base – Cyan
    Shaft – Yellow
    Key – Magenta

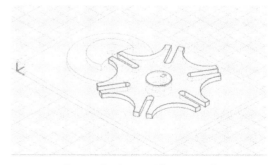

**Part Colors Changed**

16. To see the parts clearer, you may change the display style to Shaded with Edges.

    This may be done by clicking on the display setting at the upper left corner of the view.

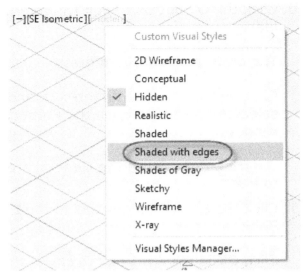

**Shaded with Edges Visual Style**

17. The parts will now appear shaded.

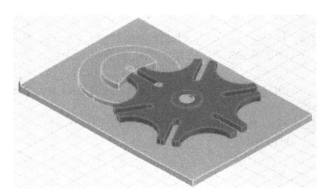

**Parts are Shaded**

18. This concludes this section of the tutorial.

    You may wish to create a 2D version of the assembled parts.

    In the next section you will create an exploded version of the assembly.

## Creating the Exploded View

In this section you will create a second version of the assembled parts. The parts will be moved away from one another as if they were exploded. This will make it easier to see the individual parts and how they are to be assembled.

1.  If needed, open the PROJ-08-3D-Assembled.dwg file.

    Save the file as: PROJ-08-3D-Exploded.dwg file.

2.  In the Isometric view, move each of the parts away from each other as indicated in the example.

    Leave the Base part in the original location.

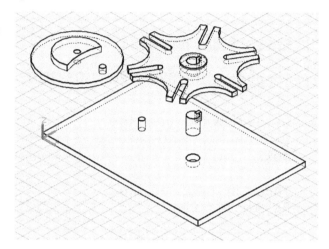

**Parts Moved**

3.  Open the 2D Sheet layout tab.

    Use the Solid View tool to create a view of the parts.

    Use the saved Ucs, Iso when placing the view.

    Use 1.000 for the view scale and name the view Iso.

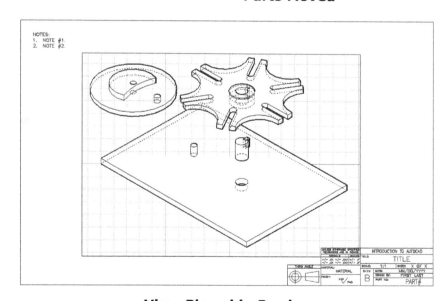

**View Placed in Border**

4.  For the next step you will first need to remove the attachment of the parts to the file.

    This is done by binding the reference files to the assembly file.

    The result will be that the individual files will become part of the assembly file and their link back to the part drawing will be lost.

    Before doing this, you will create a backup of the file.

5.  Save the drawing file.

    Then, save the file as PROJ-08-3D-Exploded-Bound.

6.  In the new file, open the External References dialog box.

    This is in the Insert tab, Reference panel.

    Click on the small arrow at the bottom right of the panel.

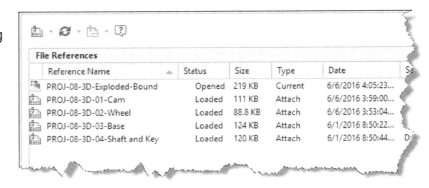

**Reference Files Attached**

7.  Select the four reference files.

    Right click and select Bind... from the menu.

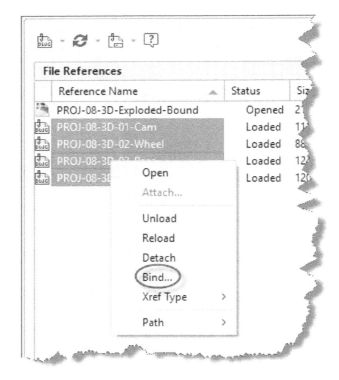

**Bind... Selected**

8. The Bind Xrefs/DGN underlays dialog box opens.

   Select the Insert option.

   **Note:** The Insert option is used to strip the layer name from each individual part and combine them when the file is bound. This makes the layer names easier to manage.

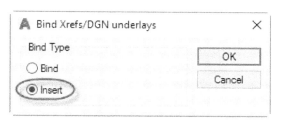

**Bind Xrefs/DGN underlays Dialog Box**

9. The part drawing files are now merged into the assembly file.

   Close the External References dialog box.

10. Next you will need to explode the parts.

    Select the four parts in the Modelspace viewport and click the Explode tool.

    **Note:** When an xref file is attached it becomes a Block Reference. The Explode tool is used to remove the block reference and allow the Solid View tool to create the hidden line views.

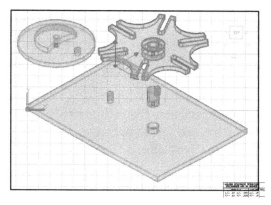

**Four Parts Selected**

11. The parts are now changed to 3D Solids.

12. Use the Solid View tool to create the hidden line views.

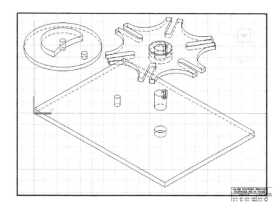

**Hidden Line Views Created**

13. Change the Object Lines and the Hidden Lines layers to the appropriate attributes.

## Modifying the View Scale

Even though the view scale was set to 1.000 when the view of the assembly was added, the view is not at the correct size.

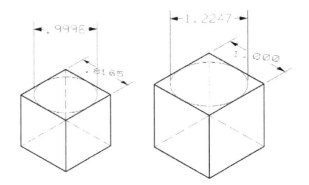

The graphic shows a one-inch cube that was converted from 3D to 2D. When the line dimensioned at 1.000 was measured after the cube was converted it changed to .8165.

**One Inch Cube Before and After Scaling**

The reason for the difference in sizes is that a 3D isometric view is foreshortened when projected onto a flat plane such as a computer monitor.

To compensate for this, the view will be scaled to 1.2247. This is the ratio between a full scale 3D view and a 2D isometric view.

Since changing the view scale to 1.2247:1.000 would make the parts too large for the border size, you will use 3/4 scale for your project.

1. Switch to modelspace if needed.

   Click on the Viewport Scale control in the status bar.

**Viewport Scale Control**

2. Scroll down to the bottom of the scales and click the Custom... option.

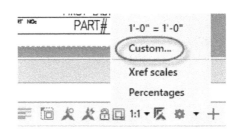

**Custom... Option**

3.  The Edit Drawing Scales dialog box
    opens.

    Click the Add... button to add a new
    drawing scale.

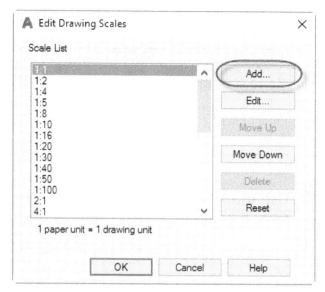

**Edit Drawing Scale Dialog Box**

4.  The Add Scale dialog box opens.

    Type in the name of the new drawing scale as
    shown.

    Type in the Paper units and Drawing units.

    Note: If the new drawing scale were Isometric
    Full Scale, the paper units would still be
    1.2247 but the drawing units would be
    1.0000.

**Add Scale Dialog Box**

5.  Press Ok to close each dialog box.

    Click on the Viewport Scale control and select
    the new scale you created.

    The view will be slightly smaller.

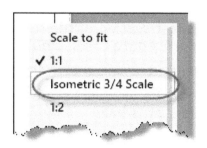

**Isometric 3/4 Scale**

6. To check to see if the scale has been set up correctly, switch to Paperspace and draw a line on top of the edge of the base part.

   Move the line away from the edge of the part.

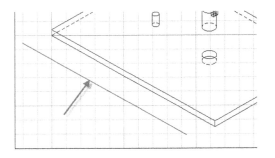

**Line Drawn and Moved**

7. Use the MEASUREGEOM key-in to measure the new line.

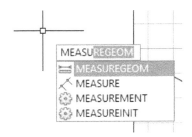

**MEASUREGEOM Key-in**

8. Snap to the endpoints. The line should be 5.999 long.

   If you round the value to 6.000, this is 3/4 of the full scale length of the base which is 8.000.

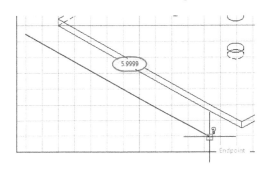

**Line Measures at 5.999**

Adding the Assembly Drawing Annotation Information

In this last section of the tutorial you will add a parts list, part bubbles (find numbers), and a procedure to assemble the parts.

1. Delete the line that was drawn in the previous section.

2. Lock the viewport scale using the lock tool in the status bar.

**Viewport Scale Lock**

   This will prevent you from accidentally changing the viewport scale.

3. Move and resize the viewport so that it is to the left of the title block.

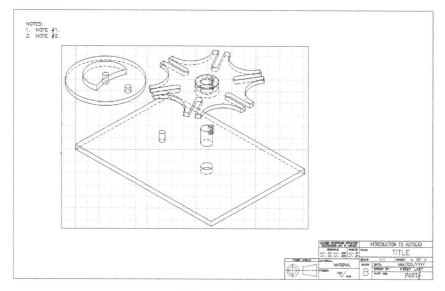

**Viewport Moved and Resized**

4. Delete the text for the general notes, you will not need it for this drawing.

   Also, turn off the VPORTS layer to hide the outline of the viewport.

5. Next you will add the Part Balloons to identify the parts in the assembly.

   The circle is .50 in diameter and the text is .25 high.

   Use Romans.shx for the font and Middle Center for the justification.

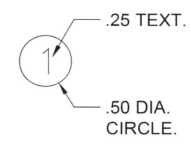

**Part Balloon**

6. Use the Multileader tool to place the arrows and leaders to point at each part.

   Do not add text for the leader. You will be using the tool for the arrow and the line only.

   Snap the balloon to the end of the leader line.

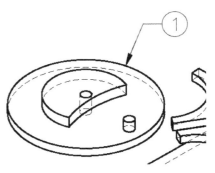

**Part Balloon for Cam**

7. Add the part balloons for the other parts.

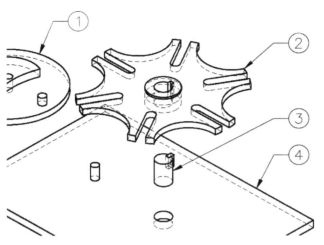

**Part Balloons Added for Remaining Parts**

8. Use the Insert Block command to insert the block for the Parts List.

   This file is located in the Support Files folder.

9. Place the Parts List above the Title Block.

| 4 | XXXX | X | | |
|---|------|---|-------------|----------|
| 3 | XXXX | X | | |
| 2 | XXXX | X | | |
| 1 | XXXX | X | DESCRIPTION | MATERIAL |
| ITEM | PART# | QTY. | DESCRIPTION | MATERIAL |

PARTS LIST

UNLESS OTHERWISE SPECIFIED TOLERANCES ARE IN INCHES — INTRODUCTION TO AUTOCAD

DECIMALS / ANGLES  TITLE: TITLE

+/- XX +/- XXX +/- .X°
+/- .XX +/- .XXX +/- .X°

THIRD ANGLE

MATERIAL:      MATERIAL

FINISH:   XXX / FAO

SCALE:  1:1  SHEET:  X OF X

SIZE  DATE:  MM/DD/YYYY

B   DRAWN BY:  FIRST LAST

PART NO:  PART#

**Parts List Block Placed**

10. This block does not use block attributes for the text.

    You will fill out the table using text editing.

    **Note:** The item numbers start at the bottom and go upward so that new parts may be added to the list easily.

| 4 | P8-03 | 1 | BASE | 6061-T6 |
|---|-------|---|--------------|----------|
| 3 | P8-04 | 1 | SHAFT AND KEY | 1018 |
| 2 | P8-01 | 1 | CAM | PLASTIC |
| 1 | P8-02 | 1 | DRIVE WHEEL | PLASTIC |
| ITEM | PART# | QTY. | DESCRIPTION | MATERIAL |

PARTS LIST

UNLESS OTHERWISE SPECIFIED TOLERANCES ARE IN INCHES — INTRODUCTION TO AUTOCAD

DECIMALS | ANGLES | TITLE

**Parts List Filled Out**

11. Add the assembly sequence and the description above the parts list on the left side of the sheet.

   Use .125 inch text with Top Left justification.

ASSEMBLY SEQUENCE
1.  ATTACH DRIVE WHEEL TO PIN ON BASE.
2.  PRESS FIT CAM ONTO KEY END OF SHAFT.
3.  INSERT OTHER END OF SHAFT INTO BASE.

GENEVA CAM DESCRIPTION
THE PURPOSE OF THE GENEVA CAM IS FOR INCREMENTAL ROTATION.

THE DRIVE WHEEL IS USED TO TURN THE CAM PORTION OF THE ASSEMBLY. DUE TO THE SHAPE OF THE CAM AND THE NUMBER OF SLOTS, THE CAM TURNS 60 DEGREES FOR EVERY REVOLUTION OF THE DRIVE WHEEL.

**Text for Assembly Sequence and Description**

12. The assembly drawing is finished.

   Create a new 2D file for the Base, Shaft & Key.

13. Since the Base, Shaft & Key drawing has multiple parts, you will need to include a view label under each set of parts.

   Use the example to the left for the text sizes. Use Middle Center justification.

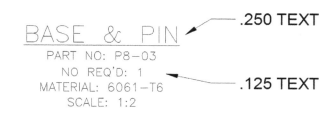

BASE & PIN
PART NO: P8-03
NO REQ'D: 1
MATERIAL: 6061-T6
SCALE: 1:2

.250 TEXT

.125 TEXT

**View Label**

14. To avoid confusion, for each of the three sheets change the Part No: field in the title block to Drawing No:

   **Note:** You do not need to change the sheets for the other 2D drawings.

DRAWN BY:        DAVE MARTIN
DRAWING NO:      PROJ-08-01

**Part No: Changed to Drawing No:**

15. If creating PDF files, save the files as: PROJ-08-01-Assembly, PROJ-08-02-Cam & Wheel, and PROJ-08-03-Base, Shaft & Key

    You will also need to modify the original Geneva Cam drawing to make this the second sheet in the set.

    See example drawings at the end of this tutorial for the three 2D sheets.

    **Note:** When plotting the Assembly drawing from the 2D Sheet layout, you will need to change the color of the object lines to black.

16. This concludes the tutorial.

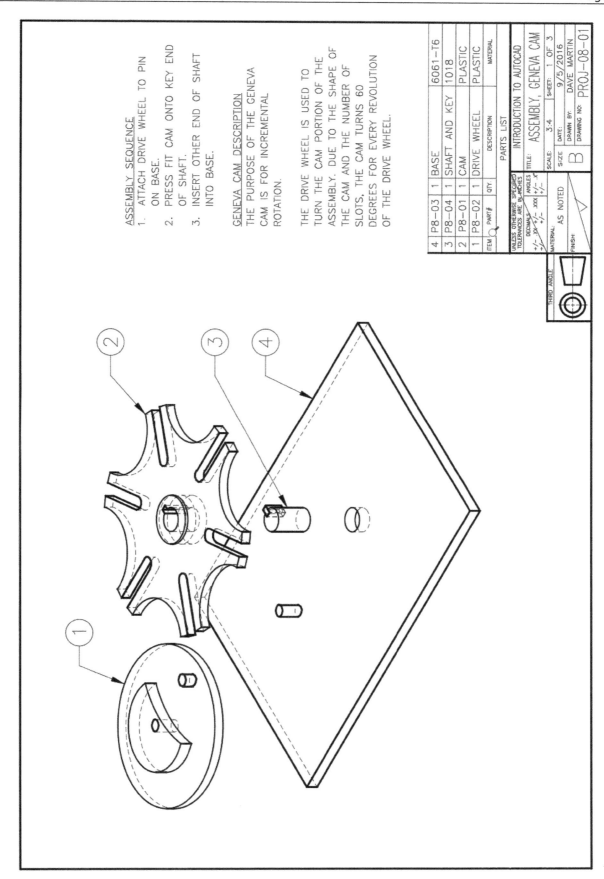

ASSEMBLY SEQUENCE
1. ATTACH DRIVE WHEEL TO PIN ON BASE.
2. PRESS FIT CAM ONTO KEY END OF SHAFT.
3. INSERT OTHER END OF SHAFT INTO BASE.

GENEVA CAM DESCRIPTION
THE PURPOSE OF THE GENEVA CAM IS FOR INCREMENTAL ROTATION.

THE DRIVE WHEEL IS USED TO TURN THE CAM PORTION OF THE ASSEMBLY. DUE TO THE SHAPE OF THE CAM AND THE NUMBER OF SLOTS, THE CAM TURNS 60 DEGREES FOR EVERY REVOLUTION OF THE DRIVE WHEEL.

| ITEM | PART # | QTY | DESCRIPTION | MATERIAL |
|------|--------|-----|-------------|----------|
| 4 | P8-03 | 1 | BASE | 6061-T6 |
| 3 | P8-04 | 1 | SHAFT AND KEY | 1018 |
| 2 | P8-01 | 1 | CAM | PLASTIC |
| 1 | P8-02 | 1 | DRIVE WHEEL | PLASTIC |

PARTS LIST

UNLESS OTHERWISE SPECIFIED
TOLERANCES ARE IN INCHES

DECIMALS
+/- .XX +/-
+/- .XXX +/-

ANGLES
+/- .X°
+/-

MATERIAL:
AS NOTED

FINISH:

THIRD ANGLE

TITLE:
INTRODUCTION TO AUTOCAD
ASSEMBLY, GENEVA CAM

SCALE: 3:4   SHEET: 1 OF 3
DATE: 9/5/2016
SIZE B   DRAWN BY: DAVE MARTIN
DRAWING NO: PROJ-08-01

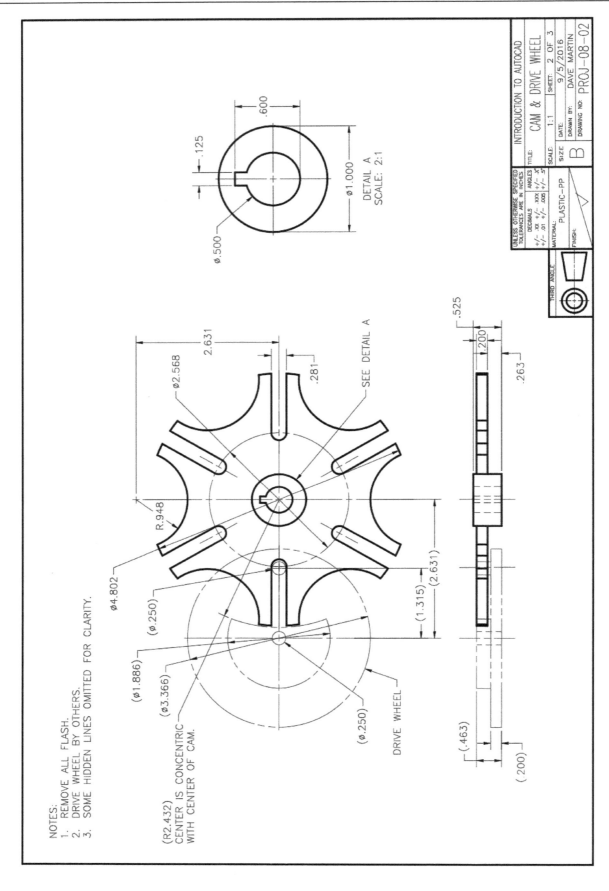

NOTES:
1. REMOVE ALL FLASH.
2. DRIVE WHEEL BY OTHERS.
3. SOME HIDDEN LINES OMITTED FOR CLARITY.

DETAIL A
SCALE: 2:1

SEE DETAIL A

DRIVE WHEEL

INTRODUCTION TO AUTOCAD

TITLE: CAM & DRIVE WHEEL

SCALE: 1:1    SHEET: 2 OF 3

DATE: 9/5/2016

DRAWN BY: DAVE MARTIN

DRAWING NO: PROJ-08-02

SIZE: B

UNLESS OTHERWISE SPECIFIED
TOLERANCES ARE IN INCHES
DECIMALS        ANGLES
+/- .XX +/- .XXX   +/- .X°
+/- .01 +/- .005   +/- .5°

MATERIAL: PLASTIC-PP

FINISH:

THIRD ANGLE

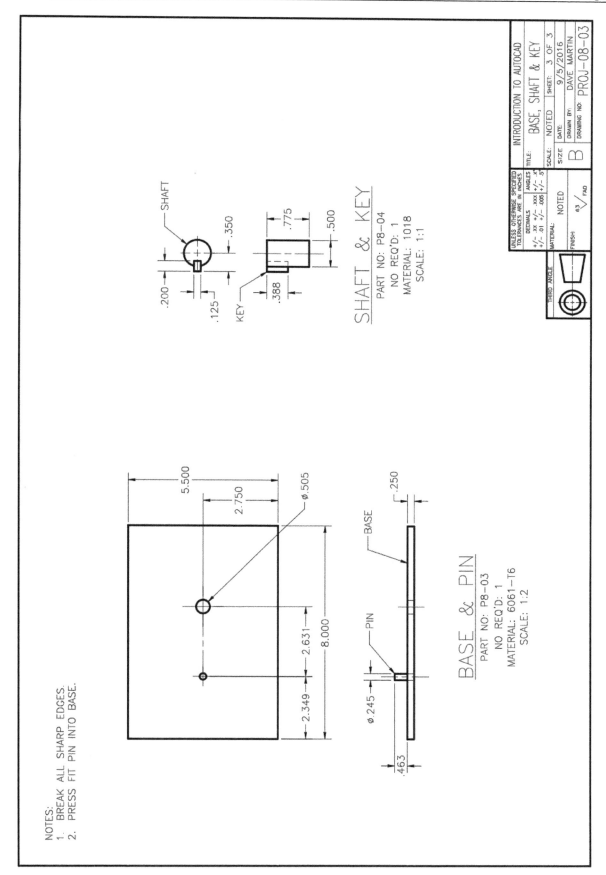

NOTES:
1. BREAK ALL SHARP EDGES.
2. PRESS FIT PIN INTO BASE.

SHAFT & KEY
PART NO: P8-04
NO REQ'D: 1
MATERIAL: 1018
SCALE: 1:1

BASE & PIN
PART NO: P8-03
NO REQ'D: 1
MATERIAL: 6061-T6
SCALE: 1:2

INTRODUCTION TO AUTOCAD
TITLE: BASE, SHAFT & KEY
SHEET: 3 OF 3
DATE: 9/5/2016
DRAWN BY: DAVE MARTIN
DRAWING NO: PROJ-08-03
SIZE B
SCALE: NOTED
MATERIAL: NOTED
THIRD ANGLE

# Project #9 – 3D – Hole Guide

**File Name:** PROJ-09-3D.dwg

Note: All screenshots are from the Autodesk® AutoCAD® software.

**Description:** This project will use the primitive method. A box (cube) will be drawn and then material will be removed to form the cut and the holes. This will be the first project to have an auxiliary surface. You will also create a set of 2D views using third angle projection.

## Beginning the Project

1. Open PROJ-08-3D-Exploded-Bound.dwg and save the drawing as PROJ-09-3D.dwg.

   If you just completed PROJ-08-3D-Exploded-Bound.dwg, save the file before saving it under a new file name.

2. Delete all the objects in the file. You will not need any elements from the previous project.

   Use Ctrl+A to select any elements that may be hidden or frozen.

3. Merge the layers generated by the Solid View tool into the Object Line, Hidden Line, Dimension layers, and Section Lines layers.

4. This is a metric drawing.

   Change the grid spacing to 5.000 with a major line every 4 grids.

## Creating the Model

1. Since this model will be created using the primitive method, you will begin by adding a box for the overall dimensions of the solid.

   Click on the Box tool in the Modeling panel.

2. Start the first corner of the solid at the origin of the drawing in the top view.

   The base of the box will be 78.41mm wide and 50.40mm deep.

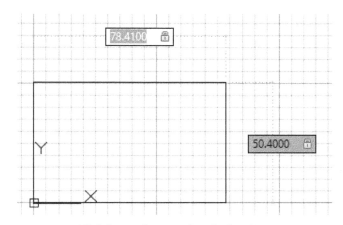

**Width and Depth of the Box**

3.  The height of the box is 63.17mm.

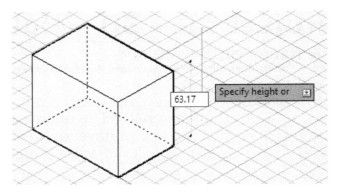

**Height of Box**

4.  The next feature will be the notch on the left side.

    Draw a shape using these dimensions in the top view.

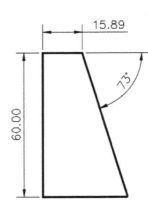

**Shape Dimensions**

5.  Create a region from the shape and extrude it 45.56mm.

    This dimension came from 63.17 (Overall Height) – 17.61 (Height of Step).

    Move the extrusion so that the top left corner is at the top left corner of the box.

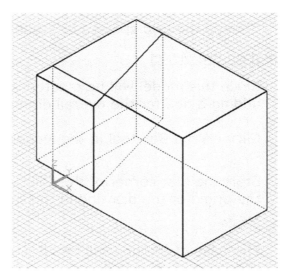

**Extrusion Moved to Top Left Corner**

6. Use the Solid, Subtract tool to create the notch.

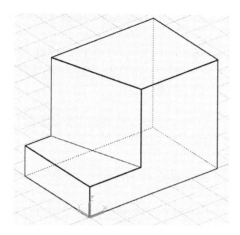

**Notch Created**

7. To place the cylinder at the correct angle, you will need to create a new UCS at the face of the angled surface.

   Click on the 3-Point tool in the Coordinates panel.

   This will use three snapped points to create a new UCS plane.

**3 Point Tool**

8. Snap at the lower left, lower right, and upper left corner of the angled face.

   You will see the UCS icon rotate as you snap the points.

   The grid squares will reorient to lay along the face of the surface.

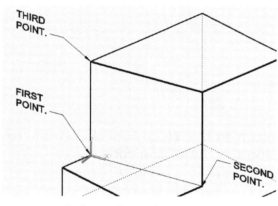

**Points for UCS Plane**

9. After reorienting the UCS, click on the Top surface in the ViewCube to rotate the view.

   The angled surface is now parallel to the screen and is true size.

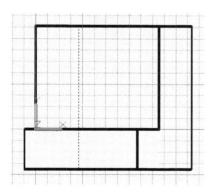

**View Rotated**

10. Click on the Cylinder tool.

    Use the FROM option to locate the origin of the
    cylinder at the bottom left corner of the
    surface.

    The distance will be 26.35 on the X axis and
    22.78 on the Y axis.

    Set the diameter to 25.4mm.

    Rotate the view and drag the end of the
    cylinder through the solid and click to place the
    other end.

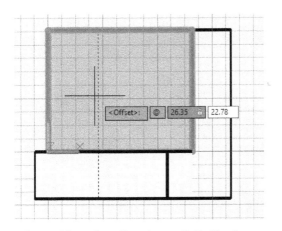

**Location for Center of Cylinder**

11. Use the Solid, Subtract tool to create the hole.

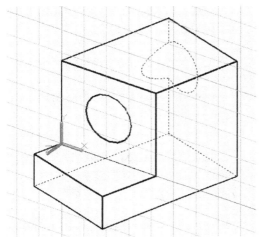

**Hole Created**

12. Return to the WCS (World Coordinate System)
    using the ViewCube controls.

**WCS**

13. Create two cylinders for the counterbored hole.

    Make the smaller cylinder with a height of 20mm so that it extends below the bottom edge of the solid.

    Locate the cylinders near the solid.

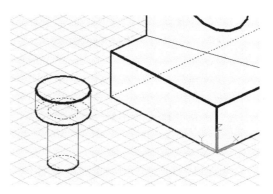

**Cylinders Added**

14. Move the cylinders onto the lower left corner of the solid.

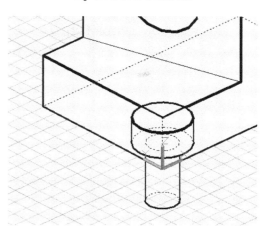

**Cylinders Moved**

15. Rotate the view to the top orientation.

    Move them into location using the Move tool and keying in the coordinates.

    The X-Axis distance is 13.65mm and the Y-Axis distance is 13.95.

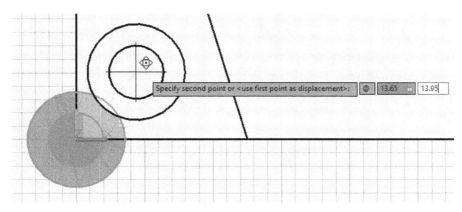

**Moving the Cylinders**

16. Use the Solid, Subtract tool to create the counterbored hole.

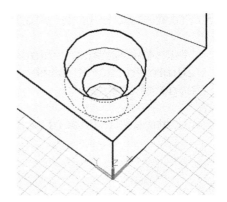

**Counterbored Hole Created**

17. The solid is completed.

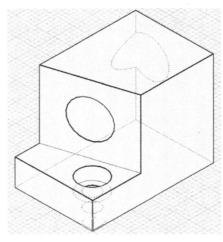

**Solid Completed**

18. Use the VOLUME command to check the volume.

The volume should be 163987.3199 cubic millimeters.

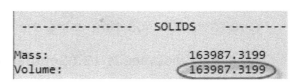

**Volume of Solid**

19. This concludes the 3D portion of the tutorial, the next section will cover creating the 2D hidden line views.

## Setting up the 2D and Isometric Views

Since this is a metric drawing, you will need to change the 2D Sheet layout for an A3 size drawing. If you are dimensioning the drawing, you may use the Autodesk Design Center to bring over the dimension styles used in the 2D version of the project.

1.  Click on the 2D Sheet layout tab to open it.

2.  Confirm that the drawing is in Paperspace.

    Delete all of the elements in the layout tab.

3.  Right-click on the 2D Sheet tab and choose Page Setup Manager.

    Click the Modify... button to modify the page setup settings.

**Page Setup Manager...**

4.  Make or verify the following changes:

    Change the paper size to: ISO full bleed A3 (420.00 x 297.00 MM).
    Set the Plot Area to Extents.
    Set the Plot Scale to 1:1.

    Press OK to save the changes and close the dialog box.

5.  Open the A3 border file and copy the elements to the clipboard.

6.  Switch back to PROJ-09-3D and paste the elements to the original coordinates.

    The points at the top left and the bottom right will be at the corners of the sheet.

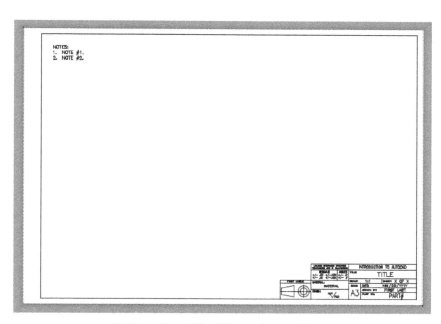

**A3 Border File Placed on Sheet**

7.  Now that the border is placed, use the Solid View tool to add the top view of the solid in the Layout view.

    Even though the border show First-Angle as the projection method, you will be using Third-Angle when placing the views.

    Use the World UCS for the rotation.

    Name the view: Top.

    Use the Ortho option to place the front view below the top view.

    Name the view: Front.

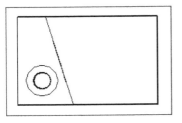

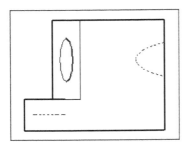

**Top and Front Views Placed**

8.  For the Auxiliary view, you will use the Auxiliary option in the Solid View tool.

    When projecting the view, use the top view as the originating view.

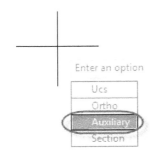

**Auxiliary Option**

9.  The command will ask for the first and second point of the inclined plane.

    To pick the points, click in the top view and then snap at the top and bottom edge of the angled surface.

    You will need to turn on the Object Snap toggle in the status bar and set the snap mode to Endpoint.

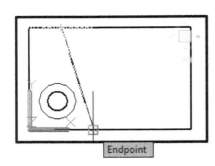

**Second Snap Point for Inclined Plane**

10. After the second point has been selected, pick a point to the left of the top view within the viewport.

    Then click a point for the center of the auxiliary view.

    You will see the paperspace icon rotate to the new angle.

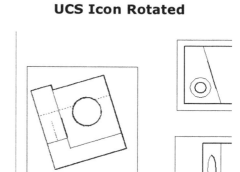

**UCS Icon Rotated**

11. Click to place the view and then draw the edges of the viewport.

    Name the view: Aux

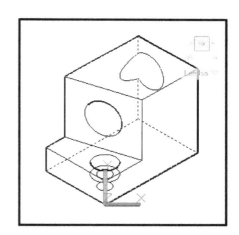

**Auxiliary View Placed**

12. Create an Isometric view at the upper right corner of the sheet.

    Used the named UCS, Left Iso for the rotation.

    Name the view: Iso

    After placing the view, set the scale to the Isometric 3/4 Scale setting that was created in the last tutorial.

**Left Isometric View**

13. Use the Solid Draw tool to create the hidden line views.

   To see the hidden lines correctly, use the LTS key-in to set the linetype scale to
   25.4.

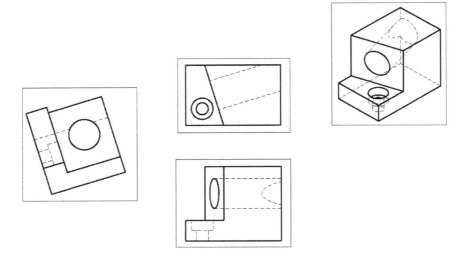

**Top, Front, Auxiliary, and Isometric Views (Third-Angle Projection)**

14. Since the views appear that same as the 2D version of PROJ-09, you can move the
    viewports to the opposite sides of the front view to create a First-Angle Projection
    version of the drawing.

15. This concludes the tutorial, dimension the drawing if needed.

# Project #10 – 3D – Cover Plate

**File Name:** PROJ-10-3D.dwg
Note: All screenshots are from the Autodesk® AutoCAD® software.

**Description:** This tutorial will introduce you to some of the Solid Editing tools. With these
tools you can move, delete, taper, and copy portions of the 3D solid. You
will also be instructed on how to extract faces from the solid.

## Beginning the Project

1.  Open PROJ-07-3D.dwg and save the drawing as PROJ-10-3D.dwg.

2.  Delete all the objects in the file. You will not need any elements from the previous
    project.

    Use Ctrl+A to select any elements that may be hidden or frozen.

3.  If needed, merge the layers generated by the Solid View tool into the Object Line,
    Hidden Line, Dimension layers, and Section Lines layers.

## Creating the Model

1.  Open the 2D version of PROJ-10.

2.  Select the object lines portion of the drawing.

    Use the Isolate tool to isolate the Object Lines
    layer.

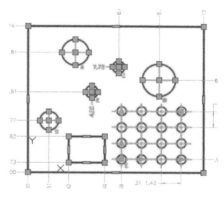

**Elements to be Copied**

3.  Switch to the PROJ-10-3D file.

    Paste the elements in the top view.

    Locate the objects with the origin at the lower left
    corner of the object.

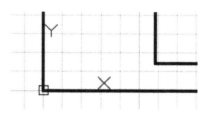

**Lower Left Corner at Origin**

4.  Use the Explode tool to explode the rectangular array into individual circles.

5.  Set the Object Lines layer as the current layer.

    Click the Region tool in the Draw panel.

    Select all of the objects to create 23 regions.

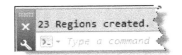

**23 Regions Created**

6.  Use the Extrude tool to extrude the regions vertically .0598 inches.

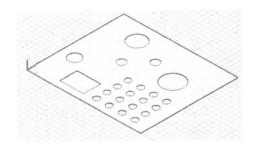

**Regions Extruded**

7.  Use the Solid, Subtract tool to create the voids.

    After selecting the outside rectangular solid, you may select all of the interior solids at one time.

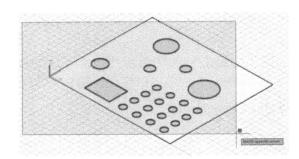

**Selecting the Interior Solids**

8.  This completes the Cover Plate.

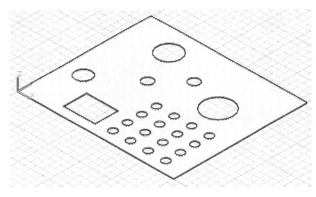

**Cover Plate Completed**

9.  Use the VOLUME command to check the volume.

    The volume should be 6.8571 cubic inches.

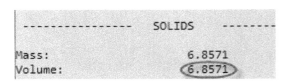

**Volume of Solid**

10. This concludes this portion of the tutorial, create a hidden line view and dimension the drawing if needed before continuing.

## Modifying the Solid (Moving 3D Faces)

1. Before modifying the solid, make a copy and position it away from the original solid.

   You will need to be in the Isometric view when modifying the solid.

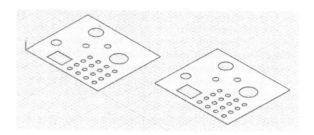

**Solid Copied**

2. You will start with moving one of the holes.

   Zoom in the far left hole.

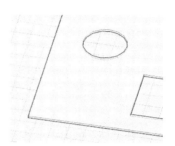

**Far Left Hole**

3. Click on the Move Faces tool.

   This tool is located in the Solid Editing panel.

   Click on the down arrow to find the tool.

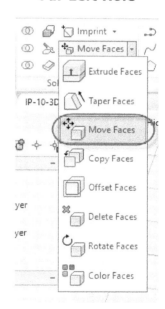

**Move Faces Tool**

4. Hold down the CTRL key and mouse over the inside edge of the hole.

   Do not pick the corner.

   The entire inside face will highlight.

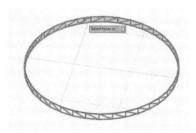

**Face of Hole Selected**

5.  Press the Enter key.

    Click a point near the hole for the Base Point.

    Click a second point to move the hole. Use the Polar tracking tool to make sure that the hole moves in a specific direction.

    You may also use the coordinate key-in with the @ symbol to move the hole a specific distance.

    Using either method, move the hole .500 inches vertically.

    **Note:** If the edge of the solid is still highlighted after completing the operation, select the entire solid and then press the ESC key.

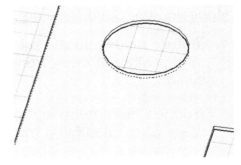

**Hole Moved**

Modifying the Solid (Deleting Faces)

1.  Next you will delete the rectangular hole.

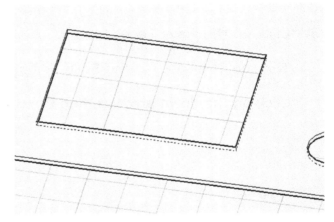

**Rectangular Hole**

2.  Since the hole consists of four sides, you will need to select the four inside faces to delete the hole.

    Click on the Delete Faces tool in the Solid Editing panel.

**Delete Faces Tool**

3.  Hold the CTRL key and click on the two faces that are facing you.

    Rotate the view and select the other two faces.

    When picking the faces, make sure that no other part of the solid is highlighted. You will need to zoom in to pick the inside of the face, do not pick the corner.

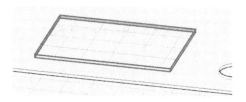

**Four Faces Selected**

    **Note:** You cannot pick faces that are hidden.

4.  This tool can also be used to delete rounded or filleted corners of holes.

    Use the Undo command to bring back the deleted rectangular hole.

    Add a filleted corner to the inside edge of the rectangular hole and then delete it by deleting the rounded face.

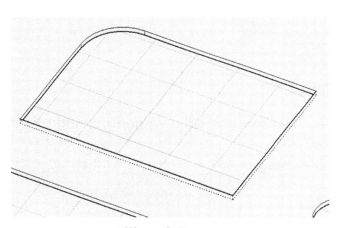

**Filleted Corner**

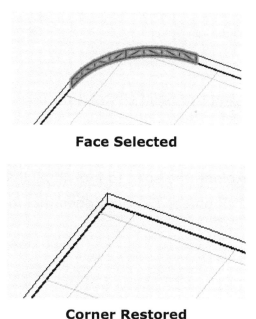

**Face Selected**

**Corner Restored**

## Modifying the Solid (Copying Faces)

1.  Next you will copy the hole at the top right corner of the solid.

    This tool can be used to create a surface from a solid.

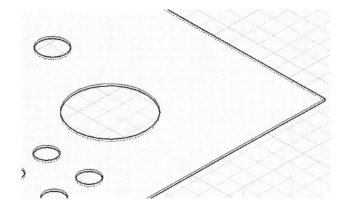

**Top Right Hole**

2.  Click on the Copy Faces tool in the Solids Editing panel.

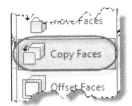

**Copy Faces Tool**

3.  Select the inside face of the hole and press Enter.
4.  Click a point for the base point and drag away from the solid.

    Click to place the face.

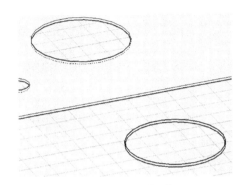

**Face Copied**

Modifying the Solid (Extracting Edges)

1.  Next you will extract the edges of the solid.

    This can be used to create a set of lines from an existing solid without having to explode the solid to individual lines and surfaces.

2.  Click on the Extract Edges tool in the Solid Editing panel.

**Extract Edges**

3.  Select the solid and press Enter.
4.  Move the solid away from its original location to expose the lines.

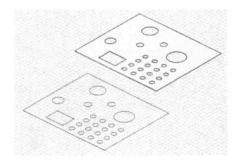

**Lines Created**

## Modifying the Solid (Extruding a Face)

1.  The last modification will be to increase the thickness of the solid by extruding the top face.

2.  Click on the Extrude Faces tool in the Solid Editing panel.

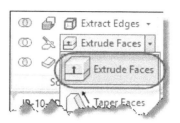

**Extrude Faces Tool**

3.  Select the top face of the solid and press Enter.

4.  Type in a value to select the height of the extrusion.

    Type in .50 for the height. This will add an additional thickness for a total of .5598 inches.

    Press Enter to accept 0 degrees for the angle of the taper for the extrusion.

    **Note:** Try entering a value for the angle to see the results.

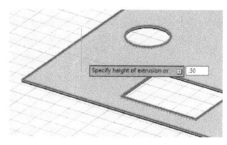

**Specifying the Height of the Extrusion**

5.  The solid is now thicker.

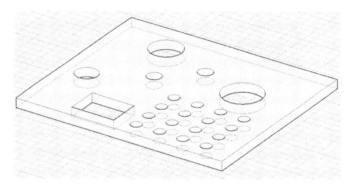

**Solid Thickness Increased to .5598 inches**

6.  This concludes the tutorial.

# Project #11 – 3D – Weldment

**File Name:** PROJ-11-3D.dwg

Note: All screenshots are from the Autodesk® AutoCAD® software.

**Description:** This project will show you the method to create a three dimensional version of the weldment completed in Project #11b. The parts will be created separately and then assembled within the file.

Unlike Project #8, you will not be referencing the parts from other files, all of the parts will be created in this file.

## Beginning the Project

1. Open PROJ-10-3D.dwg and save the drawing as PROJ-11-3D.dwg.

2. Delete all the objects in the file. You will not need any elements from the previous project.

   Use Ctrl+A to select any elements that may be hidden or frozen.

3. If needed, merge the layers generated by the Solid View tool into the Object Line, Hidden Line, Dimension layers, and Section Lines layers.

## Creating the Model

1. Open the 2D version of the Weldments project, PROJ-11b.dwg.

2. Select the object lines for the edge of the object in the top view portion of the drawing.

   Also include the outline of the existing part except for the break lines.

   Use the Isolate tool to isolate the Object Lines, Hidden Lines, and Phantom Lines layers.

   **Note:** You will be using the 2D lines to create the regions for the extrusions instead of creating them in the 3D file only. This will make the drawing of the solids go quicker.

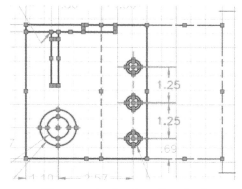

**Elements to be Copied**

3. Switch to PROJ-11-3D and paste the elements into the top view.

   You may need to use the Paste to Original Coordinates option.

4. Repeat the process for the elements in the front view and the right side views.

   Paste the elements into their respective views in the 3D file. Before pasting you will need to change the UCS for each view.

5.  After pasting the three sets of
    views, move them closer to one
    another.

    They do not need to be aligned
    with each other.

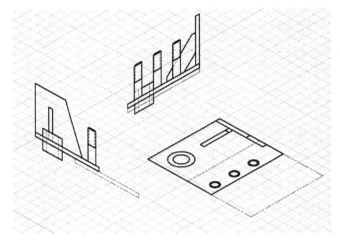

**Three Views Pasted into the 3D File**

6.  Begin with the base.

    Create a region from the four lines
    and extrude to a thickness of .25
    inches.

    As you create the parts, locate
    them away from the 2D lines.

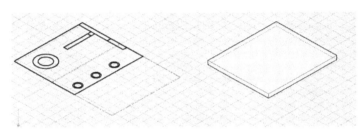

**3D Solid Created from 2D lines**

7.  Create the extrusion for the existing portion of
    the weldment.

    Locate it beneath the base.

    Locate it so it overlaps 1.56 inches.

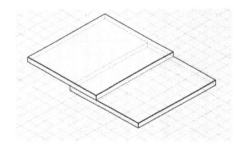

**Existing Portion Overlapping**

8.  Move to the front view to create the next part.

    Place the part at the corner of the base.

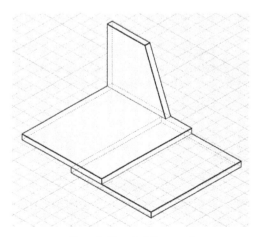

**Next Part Placed**

9.  When placing Part A, you will need to use the Object Snap Tracking function to select the part from the intersection of the right and bottom surfaces.

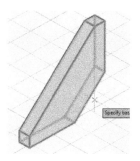

**Object Selected at the Intersection of Surfaces**

10. Place the part at the corner first and then use the Gizmo tool to move it .88 inches along the corner.

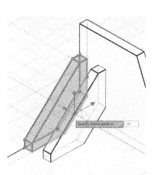

**Moving the Part .88 Inches**

11. Copy the circles from their original locations to the base.

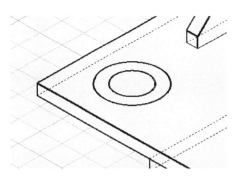

**Circles Copied**

12. Select both circles and use the Gizmo to move them .46 vertically.

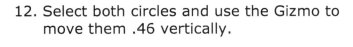

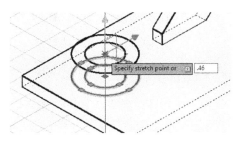

**Circles Moved .46 Inches Vertically**

13. Extrude both circles downward 1.25 inches.

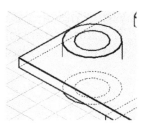

**Circles Extruded**

14. Union the larger cylinder with the base.

    Subtract the smaller cylinder to create the hole.

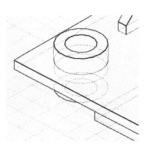

**Cylinders Unioned and Subtracted**

15. The last parts that you will create will be the three studs.

    You will create a shape with V-grooves to simulate the threads.

    Use the profile of the stud in the front view to start the shape.

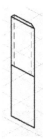

**Profile of Stud**

16. Draw the shape as shown.

    The V-grooves are 1/13 (.077) inches apart from one another.

    This is equal to the pitch of the threads.

    You may wish to switch to the front view to draw the shape.

    Use the Array tool for the V-grooves.

    Explode the array after placement or you will not be able to create the region.

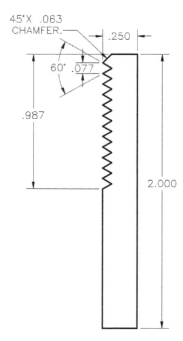

**Dimensions for Profile**

17. Create a region from the shape.

**Region Created**

18. You will use the Revolve tool to revolve the shape into a solid.

Click on the Revolve tool in the Modeling panel.

It is located in the drop-down under the Extrude tool.

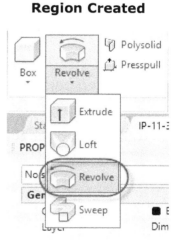

**Revolve Tool**

19. Select the region first and then snap on the bottom corner of the shape.

Then snap at the top corner of the shape.

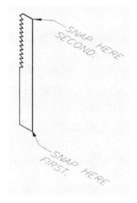

**Snap Points for Revolve**

20. After snapping the second point, press Enter to accept the 360 degree rotation.

The stud is created.

**Stud Created**

21. Move the stud into the correct location on the base and make two copies.

    Refer to the 2D drawing for locations.

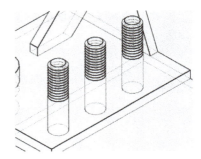

**Studs Placed**

22. This completes the weldment.

    To check the volume, copy the assembly and then union the parts together.

    Do not delete the original assembly this will be used for the 2D hidden line views in the next section.

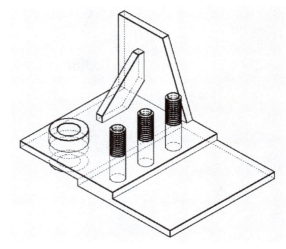

**Unioned Version of Weldment**

23. Use the VOLUME command to check the volume.

    The volume should be 13.5996 cubic inches.

```
-------------- SOLIDS  ---------
Mass:                  13.5996
Volume:                13.5996
```

**Volume of Solid**

24. This concludes the 3D portion of the tutorial.

Creating the 2D Views

1. Click on the 2D Sheet tab to open the layout tab.

2. Delete the viewports.

3. Select the Border and scale it to twice the size.

**Border Scaled to Twice Size**

3. Since this project is at half scale (1:2) you will need to modify the page setup of the 2D layout tab to a scale of 1:2.

**Plot Scale Changed to 1:2**

4. Use the Solid View to place the views.

When placing the views use a scale of 1.000.

Since the border has been doubled, the views will appear at 1/2 scale on the sheet.

Place the Top, Front, Right, and Isometric Views.

Lock the viewports when finished.

Use the Solid View tool to create the hidden line views.

5.  To show the threads of the studs correctly in the right side and front views, delete the V-grooves and show the threads in simplified form after creating the hidden line views.

    Do not do this in the isometric view.

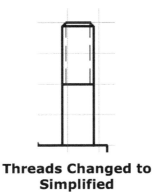

**Threads Changed to
Simplified**

6.  Delete the lines for the existing part in the top, front and side views.

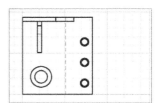 

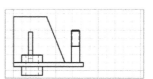 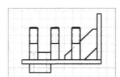

**Lines Deleted**

7.  Switch to Paperspace.

    You may wish to turn off the VPORTS layer.

    Add the break lines and phantom lines for the existing part.

    Add the dimensions and welding symbols.

8.  This concludes the 2D portion and the tutorial, dimension the drawing if needed.

# Conclusion

Congratulations on completing the book! You now should have a basic understanding of the 2D and 3D capabilities of the AutoCAD 2017 software program. With these skills you possess a valuable commodity.

Many companies, municipalities, and government agencies use the AutoCAD software. This software is used in the fields of Manufacturing, Architecture, Civil, Geospatial, and Plant Management.

If you enjoyed this book, please feel free to share your comments with me via email and/or the Amazon.com site.

## *Once Again, Congratulations!*

Sincerely,

David Martin
Author
mechdrawautocad@gmail.com
http://mechdrawautocad.com
September 2016

# Glossary

| | |
|---|---|
| **2D** | Two Dimensional |
| **3D** | Three Dimensional |
| **Absolute Coordinates** | Coordinates on the drawing that are based on a fixed point or origin. |
| **All-Around** | Indicates a condition that effects a feature that goes the entire distance of an intersection with another feature. Used in weld symbols. |
| **ANSI** | American National Standards Institute |
| **Array** | A group of elements that are copied in a rectangular or circular (polar) direction. The copies are located by the row and column spacing in a rectangular array or by their angular and distance from the center of the copies in a polar array. |
| **Attribute** | Properties of an element such as: color, linetype, or lineweight. |
| **Auxiliary View** | A view of an inclined or oblique surface that is projected 90 degrees. This is used to shown the true size of a surface that is not one of the six standard views. See Orthographic Projection. |
| **Break All Sharp Edges** | A note placed on the drawing to indicate that sharp corners are to be de-burred or smoothed after machining. |
| **Block** | The AutoCAD term used to describe a symbol. These are groups of elements that are created and used for different projects. |
| **Break Line** | A type of line placed on the drawing used to indicate that the part is larger than its size on the drawing. |
| **Chamfer** | An angled corner of an object. Indicated by the angle and distance of the angled surface. |
| **Coordinate** | A point in space. X and Y for 2D coordinates and X, Y, and Z for 3D coordinates. |
| **Counterbore** | A hole that has another hole placed inside. This type of hole may be used for a cap screw or other fastener. |
| **Detail View** | A view that is used to shown extra detail of a part. May be drawn at a larger scale than the main drawing. |
| **Element** | An individual part of the drawing such as a line, circle, arc, or text. |
| **Extrusion** | The process of converting a 2D shape to a 3D solid by thickening the shape. |

| | |
|---|---|
| **Feature** | A 3D element of a solid. Examples would be a hole, fillet, round, or surface. |
| **Fence** | A temporary box or other shape that is placed around objects to aid in modification. |
| **Field Weld** | A weld that takes place in the field, not in a fabrication or manufacturing facility. Indicated with a flag on the weld symbol. |
| **File Extensions** | The following filename extensions are used for the different type of AutoCAD files: |

.dwg   AutoCAD Drawing Files

.dwt   Template Files (e.g. acad.dwt)

.lin    Linetype Files containing information for different linetypes.

.pat   Pattern Files used for hatching.

| | |
|---|---|
| **Fillet** | An inside corner of an object that has been rounded with a radius. Also a type of weld that is used to join parts that are perpendicular or angled to one another. |
| **Finish Mark** | A symbol placed on the drawing to indicate the surface roughness of a feature or if a surface is to be machined after a casting operation. |
| **First Angle Projection** | A type of projection where the view is projected through the object rather that from it. Used primarily in Europe and Asia. |
| **GA** | Abbreviation for Gauge. Used to indicate the thickness of sheet metal. |
| **GDT** | Geometrical Dimensioning and Tolerancing. A type of dimensioning symbol used to show the relationship between two mating parts or a condition of a feature. |
| **Hatch** | A pattern added to the drawing to indicate an area of a part in section. |
| **Hole Chart** | A table on the drawing used to indicated the size, quantity, and letter designation of a hole. |
| **Isometric Projection** | A type of projection that shows the height, width, and depth of an object. Horizontal edges are typically rotated to a 30-degree angle. Edges are drawn at true size or at a standard scale. |
| **Kerf** | A narrow slit made by a saw blade. |
| **Layer** | A category of similar elements in a drawing. Layers may be categorized by their attributes such as color, line style, or line weight. |
| **Limit** | A type of tolerance dimension that shows to upper and lower limit of size and location. |

| | |
|---|---|
| **Linetype** | A line that contains fixed dash and gap lengths. Used to indicate different types of lines on a drawing. Examples include: Hidden, Phantom, and Center lines. |
| **Mirror** | To create a reversed image of an element or a group of elements. |
| **Modelspace** | A portion of the drawing that contains elements located in the Model tab. These elements are typically the drawing views and dimensions. Depending on the set-up of the drawing, all elements may be placed in modelspace. |
| **Ordinate Dimensioning** | A type of dimensioning that does not use extension or dimension lines. Also known as Arrowless Dimensioning. |
| **Origin** | The base point of a project or the 0,0 coordinate. The origin may be changed through the use of the Auxiliary Coordinate System (ACS) tool. |
| **Orthographic Projection** | Views of a single object that are projected 90 degrees from one another. Consists of six standard views: Top, Front, Right, Bottom, Rear, and Left. |
| **Paperspace** | A portion of the drawing that contains elements not located in the Model tab (Modelspace). Access to these elements are through the Layout tabs. Sometimes the title block and dimensions of viewport elements are placed in paperspace. |
| **PDF** | Portable Document Format. A type of file that is used to show 2D and 3D drawings without the use of the AutoCAD program. |
| **Plus/Minus** | A type of tolerance that indicates the maximum and minimum size or location of a dimension. |
| **Primitive** | A basic type of solid such as a slab, sphere, torus, wedge, cylinder, or cone. |
| **Region** | A group of linear elements that are joined together to create a single shape. |
| **Reference (File)** | To link a file from another location to another file. The AutoCAD term is "xref". |
| **Relative Coordinates** | Coordinates on the drawing that are based on a movable point or origin. |
| **Resolution** | Associated with the Working Units of the file. This controls the accuracy of the model and is changed based on its overall size. |
| **Revolve** | A 3D tool used to project a shape in a cylindrical direction |
| **Round** | An outside corner of an object that has been rounded with a radius. |
| **Scale** | The relationship between the size of the drawing on paper/screen and its actual size. |

| | |
|---|---|
| **Section** | A simulated cut made in the object to show additional interior detail. |
| **Slab** | A flat 3D solid with height, width, and depth. |
| **Slot** | An opening in a flat part with parallel sides. May have rounded corners. |
| **Solid** | A three dimensional object with height, width, and depth. |
| **Spline** | An arc that does not have a fixed center. Also known as a Bezier Curve. Also is a term for slots that are cut on a cylindrical part for a mating part. |
| **Stud** | A threaded metal part. May be welded to another component of a weldment. |
| **Tag** | A type of element that is used as a placeholder to add text to a drawing. In this book tags are used to aid in filling out the title block on a drawing. |
| **Third Angle Projection** | A type of projection where the view is projected from the object. Used primarily in the United States. |
| **Tolerance** | The amount that a feature is allowed to deviate from perfect or design size. |
| **Union** | To join two or more solids into one solid. |
| **U.N.O.** | Unless Noted Otherwise. |
| **Weldment** | A group of parts that are welded together. |

# Index

## #

\# Symbol Use ...............................................15

## %

%%c Symbol ................................................ 115

## @

@ Symbol Use ...................................29, 37, 49

## 3

3D Layout View ........................................... 230
3D View of Weldment................................. 183
3-Point Tool, UCS ....................................... 289

## A

acad-md.lin File ............................................43
Add Page Setup Dialog Box............................73
Add Scale Dialog Box ................................... 277
Add... Button, Printing ..................................73
Additional Format Dialog Box (Table Tool) ...... 168
Aligned Dimension Tool..................................84
Alignment Tool (Table Tool) .......................... 169
All-Around Symbol........................................ 176
Alternative Method to Access Videos ............... 3
AMGDT Font .............................................. 116
Angular Dimension Tool..................................85
Annotate Tab ...............................................56
ANSI131 Hatch Pattern ................................ 113
Apply to Layout ............................................73
Apply to Layout Button...................................71
Array Tool .................................................. 127
Arrow Size, Multileader ..................................89
Arrowhead Settings .......................................33
A-Size Border File.........................................45
Assembly Sequence ..................................... 281
Associative Tool (Hatch Tool) ........................ 113
Attach External Reference Dialog Box ............ 269
Attach Tool, Reference Panel........................ 268
AutoCAD Educational License .......................... 5
Autodesk DesignCenter ................................ 188
Auxiliary Option, New Viewport ..................... 294
Auxiliary View Projection ............................. 150
AWS Standard ............................................ 189

## B

Before Beginning to Draw ............................... 4
Bind Xrefs/DGN underlays Dialog Box ........... 275
Block Definition Dialog Box .......................... 178
Book Website Address.................................... 4
Break Tool...................................................54
Break Tool (Dimensioning) ..............................83

Break-line Symbol Tool ................................ 186

## C

Cell Border Properties Dialog Box .................. 170
Cell Names and Descriptions......................... 177
Center Lines Layer .......................................61
Center Mark .............................................. 128
Center Mark 1-2 Dimension Style .................. 162
Center Mark Tool...........................................61
Center Marks Dimension Style ........................60
Center, Start, Angle Option (Arc Tool) ............95
Center, Start, End Option (Arc Tool) ...............78
CENTER-Short Linetype..................................62
Chain Option (Fillet Tool) ............................ 239
Chamfer Tool .............................................. 185
Chamfer Tool (3D Corner) ............................ 249
Changing the Later of Elements ......................23
Chart for Project #1 .....................................15
Circle Tool............................................ 17, 48
Clipboard Panel ............................................46
Close Preview Window ...................................72
Conclusion................................................. 313
Continue Dimension ......................................64
Continue Option .......................................... 104
Copy Clip Tool...............................................46
Copy Faces Tool ......................................... 302
Copy Tool....................................................28
Counterbore Symbol..................................... 116
Create New Dimension Style...........................56
Create New Multileader Style Dialog Box ..........32
Create New Table Style Dialog Box ................ 171
Create Tool (Blocks) .................................... 177
Creating Hidden Line Views of Viewports ........ 225
Creating Slots ..............................................79
Custom Viewport Scales................................ 276
Cylinder Tool .............................................. 214

## D

Data Format Tool (Table Tool) ...................... 167
DDUNITS Key-in Command ............................38
Delete Faces Tool ....................................... 300
Depth Symbol.............................................. 116
Description Window (Block Definition)............ 179
Detail View ................................................ 141
Diameter Dimension Tool ......................... 65, 87
Dimension Style Setup...................................56
Dimension Styles Manager Dialog Box ............56
Dimension Tool .............................................63
Dimensioning Hole Centers.............................64
Dimensions Panel .........................................56
Drafting Settings ..........................................20
Drawing Grids ..............................................20
Drawing Notes .............................................66
Drawing Orientation (Printing) ........................70
Drawing Setup for 2D Projects .........................6
Drawing Tabs ...............................................46
Drawing Units, Angle Precision...................... 38

DWT Files ..................................................... 13
DYNMODE Key-in ..................................... 14

## E

ECS Key Use ............................................... 15
Edit Borders ............................................. 169
Edit Drawing Scales Dialog Box .................... 277
Edit Reference Panel ................................. 271
Ellipse Tool .............................................. 149
Email Contact ............................................ 4
Enhanced Attribute Editor ........................... 66
Explode Tool ..................................... 181, 257
Exploded View .......................................... 273
Extend Tool ............................................... 54
Extension Line Break .................................. 104
Extension Snap Mode .................................. 102
External References Files Have Changed ........ 271
Extracting Edges Tool .................................. 302
Extrude Faces Tool ..................................... 303
Extrude Tool .............................................. 201
Extruding a Shape ...................................... 201
Extrusion Method ....................................... 193

## F

Field Weld Flag ........................................... 176
File Management ........................................... 4
Fillet Tool ................................................... 47
Fillet Tool (3D Corners) .............................. 239
Fillet Weld Symbol ..................................... 175
First Angle Projection .................................. 148
Fit Options (Dimension Setup) ..................... 105
Fit Tab, New Dimension Style ........................ 59
Folder Structure .......................................... 11
Font Setting ............................................... 27
Font Settings .............................................. 34
FROM Command Modifier .......... 48, 75, 80, 125

## G

Geneva Cam Part Colors ............................. 271
Gizmo Tool ................................................ 261
Grid Spacing, Metric Drawings ..................... 146
Grids .......................................................... 20
Group Manager Tool ................................... 118
Group Tool ................................................ 117

## H

Hatch Tool ................................................ 112
Hidden Line Views ...................................... 225
Hole Chart ......................................... 160, 166

## I

Inscribed in Circle Option ............................. 16
Insert Dialog (Blocks) ................................. 180
Insert Option, Reference Files ...................... 275
Insert Table Dialog Box ............................... 166
Insert Tool (Blocks) .................................... 180

Inserting the Border into Layout View ............ 227
Introduction ................................................ 3
Isolate Tool ............................................... 207
Isometric 3/4 Scale ..................................... 277
Isometric Orientation (ViewCube) ................. 198
Isometric View Scale ................................... 276

## L

Landing Distance, Multileader Style ........... 33, 89
Layer Area (Autodesk DesignCenter .............. 218
Layer Properties Manager ............................. 18
Layer Properties Manager Dialog Box ............... 5
Layer Setup .................................................. 5
Layer Setup (Project #1) .............................. 18
Layout Tab ................................................ 219
Layout View Page Setup .............................. 242
Leader Tool ................................................ 31
Legal ........................................................... i
Lengthen Option .......................................... 82
Linear Tool ................................................. 63
Lines Tab, New Dimension Style ..................... 58
Linetype File ............................................... 43
Linetype Manager ....................................... 218
Linetype Manager Dialog Box ......................... 43
Linetype Scale Factor, Half Scale Drawings ..... 184
Linetype Scale Setting for Metric Drawings ..... 296
Linetype Scale, Metric Drawings ................... 148
Loading Linetypes ........................................ 44
Local Notes .......................................... 88, 118
LWDISPLAY Variable .................................... 23

## M

MASSPROP Command ................................. 203
MEASUREGEOM Key-In Command ................ 278
Mech 1-1 Dimension Style ............................. 57
Mech 1-2 Dimension Style ........................... 162
Menu Bar .................................................. 199
Merging Layers .......................................... 235
Metric 1-1 (Radial) Dimension Style .............. 156
Metric 1-1 Dimension Style .......................... 154
Metric Drawing Grid Spacing ........................ 287
Metric Drawing Page Setup .......................... 293
Metric Drawing Units .................................. 146
Mirror Tool ................................................ 125
Miter Line Technique .................................... 52
Modify Multileader Style Dialog Box ................ 32
More Options... (Blocks) ............................. 180
Move Faces Tool ......................................... 299
Move Tool .................................................. 29
Move with Dim Line Option .......................... 103
Multileader Arrowhead Settings ..................... 33
Multileader Style Manager ........................ 31, 88
Multileader Style Tool .............................. 31, 88
Multiline Text Tool ....................................... 26
MVSETUP Key-In Command ......................... 224

## N

Named UCS ............................................... 220
Naming Groups .......................................... 117

**N**

Navigation Wheel ......................................... 198
New Dimension Style Dialog Box ..................... 57
New Layer Tool ............................................. 18
New Style Table Dialog Box ......................... 172
New Viewport, Section Option ...................... 250
No Trim Option (Fillet Tool) ......................... 100
Notes Weld Symbol ..................................... 176
Number of Items (Array Tool) ...................... 127

**O**

Object Grouping Dialog Box .......................... 118
Object Line Layer Attributes ........................... 19
Object Snap Settings ..................................... 22
Object Snap Tracking ..................................... 80
Offset Tool .................................................... 24
One Inch Cube ............................................. 276
On-Line Video Tutorials .................................. 4
Opening Screen ............................................. 12
Ordinate Dimension Tool .............................. 164
Ortho Option (Solid View Tool) ..................... 222
Orthogonal Triangle ..................................... 197

**P**

Page Setup Manager ..................................... 242
Paper Size for B-Size Drawings .................... 106
Paperspace Toggle ...................................... 228
Paperspace View .......................................... 219
Paragraph Dialog Box ..................................... 28
Paragraph Settings ........................................ 28
Part Balloon ................................................. 279
Parts List .................................................... 280
Paste to Original Coordinates ......................... 46
Perpendicular Snap Mode ............................. 103
PH and PV Layers ........................................ 245
Phantom Linestyle ....................................... 184
Pick Point Tool (Block Definition) ................. 178
Placing Section Lines .................................... 112
Plot Area ...................................................... 72
Plot Offset .................................................... 71
Plot Scale ..................................................... 70
Plot Style Table ............................................. 70
Point Style Dialog Box .................................... 71
Polar Array .......................................... 127, 135
Polar Tracking Settings ................................... 22
Polygon Tool .................................................. 16
Preview Area, Printing .................................... 72
Preview Button .............................................. 72
Primary Units Tab, New Dimension Style .......... 60
Primitive Method .......................................... 193
Primitive Solids ........................................... 193
Print Dialog Box ............................................ 69
Print Tool ..................................................... 69
Printing to a PDF File ..................................... 74
Printing Your Drawing ..................................... 69
Project #1 – Table Dimensions ........................ 24
Projecting Orthographic Views ........................ 50
Projection Lines ............................................. 50
Properties Window .......................................... 38
PROPS Key-in Command ................................. 38
PTYPE Key-In Command .................................. 71

**Q**

Quick Access Toolbar (QAT) ........................... 20

**R**

Radius Dimension Tool .................................... 86
Rectangle Tool ............................................... 30
Rectangular Array ........................................ 161
Reference Dimension .................................... 129
Reference Edit Dialog Box ............................. 270
Reference File Fading ................................... 269
Region Tool ................................................. 200
Renaming Layout Tabs .................................. 230
Revolve Tool ................................................ 309

**S**

Save Changes, Edit Reference Panel .............. 271
Save Tool ...................................................... 14
Saving a UCS Setting .................................... 198
Saving Page Setup, Printing ............................ 74
Saving the Print Settings ................................ 73
Saving the UCS ............................................ 224
Scale Factor (Dimension Tool) ...................... 142
Scale Setting for Metric Dimensions .............. 154
Scale Tool .............................................. 141, 159
Select Objects Tool (Block Definition) ........... 178
Select Reference File Dialog Box .................. 268
Selecting a Custom Linetype File ..................... 44
Setting Up Metric Drawings .......................... 145
Simulated Threads for 3D Parts ..................... 308
Snaps ........................................................... 20
Solid Drawing Tool ....................................... 225
Solid Profile Tool ......................................... 245
Solid View Tool ............................................ 219
Solid, Subtract Tool ..................................... 203
Solid, Union Tool ......................................... 248
Splash Screen ............................................... 12
Start Drawing Icon ......................................... 13
Starting the Software ...................................... 12
Stretch Tool .................................................. 39
Stud Weld Symbol ........................................ 189
Support File Downloading ............................... 45
Surface Texture Symbol ................................ 117
Symbol Tool, Text Editor .............................. 115
Symbols and Arrows Tab, New Dimension Style 58
Symmetry Mark ............................................ 129

**T**

Table Cell Format (Table Tool) ...................... 168
Table of Contents ............................................ 1
Table Style Dialog Box .................................. 171
Table Tool ................................................... 166
Tangent Snap .............................................. 110
Temporary Snap Modes ................................ 102
Text Alignment for Metric Dimensions ........... 154
Text Editor Box .............................................. 26
Text Justification ........................................... 27
Text Style Font .............................................. 34
Text Tab, New Dimension Style ....................... 59

Text Window (VOLUME Command) ................. 204
Title Block .........................................................45
Trim Tool............................................................25

## U

UCS Drop-down in ViewCube ........................ 199
UCS Icon.............................................................14
UCS Key-in Command.................................... 160
Ucs Option (Solid View Tool) ........................ 220
UCS Options ................................................... 198
Underline Toggle ...............................................31
Unisolate Tool ................................................ 208
User Interface ...................................................13

## V

V-Grooves ..................................................... 308
View Option (UCS Tool)................................. 223
View Tools ...................................................... 197
ViewCube ....................................................... 197
Viewport Freeze ............................................ 229
Viewport Lock Tool ....................................... 221

Viewport Scale............................................... 220
Viewport Scale Control................................... 276
Viewport Scale Lock....................................... 278
Viewport Scale Tool ...................................... 244
Viewports Dialog Box ..................................... 231
VIEWRES Command ....................................... 238
Visual Styles Manager Dialog Box.................. 202
VOLUME Key-In .............................................. 203
Volumes for 3D Projects...................................7
VPORTS Command ......................................... 244

## W

Weld Chart Dimensions............................... 177
Weldment .................................................... 175
Workspace Switching ................................... 195

## X

Xref Fading.................................................... 269

www.ingramcontent.com/pod-product-compliance
Lightning Source LLC
Chambersburg PA
CBHW080352060326
40689CB00019B/3985